How to Hike the AT

How to Hike the AT

The Nitty-Gritty Details of a Long-Distance Trek

MICHELLE RAY

STACKPOLE
BOOKS

Copyright © 2009 by Stackpole Books

Published by
STACKPOLE BOOKS
5067 Ritter Road
Mechanicsburg, PA 17055
www.stackpolebooks.com

Printed in the United States of America

10 9 8 7 6 5 4

First edition

Cover design by Wendy A. Reynolds

Library of Congress Cataloging-in-Publication Data

Ray, Michelle.
  How to hike the AT : the nitty-gritty details of a long-distance trek / Michelle Ray. — 1st ed.
    p. cm.
  Includes bibliographical references.
  ISBN-13: 978-0-8117-3542-1
  ISBN-10: 0-8117-3542-7
  1. Hiking—Appalachian Trail. 2. Appalachian Trail—Description and travel. I. Title. II. Title: How to hike the Appalachian Trail.
GV199.42.A68R39 2009
796.510974—dc22

2008025800

Contents

Preface

Everywhere is walking distance if you have the time.

—Steven Wright

It was the summer of 2005 when I first discovered that the Appalachian Trail, more familiarly known as the AT, was a relatively short train ride from my New York City apartment. Sweltering summer days, the high price of entertainment in the city, and a need for space and fresh air guided me to the woods. After backpacking a couple hundred miles or so of the AT by the end of summer, I was completely enchanted with it and decided to plan for a long hike in 2007.

Upon making this decision, I became obsessed with the beauty, culture, and challenges of the trail, and I dove headfirst into examining every aspect of it. I had a lot of logistical questions but was also very interested in the people, traditions, and history behind long-distance hiking on the AT. There's a wealth of information available on hiking the AT, but I wasn't able to find any single truly comprehensive resource geared toward planning a long-distance hike. There was also a missing link between the ideal hiking conditions found in the existing how-to guides and the bona fide day-to-day duct tape and ramen existence of long-distance hikers. I decided to compile all of the information I could lay my hands on prior to my trip and revise it, where necessary, after my long hike was completed. Since then, I've hiked in every state and logged thousands of miles on the AT, testing my ideas about long-distance hiking while learning from my experiences and those of other hikers. I completed all but a hundred-some miles of the trail in a single hike, and I've done numerous section hikes.

If you're reading this book, odds are that you have already decided to do a long-distance hike of your own. Or, possibly, you are a backpacking enthusiast and would like to get a better idea of what long-distance hiking is all about. This book is geared toward prospective AT long-distance hikers with all ranges of backpacking experience. Whether you've spent one night out on the trail or a hundred, this book has something to add to your backpacking knowledge.

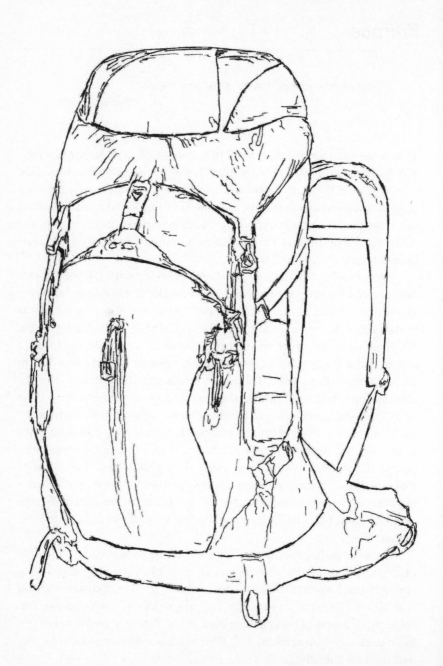

I hope this resource will assist you in making good decisions when planning for your trip or, if you haven't seriously considered attempting a long-distance hike, help you decide if a long hike is a good option for you (and, in my opinion, it's a great option for just about everyone who is able to walk). Thousands of people have completed long-distance hikes since Earl Shaffer's pioneering thru-hike in 1948, and the success rate for long-distance hikers is increasing thanks to better gear, on-trail support, and the widespread availability of information on the web, in magazines, and in books such as this one.

Introduction

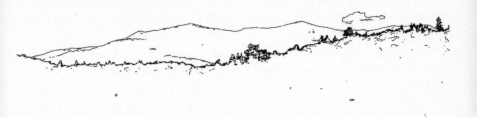

The longest journey begins with a single step.
—Lao-tzu, *Tao Te Ching*

Long-distance hikers cannot be placed in the same category as other athletes. They sleep half of the day, eat their body weight in fatty foods, rarely shower, and typically move about two to three miles per hour. In this sport, all-you-can-eat buffets and naptime reign supreme. Yet hikers are regarded with awe and the Appalachian Trail long-distance hiker is a modern day enigma. Perhaps this has something to do with climbing mountains or dealing with bears.

So what, exactly, *is* a long-distance hike? The definition varies according to whom you ask, but generally it's considered to be a hike of days, weeks, or months that necessitates complex logistics such as resupply or seasonal gear replacement. Long-distance hikes include anything from a hundred-mile hike to a thru-hike, when a hiker travels the entire length of the trail in a single year.

Typically, a long-distance hiker is not a corporate-sponsored athlete. He or she doesn't spend extensive time training or attending competitions. Though thru-hiking speed records do exist, most hikers on the AT have no time concerns other than completing their hike before the winter weather hits and the hiking season officially ends. They literally mosey their way along the 2,175-mile-long path, stopping frequently to snack and enjoy the scenery—not that the moseying doesn't get decently strenuous in spots.

Appalachian skyline in New England

Appalachian Trail long-distance hikers are representative of all walks of life: extreme athletes, recent high school or college graduates, those with career burn-out, refugees from failed relationships or midlife crises, and retirees. This ragtag assortment assembles year after year at the northern and southern ends of the Appalachian Trail and at all points in between to begin the journey.

Hiking any of the 2,175 miles between Springer Mountain in Georgia and Katahdin in Maine is no easy task. A long hike can be a downright brutal experience, complete with poor weather, rough terrain, and wear and tear on the body. However, on the trail you will likely encounter beauty, camaraderie, and other pleasures that more than compensate for the difficult days. And, at the end of the trail, you will have an experience that will be one of the most positive and memorable of your lifetime.

The Short History of a Long Trail

Little did I dream more than fifty years ago when I sat down with two men in the New Jersey Highlands and outlined to them my idea of a footpath through the Appalachians, that such a plan would be translated into the institution that has now come to pass.
—Benton MacKaye

The Appalachian National Scenic Trail, more commonly known as the Appalachian Trail or the AT, is a 2,175-mile-long footpath running from Springer Mountain in Georgia to Katahdin in Maine. The trail winds its way up and down mountains through the states of Georgia, North Carolina, Tennessee, Virginia, West Virginia, Maryland, Pennsylvania, New Jersey, New York, Connecticut, Massachusetts, Vermont, New Hampshire, and Maine. It is populated by periodic shelters and is marked along its full length with two-by-six-inch white painted blazes.

The story of this trail begins with the idealistic concepts of Benton MacKaye and the tenacity of Myron Avery. The utopian ideals on which this large-scale project was founded are associated with the trail to this day.

BENTON MACKAYE'S BIG IDEA

Harvard graduate and former U.S. Forest Service employee Benton Mac-Kaye proposed the Appalachian National Scenic Trailway plan in 1921. MacKaye thought of the AT as an escape from the polluted and congested urban areas on the East Coast and as a tool for responsible land and wildlife management. It was to be accessible to those living in the urban centers along the East Coast.

The AT is not fully wilderness; towns or major metropolitan centers are never more than a few days' hike away. On average, hikers encounter resupply points such as towns every few days, and the longest stretch a

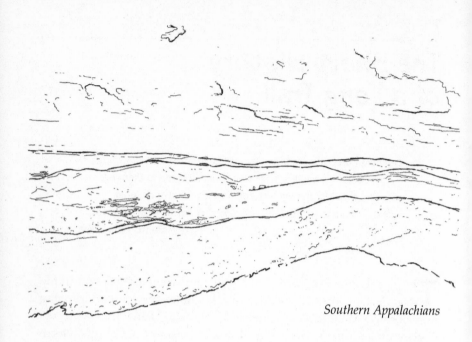

Southern Appalachians

hiker will have to walk between resupply points is four or five days. Long stretches of wilderness are not found on the AT. Even in the Hundred Mile Wilderness, logging roads, inexpensive float planes services, and hunting camps make the area accessible to the outside world.

The first Appalachian Trail Conference (ATC) was held in Washington, D.C., in 1925 and established a group of advocates intent on constructing the trail (the Appalachian Trail Conference was renamed the Appalachian Trail Conservancy in the summer of 2005). The trail was slowly created by scouting and constructing short sections, which were later connected.

Completed in 1937, the AT was the longest marked footpath in America at that time, and it was later designated as the country's first national scenic trail in 1968. The 2,175 miles of the trail (a distance that changes slightly year to year due to relocations and general debate) pass alongside or through fourteen states and six national parks, and have elevations ranging from 124 to 6,625 feet.

MacKaye proved himself to be a better abstract thinker than project leader, and eventually the project's more pragmatic aspects were taken over by Arthur Perkins and Myron Avery. Avery fully took over when

Perkins's health failed, and he aggressively led the project to its completion. We have Avery to thank for the AT's northern terminus at Katahdin, as Maine was his native state. Unfortunately, Avery and MacKaye had some serious differences in their goals, prompting MacKaye to leave the ATC in 1935. MacKaye was not involved with the organization again until after Avery's death in 1952.

The AT has undergone many phases in its existence. World War II left it poorly maintained due to a lack of available volunteer workers, but the trail was rehabilitated and maintained in the post-war era. To this day, volunteer labor is used to build and maintain shelters, clear brush and blow-downs, construct new trail, and paint blazes. After congress declared the AT a national scenic trail, the government began buying land for trail use, eliminating the problematic need of negotiating for sections of the trail that ran through private property. In 1978, the National Trails System Act was amended with the Appalachian Trail Bill, which authorized an initial $90 million budget for purchasing trail corridor lands with additional funds appropriated for it during later presidential administrations. Now all but a few miles of the AT run through public land. Though some sections of the original trail have been relocated, it is more or less the same as it was in 1971 when it was permanently blazed with the help of volunteers and the National Park Service.

LONG-DISTANCE HIKERS AND THE AT

Initially, the AT was intended as a retreat for urban day hikers, a way for the masses to get fresh air and exercise and to revel in nature's beauty. True, Myron Avery had walked the entire length of the trail in sections, but this was not done as an official hike of the entire trail. It wasn't until Earl Shaffer, a war veteran and Pennsylvania native, made his pioneering thru-hike in 1948 (of which he wrote an account entitled *Walking with Spring*) that the concept of thru-hiking came into being.

Known as "the Crazy One" by those who had heard of his travels, Shaffer's hike from Georgia to Maine was met with much skepticism. At the time of his historic hike, the AT was in a state of neglect due to the recent war. After an intense interview headed by Myron Avery at the Appalachian Trail Conference's headquarters in Washington, D.C., Shaffer was officially declared the first Appalachian Trail thru-hiker. In 1965, Shaffer upped the ante by completing a southbound thru-hike, becoming the first person to hike the trail in both directions (his fascinating 1965 trail journal may be found at www.trailjournals.com/earlshaffer).

Many years passed after Shaffer's hike before long-distance hiking culture fully developed. With the 1970s came a large rise in the number of thru-hikers, and the term "2,000 miler" was coined. Ed Garvey, a 1970 thru-hiker, published *Appalachian Hiker: Adventure of a Lifetime,* which generated publicity for the AT and increased the number of long-distance hikers on the trail (much like what happened with the more recent Bill Bryson book, *A Walk in the Woods,* when it was published in the late nineties). The increase in long-distance hikers continued dramatically until 2000, when it saw a slight decline. However, thanks to Earl Shaffer and other long-distance hiking pioneers, there are to this day a significant number of eager long-distance hikers who start their journeys every year.

2

Why Hike the Trail?

*Who can say where a voyage starts—not the actual passage but
the dream of a journey and its urge to find a way?*
                    —William Least Heat-Moon, *River-Horse*

"Springer fever" is the term used to describe the magnetic pull that draws
hikers to Springer Mountain, the southern terminus of the Appalachian
Trail, at the start of each hiking season. Thousands of hikers have their
hearts trained on the Appalachian Mountain range and feel the subtle stir-
ring and pulling, the need to travel the trail. And, like a flock of migrating
birds, they collect in bunches and move off through the mountains on an
annual basis.

THE MOTIVATION BEHIND THE HIKE

Why hike the Appalachian Trail? Why not take a cruise, get a degree, or
learn a new craft for personal fulfillment? This is an essential question that
most hikers are aware of, if not fully able to answer, and is the question
you'll be asked most when declaring your intent to undertake a long-distance hike. The answer to this question is a personal one and varies from
hiker to hiker. Many feel that the journey of a long-distance hiker begins
once that person commits to doing the trip, when he or she decides on
some level that there is a reason to make the trip. For the long-distance-
hiker-to-be, this is the point of psychological commitment, of deciding to
leave a familiar life behind.

Some hikers head to the mountains with a mixed bag of motivations:
they might enjoy nature's beauty, the physical experience of hiking, the
challenge of the trip, or the appeal of self-reliance. Some people are even
drawn to the idea of an archetypal heroic journey or spiritual pilgrimage,
and many long-distance hikers go to the mountains looking for some sort
of enlightenment or sense of accomplishment.

Shenandoah River at Harpers Ferry, West Virginia

Many of us exist in a state of disenchantment with the contemporary world. We are tired of bills, crowds, pollution, and consumerism. The onslaught of technological and commercial intervention in our lives is a motivational force that drives some people to the refuge of the woods for a prolonged break. Rather than looking at this as an escapist retreat from society, a long hike should be viewed as a healthy exploration of an alternative lifestyle. Indeed, some hikers go through radical life changes after completing their hikes. Some leave cities to adopt a simpler way of living, while others may enter school for environmental studies.

An appreciation of nature factors heavily into the long-distance hiking experience. The Appalachian Trail is, after all, a vestige of wilderness in the heavily developed eastern United States. The AT possesses natural wonders not found anywhere else in the world and hosts a surprisingly large number of species of flora and fauna.

Hikers may head to the mountains in order to seek an authentic life experience. Using the words of Henry David Thoreau, a person may rationalize hiking as going to the woods ". . . to live deliberately." In a world full of mediated spaces and experiences, a trip to the backcountry allows an individual the sort of autonomy he or she craves. A life temporarily devoid of meetings, deadlines, ringing phones, and other distractions enables a hiker to connect with the essential components of the self. Life on the AT can be brutal, direct, and devoid of sentimentality, and long-distance hiking is one of the most in-your-face experiences found in contemporary life.

WHAT MAKES A LONG-DISTANCE HIKER TICK?

There's a breed of individual found on the AT that is plagued by insatiable wanderlust. This person is the nomad, the contemporary gypsy, the displaced. Bruce Chatwin's *Songlines*, a book about the nomadic aboriginal culture, makes the bold statement that a lot of problems in contemporary society are a direct result of leading sedentary lives. He champions a life of healthy restlessness, of travel and exploration. His words appeal to those individuals out there who are only fulfilled when on the move. For these people, the AT is a wonderful way to stimulate the mind and heart.

A long-distance hike proves to be the ultimate challenge for the type-A go-getter, the record breaker on the high school sports team, and the survivalist. These are people who thrive in demanding physical and psychological situations. A twenty-five-mile slog through the rain is a day of rewarding tests for them. It's difficult to say why some people seek out challenges like this while others do not, but one could claim that no one on the AT is fully free of a self-testing bent. Practically every long-distance hiker claims that one of the big appeals of hiking is its inherent challenges.

> "**W**hy hike?" is one of the most essential questions asked of hikers. There are many different answers to why someone would pick up and head off to the woods for weeks or months on end. ADHD of the soul, a spiritual quest, disenchantment, or a case of Springer fever are but a handful of the complex answers to this question.

Some long-distance hikers are labeled as escapists. This group includes the person who lost a job, ended a painful relationship, or entered a phase in life seemingly unrealized by any option other than taking a prolonged hiking hiatus. For this group of people, the trail provides a buffer between them and their problems. Personal motives and past decisions can be dissected during hours of solitary walking. Activities such as outrunning a lightning storm, finding water during a drought, or staying warm on a freezing night can provide perspective on life's predicaments.

Nature photographer Glenn Randall states that "Living simply in the woods is good practice for living in civilization." Some hikers worry that taking months away from work and loved ones to hike is selfish or un-productive. This is debatable on the grounds that hiking is relatively easy on the environment and usually improves a person, an improvement that is spread to others off the trail. After all, interpreting spreadsheets or flip-ping hamburgers is no more useful in the larger sense than walking over a mountain. In fact, hikers often leave their mark on those around them by providing inspiration and entertainment, something an accountant or sales clerk doesn't necessarily do.

Regardless of your rationale for undertaking a long-distance hike, it's important to be in touch with the root of your desires. Through this sense of awareness, you will be able to acknowledge and communicate the pur-pose of the hike to others. And by having an idea of why your hike is es-sential, you will get closer to fulfilling the purpose of your journey.

3

Behind-the-Scenes Planning

*He who starts on a ride of two or three thousand miles may experi-
ence, at the moment of departure, a variety of emotions. He may
feel excited, sentimental, anxious, care-free, heroic, roistering, pica-
resque, introspective, or practically anything else; but, above all, he
must and will feel like a fool.*

—Peter Fleming, *News from Tartary*

So, you've decided to hike a large portion of the trail or perhaps even its entire length? There are many details to which you must attend before putting on your pack and heading out into the woods. Take into account the large number of day-to-day activities in which a typical person engages. There are bills, employment, housing, taxes, automobile and health insurance, and social obligations to consider. Thoughts about practical planning matters can overshadow a hike, but for some the transition into hiking life may be made simpler by virtue of age (young), marital status (single), financial situation (independently wealthy), or career (freelance, student, seasonal, or unemployed). However, for the majority of us, leaving civilization to go walk in the woods for an extended period of time requires planning.

CHEAP THRILLS: PERSONAL FINANCE FOR THE LONG-DISTANCE HIKER

Signs posted along the AT state that the trail is "open to all who walk." While this is true and hiking the AT is a relatively inexpensive adventure, there are some monetary concerns to contemplate before embarking on your trip. Currently, the average budget for hiking the Appalachian Trail totals $2.00 to $2.50 (U.S.) per mile, which is roughly $4,000 to $5,000 for a thru-hike or $150 to $175 per week for a section hike (though shorter hikes tend to cost less per mile due to the lack of need for gear repairs, hotel stays, and other similar expenses). This budget accounts for food, campsite fees, postage, laundry, motels and hostels, shuttles, miscellaneous town resupply needs, and gear purchases or repairs. There are ways to hike the trail cheaply (quite a few people have been able to thru-hike for $3,000 or less) and ways to do it extravagantly, but this base budget is a good starting point for most long-distance hikers.

Hiker at lean-to

The cost of resupply and services in trail towns increases as one hikes from south to north. The south offers many inexpensive hostels, restaurants, and resupply opportunities. Affordable lodging providing electricity, showers, and other basic amenities is especially difficult to find in the section between New Jersey and Massachusetts. Adjust your budget according to the area in which you hike, anticipating higher costs in the mid-Atlantic and southern New England regions.

A $2.00 to $2.50 per mile base budget covers costs once you already own all of your gear. Gear can be a large initial expense, so budget accordingly if you're planning on upgrading your gear inventory or if you are starting from scratch. A hiker can spend anywhere from a few hundred to well over a thousand dollars for gear. You can save a lot of money by buying used and reconditioned gear or by making your own. Starting your hike with gear that you've tested and are comfortable with is a great way to avoid the expense of gear replacement later on. It's a good idea to keep a credit card on hand or extra money in your bank account in case you need to make a major gear purchase or replacement on the trail. Also, be sure to have access to gear receipts and manufacturers' customer service information to facilitate free exchanges and repairs for items under warranty.

If you have outstanding student loans, credit card balances, or other debt, it is wise to plan on saving enough money to pay these bills during your hike unless you're willing to damage your credit rating. Remember that no matter how appealing it is to take off into the woods and forget about off-trail obligations, you have to return to civilization at some point and it's good to have solid financial footing when you do. Depending on your debtors, you may be able to consolidate, defer, or lower payments for the duration of your hike. It's also good to factor in money you need to live on after getting off of the trail. Having a small savings to pay for a few months' worth of living expenses will ease your transition back into civilization. You may want to set up a quick budget on paper or in Microsoft Excel to get a picture of your total financial situation.

CASH, CHECK, OR CHARGE?

On the trail, cash is the universal way to pay. Keep in mind that, unlike some other types of travel, hiking takes you to very rural areas, some of which have limited technology or other resources required for non-cash payments. ATMs are becoming more common in rural Appalachia as the years go by, but there are still businesses that deal only in cash. It's a good idea to always have some spare emergency cash tucked away in case you find yourself in a "cash only" situation with the closest ATM miles away. Keeping emergency cash hidden away in your pack is also a good idea in case your wallet gets lost or stolen. Avoid carrying large bills (such as $50 or $100 denominations) since not every business is able to break them.

Most hikers carry an ATM card that can be used as a credit/debit card or a credit card with a low interest rate. Make the decision of what to carry based on your financial priorities. For example, you may want to obtain frequent flyer miles by using a credit card or you may want to avoid financing charges or interest rates by using a debit card. Keep in mind that most ATMs charge a fee for use, and some banks also charge their own secondary fee for an ATM transaction at a machine that does not belong to the bank's network. Regardless of what sort of card you opt to use, make sure that the card itself is up-to-date and won't expire while you're out on the trail. Having an expired card is as useful as having no card at all, and the logistics of mail and telephone access can complicate the process of updating your card on the trail.

Along with carrying a credit or debit card, you may want to bring a few personal checks. Personal checks are accepted in a surprisingly large number of locations, some of which refuse credit or debit cards. One may also come in handy if you need access to your bank routing and account numbers, which are found at the bottom of the check. If you need to mail a bill payment but don't have personal checks with you, there's the option of purchasing a money order from a bank, cash checking business, or post office (you may also wire money at the post office).

> Some types of credit cards (such as Visa) are more universally accepted than others (American Express or MasterCard). You should consider this when deciding which card to bring on your trip.

Traveler's checks are another option for paying your way on the AT. This type of check is safer to carry than cash and is more universally accepted than credit cards or personal checks. Traveler's checks may be obtained at a bank or currency exchange office. Carry checks in $20 denominations as opposed to $50 or $100, as the lower denomination is easier to change at most businesses. Traveler's checks come with receipts that you should leave at home with your support crew in case the checks are lost or stolen. If the checks are lost, you may use the receipts for reimbursement (be sure to have the contact information of the agency where you obtained the checks on file). Not all businesses accept traveler's checks, so carry spare cash or alternate means to pay. Change for traveler's checks is given in regular bills and coins, creating a nice way to easily obtain cash while in town. Due to their built-in security, traveler's checks are a safe way to receive funds on the trail via mail drops.

DEALING WITH DEBT WHILE ON THE TRAIL

Most of us have debt, whether it is from student loans, mortgages, car payments, or credit cards. Ideally, this debt should be cleared before beginning your long hike, but this is not always a realistic goal. Make the effort to pay off as much debt as possible before hiking and develop a strategy for dealing with the remaining balance. While it's difficult to take care of debt when you have no steady income for months on end, there are ways to effectively deal with it without damaging your credit.

Credit card companies make money off of you as long as your card carries any amount of debt. This is something that can work in your favor since these companies are flexible and sometimes willing to allow you to carry debt for a longer period of time in exchange for lowered monthly payments or interest rates. Another option to lessen the blow of monthly credit bills is to transfer your existing balance to a card with a 0 percent APR (just be careful to read the fine print on the card agreement to avoid being charged excessive transfer or financing fees).

Also consider the contracts you hold with various companies. These contracts represent a legal obligation to spend money on a company's services or products. If you violate a contract such as a cell phone service agreement, you are subject to fines and fees and, in a worst case scenario, it may create legal or credit problems for you. It is ideal to terminate or suspend cable, cell, auto insurance, or other contracts for things you won't utilize while on the trail.

While it may not always be possible to fully exit a contract, you can usually lower your payments by dropping services such as extra cellular minutes or additional insurance coverage. No matter what sort of alterations you make to your contracts, *always get a paper copy of the changes* in case a conflict arises, and remember to read the fine print and understand the terms and conditions before signing off on something.

Along with contracts for services and products, you may hold loans for school, housing, or an automobile. Responsibly handling these loans strongly impacts your credit rating, so it's important to pay loans while on the trail, if possible. Some forms of loans, such as certain student loans, are flexible and fairly easy to defer (deferment is a way to postpone paying a loan during a period of economic hardship). Check with the financial organization responsible for distributing your loan to get details on lowering payments, deferment, and other options. Keep in mind that hiking the AT is a voluntary act of entering a state of financial hardship and many companies may still hold you responsible for loan repayment while you hike.

These words of advice may seem overly cautious, but you need to be careful when setting up your finances before your hike—a lot of damage can occur in even a few months' time. Attempting to resolve financial problems while on the trail is frustrating and can take away from the enjoyment of your hike. Take a trip to your local library and check out the most recently published books on personal finance; there are many user-friendly options available. Not only can this help you to save and manage your finances for your hike, it might even start a lifetime of responsible money management (allowing you to save for future hiking trips, of course).

To manage your remaining financial responsibilities while you hike, you should, ideally, have a person at home such as a parent, friend, or spouse who is willing to collect your bills and mail your payments in a timely manner. Contact companies to which you owe money well in advance of hiking, and figure out what your payment schedule will be for the duration of your hike. You can then write out personal checks or money orders according to each payment and leave them in stamped, dated, and addressed envelopes for your support person to mail. You may also opt to pay your bills online, over the phone, or through direct withdrawal from your bank account. Using a phone to check balances or pay bills using a debit or credit card is a viable option since there are many areas where cell phone service, hostel or motel phones, or pay phones are accessible. Many companies offer an electronic payment option, for which you set up automated debiting from your checking account. Whenever altering your billing activity, make sure to set up changes a few billing cycles before you leave in case problems arise or you need to make changes to your payment method.

FRUGAL HIKING

Unfortunately, many hikers are forced off the trail due to financial reasons, so you need to responsibly manage your budget while on the trail. It's easy to keep track of your finances through eight-hundred numbers and customer service web sites that most banks now provide. Check your account balances when in town and have a paper copy of your statements mailed to someone at home in case a balance dispute arises. Be prepared for unforeseeable expenses, such as major gear failure or medical bills, and have a credit card or additional sum of cash in your savings account designated for use only in emergencies (remember: buying beer and pizza is not an emergency expense!). When budgeting, plan for the maximum amount of time your hike may take. While you'll probably finish before that time, it's good to have a small cushion in case you decide to slow down or take an extended break partway through your trip.

When I decided to undertake a multi-month hike, I created a spreadsheet to help figure out my on-trail finances. Based on my budget, I calculated that I "earned" $2 per mile hiked, which meant that I could allot myself a $120 budget in town for resupply and other costs if I walked sixty miles to get there. It was a good system for me, enabling me to keep tabs on my expenses and producing motivation to walk a bit farther between towns instead of stopping every two days to resupply.

My financial Achilles' heel was spending money at places like Paddler's Pub in Hot Springs, North Carolina, where the food bill was on par with a big city grill (though well worth it). When I came off the trail into towns, I was so hungry for hot, greasy food that I'd happily pay $15 for a hamburger. In fact, I'd eat the burger, consider it a good deal, and pay the extra $5 for a side of fries. When it came to exercising financial self-control over my appetite, all bets were off.

To save money while on the trail, avoid taking too many zero days (days with zero mileage) in town. Remember, it's pretty difficult to spend cash when away from restaurants and the other temptations of civilization. That said, hiking the AT is a great way to experience small town America, so don't deny yourself the pleasures of sampling regional cuisine, taking in a festival, or sleeping in a soft bed from time to time. You don't want to kick yourself for skipping through towns like Hot Springs or Damascus in the name of saving money.

For times when you only want to go into town for a quick resupply, camp as close to town as possible so you can be in and out in a short amount of time. Sleeping on the trail rather than in a hotel is a

> Thru-hiker Weathercarrot provides a useful article on whiteblaze.net entitled "Ideas for an Inexpensive Thru-hike" (www.whiteblaze.net). His article is geared toward helping hikers with little or no thru-hiking experience and tight budgets. He emphasizes money-saving resupply strategies for specific areas on the AT and gives a good overview on where the most money is spent on a long-distance hike.

great way to enjoy town while saving money. You should also consider inexpensive alternatives to hotels and motels. There are many hiker-friendly hostels up and down the trail, and a few towns even allow hikers to camp in their parks for free.

SPONSORSHIPS

Long-distance hiking isn't a glamorous sport. It's not the sort of activity people watch on television or pay a lot of money to see in a stadium. For that reason, it's somewhat difficult to find companies who are willing to sponsor your hike. If you are a hiker with professional affiliations to an outdoors school or gear company, or have completed a long hike on another trail, your chances are much better at getting sponsored. Major outfitters such as REI, GoLite, and Sierra Designs occasionally throw cash at outdoor athletes, so it's worth contacting them if you feel that sponsorship could benefit both your hike and the company's image. You may want to approach businesses by requesting products rather than cash. Be creative. Some hikers have managed to score boxes of macaroni and cheese, energy bars, and cameras by contacting companies.

WHEN HIKING IS YOUR ONLY JOB

Though hiking the AT is a lot of work, it's a break from forty-hour-per-week drudgery. Undertaking a long-distance hike says a lot of great things about an individual. It shows that you're tenacious and motivated, which are positive qualities in any employee. Unfortunately, hiking long trails only looks good on your résumé if you live in certain European countries, and the American workplace doesn't always look favorably on those who choose to play in the woods for months on end.

Depending on the business or organization for which you work, leaving for an extended period of time to hike can really throw a wrench into your professional life. Some jobs are easily replaced, while others aren't due to a tight job market or a high level of training and specialization. Some organizations may offer a leave of absence, essentially a very long vacation, usually without pay. Others may only be willing to hire you back at the end of your hike if the same or similar position is still available.

When leaving your job to hike, you may want to pitch the hike as a form of public relations for the company by providing advertising or fund raising, buying yourself a little insurance for getting rehired once your hike is complete. Discuss your options with management or human resources to see what possibilities are available to you. And remember, while a long hike is a once-in-a-lifetime experience, you can always get another job.

PAPERWORK

A large part of being financially responsible is good record keeping. Having your paperwork in order when you hit the trail makes life a lot easier for you and whoever is helping out with logistics while you're gone. Prior to my hike, I created a document with all of my records; this included information about my bills, outstanding accounts and debt, medications and prescriptions, contact information for friends, relatives, and my trail journal transcriber, and manufacturer contacts for my major gear items. I kept a Xeroxed copy of this list in my pack and in my bounce box so I could have ready access to it.

Hang onto statements for utility, credit card, bank, and other outstanding accounts as proof of your pre-hike account status. These come in handy in case there's a billing or balance issue down the road. Leave a copy of all of these documents with a trustworthy person. Also, as mentioned earlier, have a full record of your gear receipts, warranties,

There are three major credit reporting agencies that govern credit ratings. These are Equifax Credit Information Services, Inc., 888-766-0008, www.equifax.com; Experian 888-397-3742, www.experian.com; and Trans Union 800-680-7289, www.transunion.com. If you have your credit or debit cards lost or stolen, make sure to contact these agencies as well as the financial institution from which you obtained the card. File a police report if a card is stolen to help prove the legitimacy of your claim.

and customer service numbers in a drop box or with a support person in case you need to upgrade, replace, or have repairs done.

Carry an up-to-date, widely accepted form of photo ID (you'll need it for a variety of situations from buying beer to picking up mail at the post office to cashing traveler's checks). Make copies of the fronts and backs of all of the cards (ID, credit, health insurance, etc.) that you plan on carrying with you. That way, if the cards are lost or stolen, you have all of your account information (including the eight-hundred numbers printed on the backs of the cards) and can easily report the missing cards. Bear in mind that a social security card is better left at home where it can't be damaged or lost.

THE MOUNTAINS ARE NO PLACE TO HIDE FROM THE IRS

Hikers who start in early spring should prepare taxes well in advance of their trip. Along with getting the task out of the way, a nice refund may help to fund your trip. Rather than waiting for local agencies to distribute tax forms, you may obtain them online at www.irs.gov and at state and local tax department web sites. Employers send out your tax information by January 31, so expect to be able to complete your forms and mail them by mid-February to late February. If possible, have your refund automatically deposited into your checking account so that you won't have to worry about a delayed or missing check. If you plan on an early start date and cannot complete your taxes in time, look into filing for an extension with the IRS. This automatically gives you six months (conveniently the average amount of time it takes for a thru-hike) to complete your taxes. Check with your state and local taxation departments and the IRS for details on filing forms, eligibility, and other details.

KEEPING YOUR MAIL SAFE

In some areas of the country, receiving mail presents itself as a security risk. Identity theft is on the rise and it's important to protect yourself against it while on the trail. Forward all of your mail to the address of someone you trust who can set it aside for you while you're on your hike, or request that businesses and individuals correspond through e-mail. Many companies are more than happy to switch to electronic correspondence and billing, since this saves them postage costs. Some financial institutions allow you to set up automated alarms to notify you when there are large transactions and other suspicious activity occurring with your account. These alerts can be sent to your e-mail inbox for you to periodically check while in town.

> Many of us receive preapproved credit offers through the mail. It takes very little information to set up a credit account in someone's name, and these mailings can pose a security risk. You can stop these sorts of mailings by opting out of being on the preapproved credit direct mailing lists. To opt out for a five-year period, contact the three major credit agencies at 888-567-8688 (all three major credit reporting agencies use the same number for opting out).

If you don't have an address where mail can be forwarded during your hike, you may choose to have the post office hold your mail. They will hold mail for up to thirty days, after which time special arrangements are required. A third party may collect your mail for you. Contact your local post office or go to www.usps.com for further ideas on how to deal with mail while you're away from home.

THE MOST DIFFICULT THINGS TO LEAVE

One of the great things about the AT is that it's a rent- and mortgage-free place to live. Located on public lands, most shelters and campsites on the trail cost nothing. But there's the issue of what to do about your current housing situation if you're planning a hike for multiple months. If you own, you may want to rent or sell. If you rent, subletting or breaking the lease is an option. For leased property, check with your landlord and review your lease to see what your rights are. Typically, the earlier you notify a landlord, the easier it is to make arrangements to end a lease or sublet.

And then there's all of your stuff to worry about. Most people own a lot of things: clothes, music, toys, boxes upon boxes of stuff. For many hikers, reducing personal possessions is an integral part of the trip-planning process. For others with large collections of irreplaceable things, storage is the only answer and commercial storage can be a reasonable solution. Storage is priced according to volume, so it's still a good idea to pick through your possessions and decide what you can and can't live without. The best-case scenario is finding a kind friend or relative with ample dry and cool storage space. Trimming down your possessions can be an arduous process. Start well before your hike, giving yourself as much time as possible to sort through what you do and don't want to keep. Donate useful items to charitable organizations, have a yard sale, or sell them on eBay rather than send them to the curb.

Along with leaving your space and your things, you may need to leave your best friend: your pet. Some hikers take their dog on the trail (and, in a couple of instances, cats and goats), and it's an option worth considering. For those four-footed friends who can't make the hike, find a safe place for them to stay, such as a friend's house or a commercial kennel. Make your choice wisely; you want to know that your pet will be in good hands while you hike.

STAYING IN TOUCH

Leaving loved ones is hard enough in circumstances where you have access to telephones and e-mail, but the lack of communication opportunities on the AT makes the separation even more difficult. Stay in touch while on the trail by sending postcards, e-mails, keeping an online journal, and making phone calls (hikers who don't have cell phones generally carry calling cards). Public libraries are an excellent resource for hikers who want to stay in touch. Most libraries offer free internet for patrons and may even provide air conditioning and comfy chairs to relax in. Some hikers use PocketMail devices to overcome the difficulty of keeping up with e-mail correspondence while having only limited internet time at libraries or internet cafes.

You may make plans to hike with friends and family during your trip. While this seems like an ideal solution to getting in both miles and bonding time, it can be frustrating since you will be in peak condition and ready to do big miles

An online journal is a great way to share your hike with friends and family. Trailjournals.com (www.trailjournals.com), the most popular hiking journal site, offers a blog format for hikers to upload journal entries and pictures. Journals may be regularly updated while underway by using public access computers or a PocketMail device. If you wish to write out entries in longhand, someone at home or a volunteer from trailjournals.com can transcribe and post your entries.

while your guest on the trail may struggle with the mere concept of sleeping out-of-doors and not taking showers on a regular basis. As long as you take it slow and are open about the realities of hiking with your AT guest, this can be a very rewarding venture and can give your loved ones insight into your trail lifestyle.

HEALTH INSURANCE FOR HIKERS

Your health is a major concern while out on the trail and, ideally, every hiker should carry health insurance. For the fortunate, health insurance may be freely or inexpensively secured through spouses or parents. But many hikers are forced to make the decision of whether or not they want to risk going without during their long-distance hike. Health care costs are obscenely pricey (the average emergency room visit costs about $500), and opting out of a health care plan can have long-term financial repercussions. Some companies offer special packages for travelers that provide reasonably priced coverage for major accidents and illnesses. Insurance options are too numerous to mention individually but, for quotes and insurance information, check out non-profit web pages such as HealthInsurance.org (www.healthinsurance.org).

COBRA (Consolidated Omnibus Budget Reconciliation Act) entitles employees to continue their group health care for a time after leaving their place of employment. While COBRA is generally more expensive than employer-provided benefits, it's typically less expensive than obtaining insurance through an independent provider. Check out www.cobrainsurance.com for details on COBRA coverage.

For hikers without health insurance, there are options to receive free or inexpensive health care. Some towns provide walk-in or urgent care clinics that cater to the low-income or unemployed members of the community. Some of these clinics operate on a sliding fee scale and bill a person according to his or her income. *Charity care* is an umbrella term describing the free or reduced fee rates at nonprofit hospitals given to patients who are in a low-income bracket and have no insurance. Charity care covers those who earn too much to qualify for Medicaid (and are too young for Medicare) but don't have the financial resources to deal with the costs of health care. Charity care is honored on criteria such as a person's residency and liquid assets as well as the operational decisions of the institution that is providing the care.

Emergency Medicaid (www.cms.hhs.gov/home/medicaid.asp) is provided by the U.S. Department of Health and Human Services. Medicaid is a program that pays for medical costs but may require patient co-payment in some situations. The service is based on a number of factors such as income, savings, physical condition, and age. Many states provide state-specific programs. Emergency Medicaid is available to certain people who have an acute, non-preexisting condition that requires treatment. Though this service is not applicable to all, it is worth investigating as a means of dealing with potential medical costs an uninsured hiker may encounter on the trail.

Regardless of your insurance status, you have rights as a patient. If you have a medical emergency, you are entitled to treatment without having your ability to pay questioned prior to that treatment. You should never have to fight for treatment at a hospital if it is an emergency situation (if you are in severe pain or your life is in danger). Keep in mind that these rights do not apply unless the situation is an emergency. A hiker with an ingrown toenail is *not* entitled to the same rights as a hiker with severe internal injuries, for example. Though you can be admitted to a hospital in an emergency situation without proof of ability to pay, you are still held accountable for any costs incurred during your stay.

CHARITY HIKES

Hiking the AT can be a great philanthropic act, helping to raise thousands of dollars for a worthwhile charity, or it can serve as an educational and inspirational gift to the community. While hiking for charity presents obligations such as deadlines, public speaking engagements, blogging, and other outreach responsibilities, it can add a very satisfying dimension to your hiking experience. Charity work, education, and outreach activities can be conducted with the help of a local organization such as a church, synagogue, school, or library. There are a number of organizations that facilitate hiking for charity activities. Among them is www.charityhikers.org.

A long hike involves more than throwing on a pack and stepping out into the woods. The more planning you do, the more enjoyable your trip will be. With proper planning and a little bit of luck, everyday tragedies such as bounced checks or denied access to medical care won't factor into your trip. Making sure all of your loose ends are tied up before you leave home ensures that your mind will be free of worries, enabling you to make the most of your hike.

4
Physical Conditioning

Of all exercises walking is the best.

—Thomas Jefferson

The popular belief is that nothing other than hiking long distances can prepare one for a long-distance hike. Some successful long-distance hikers engage in no physical training before a hiking trip. At the other end of extremes, there are hikers who undergo major lifestyle changes, such as losing weight, quitting smoking, or beginning a workout program to get their bodies into better shape. While you don't necessarily need to train for the AT, being in shape can make your hike much more enjoyable.

Many feel that it takes about a month of hiking to get into peak backpacking shape. Sadly, that equals about one-fifth to one-sixth of an entire thru-hike—not thru-hiking time that most would want to spend in physical discomfort. It's important to get on the trail already in decent shape in order to better enjoy your hiking experience (especially for those of us who are older or really out of shape). Being in good shape when you start your hike makes the trip more enjoyable, supports easier mileage, and helps to keep injuries at bay.

In preparation for my multi-month hike, I spent an hour in the gym six days a week doing core-strength training and cardio workouts. In addition to that, I commuted six miles to work on foot almost every day. During many weekends, I would go on overnight hikes to get my body accustomed to carrying gear while traveling over rough terrain. Once on the trail, I reaped the benefits of my hard work and enjoyed the difficult early miles much more than some of my less-prepared counterparts.

Also keep in mind that unless you already have a routine of walking high daily mileage while carrying weight, your body needs an adjustment period to become used to the demands of shouldering a thirty-plus-pound pack while trudging up and down hundreds or even thousands of feet of elevation every day. To avoid injuries, take it easy during the early stages of training and initial hiking trips. Get a lot of sleep, eat well, take frequent breaks, stay hydrated, and pay close attention to your body. Even if you think you are in great shape, impose a relaxed itinerary for the first few weeks of your trip, forcing yourself to slow down if you're the type of person prone to doing big workouts until you drop (one 2006 thru-hiker imposed a limit of about five miles a day on herself out of a fear of overdoing it the first few weeks out). For the average hiker, ten miles or less a day over easy to moderate terrain for the first week is a reasonable pace with which to begin.

BECOMING A LEAN, MEAN TRAIL MACHINE

Specific training is when you train by doing the same activity for which you plan to utilize your conditioning (such as carrying a loaded pack over mountains in order to—well, better carry a loaded pack over mountains). This is the most ideal form of training but not the most realistic since most of us don't have the option of doing eight to ten hours a day of backpacking over rugged terrain to prepare for a hiking trip. There are decent substitutes, however, such as stair climbing, trail running, and walking a few hours a day with your pack on, which will give your body an edge when starting the trail.

Hiker on Charlie's Bunion, Tennessee

Take multi-day practice trips before your long-distance hike to acclimate your body to the activity. Along with helping you get in shape, this is a great way to get used to your gear and resolve equipment issues before you begin a long hike. On these preliminary hikes, pay close attention to what your body is saying. For example, if you tend to huff and puff on the uphill terrain, you may need to increase your cardio regimen at home.

nformation for marathon walkers is available at www.marathonwalking.com/training, and the guide is also useful for long-distance hikers in training. A number of training routines are provided, catering to everyone from beginner to advanced walkers.

Join a local hiking club and accompany other hikers on outings. As well as providing motivation, these clubs are a good source of general backpacking experience and information. If possible, you may want to complete a thru-hike of a shorter trail prior to hiking the AT (this is a particularly good idea for aspiring AT thru-hikers). There are many trails in the two-hundred-mile range that would serve as good training hikes for prospective AT hikers. The American Long-distance Hiking Association-West's web site provides a great listing of long-distance trails in the United States (www.aldhawest.org/trails/ot_def.asp).

Where you live can have a large impact on your training routine. If you live in an urban area devoid of hills, you may want to join a gym in order to use weight machines to mimic the strain of hill climbing. If you live in a rural area with hiking trails, utilize them. Your training routine should have several goals: you need to get into decent cardiovascular shape in order to be able to do steep uphill climbs, you need to have decent muscle strength—particularly in your legs and abdominals (the abdominals help to support much of the weight carried on a person's back), and you need to develop the stamina to enable you to hike long hours every day. The last one is difficult to achieve with an everyday gym routine, but making periodic multi-day trips to local trails can help build up your endurance.

AM I FIT YET?

Give yourself at least three months to train for a long-distance hike. You need to have time to deal with any latent quirks in your body or training-induced injuries and soreness. You can't rush the rate at which your body becomes fit. If you get tired during your workout, stop to rest; tiredness leads to clumsiness and even injuries. It's important to take days off while you train, just as it's important to take zero-mileage days while on the trail. A periodic day of rest allows the body to heal and prevents burn-out and boredom.

Some soreness is inherent with any training program. However, there is a difference between good and bad pain. Sore muscles are normal and may be treated with heat, ice, rest, and NSAIDs (over-the-counter, nonsteroidal, anti-inflammatory medications such as ibuprofen). Acute and chronic injuries require attention, however. Due to the nature of many injuries, especially soft tissue ones, a lack of muscular support plays a big role in their occurrence. A body that is out of shape and being pushed is more likely to break down than a well-conditioned body. For this reason, someone engaging in a new exercise regimen is at significantly more risk for injuries. Pay attention to your body and, when in doubt, seek medical help.

> If you are prone to joint problems, you may want to take an over-the-counter supplement such as glucosamine or chondroitin to speed soft tissue repair. Discuss this possibility with your health care practitioner.

One of the most important aspects of your fitness routine is your cardio workout. Elevation gains and carrying additional weight are demanding on the cardiovascular system (this includes the heart, lungs, arteries, and veins). If you're in poor cardiovascular health, you'll be huffing and puffing on the climbs (that said, you will probably be huffing and puffing even if you're fit). Your *target heart rate* is your optimal "zone" for training and occurs when your body is doing the maximum amount of work without being too stressed. You can mathematically calculate your target heart rate using your age and other data, but there is also a simple commonsense way to determine it. When working at your optimal heart rate, you should be breathing more heavily than normal but should still be able to hold a conversation. You should be perspiring and able to feel your lungs and heart working harder than usual. If you'd like to more accurately calculate your target heart rate, the Mayo Clinic provides an online heart rate calculator (www.mayoclinic.com/health/target-heart-rate/SM00083). It requires entering your vital information and doing minimal math to discover your ideal heart rate zone.

Keep in mind that this heart rate number is just a ballpark figure and if you feel dizzy or faint, stop exercising immediately. If working out is exhausting you or burning you out, you're working too hard. Give yourself time to work up to your desired level of fitness. It's always advisable to consult with your doctor before you begin a workout program. A doctor is able to help you develop an approach to exercise that is right for you and give you advice on factors such as nutrition and injury prevention.

For those worried about having enough hours in the day to fit in a workout, there are small exercises that can be done throughout the day whenever you have a spare moment. Ankle rotations may be done at your desk by rotating your ankles slowly in 360-degree circles, improving strength and flexibility. Calf raises may be done by raising yourself onto the balls of your feet repeatedly. This exercise helps to strengthen the tops of the feet and calves, very important target areas for hikers. Since your abdominal muscles play such an integral role in providing back support when you carry your pack, do sit-ups and crunches to increase your carrying power, or lie on your stomach or back and do leg lifts. Exercises such as squats, calf raises, lunges, and leg lifts help to build strength and ward off injuries. Knee, quad, hamstring, and calf exercises build supportive muscle and soft tissue to reinforce joints. Stretching is also a good habit to develop, and I recommend doing it while you're on the trail as well as at home. Flexibility, especially in the hamstrings, quadriceps, lower back, and calves, helps prevent many common injuries.

There are many good fitness books outlining the above exercises in detail. You may want to schedule a session with a personal trainer or check out exercise videos to get a better sense of how to properly exercise. Technique is incredibly important since exercise can do more harm than good if done incorrectly (for example, you can do a lot of damage to your knees when doing lunges if you extend them beyond your toes). It is especially important to pay attention to form if you've never worked out before or if it's been a while since you've been in the gym.

Take an intuitive approach to your training, allowing your body to dictate the routine. Three exercise sessions a week is a good minimum. It is better to exercise in small doses on a daily basis than to do a few hard workouts during the course of a week. Whatever frequency you have with your exercise schedule, be sure to be consistent (but not rigid) with it.

Strange things happen to hikers' bodies after walking thousands of miles, and it's hard to imitate the effects of long-distance hiking in a gym environment. Many hikers complain that they lose upper-body strength and mass during their hike. Though trekking poles tend to offset this lopsided look, expect to have an imbalanced amount of muscle mass at the end of your hike. Another physical side effect of long-distance hiking is the changing ratio of body fat to muscle mass. Hikers tend to become very lean and muscled as they burn through the miles. Most weight loss on the trail occurs in the first thirty days. You should try to be at a healthy weight when you start your hike. While overweight hikers may have more bone density to help carry the excess weight of a pack, being overweight is still ultimately unhealthy.

On the trail, men tend to lose weight by losing fat and women tend to gain weight from building muscle mass. As one hiker stated, at the end of the hike the men look like they're victims of famine and the women look like supermodels. This has a lot to do with how the male and female bodies distribute, store, and use weight. I'm sure you've heard that female marathon runners are less likely to "hit the wall" than male ones. Male hikers generally run into more serious calorie deficit situations. This phenomenon, of course, varies greatly person to person.

Try to be healthy about your conditioning regimen. Avoid overtraining as this can be both mentally and physically damaging. Many injuries result from athletes pushing too hard, too fast and going beyond their physical limits. Don't play games of self-inflicted guilt if you miss a workout. On the other hand, don't make excuses for sloth. Try to do as much hiking with your pack as possible, but mix it up with trips to the gym or the pool, or with other physical activities to get your body in shape. Even a moderate exercise schedule of three sessions a week for an hour each is better than nothing at all, and you will reap the rewards once you set foot on the trail.

5
Getting Your Gear On

Good and beautiful gear is a kind of drug.
—Kevin Patterson, *The Water in Between*

Roughly thirty miles from its southern terminus, the AT runs past Mountain Crossings outfitters at Walasi-Yi (www.mountaincrossings.com), and a path winds through the store, leading the way to an exhausted credit card. At this point in northbounders' thru-hikes, not everyone feels physically great or has developed a comfortable relationship with their gear. During the early stages of a long hike, it is easy to be tempted by the false illusion that gear makes the hiker.

Although there is something very reassuring about being surrounded by hundreds of dollars worth of the latest and greatest gear, the appeal of the long-distance hiking lifestyle lies in its minimalism. Everything you need to live for weeks or months is carried on your back (not including food, water, fuel, and other consumable items). Some hikers take this minimalism to an extreme, carrying nothing but the most essential items, while others carry luxury items such as musical instruments, books, and electronic gadgets.

When preparing your gear, consider your need to be physically and psychologically comfortable, and don't skimp on vital items such as a sleeping bag and pack. While some may choose to eat only cold food and sleep under a tarp, you may want to consider the luxury of the privacy and warm space of a tent or the pleasure of making a cup of hot tea on your stove at the end of a long, cold day. There are also items of gear, such as a tent, that many hikers believe are a necessity for personal safety. This is largely a matter of personal preference and hiking style, however, and the ultralight movement demonstrates that great distances can be covered safely with minimal equipment.

It's not uncommon for nascent long-distance hikers to shed five or more pounds worth of miscellaneous belongings during their first week out. Hikers who hike light are less prone to certain stress-related injuries and may have the ability to hike faster, but if speed is not your style and you feel up to the task of carrying the additional weight, extra items may be well worth the effort. I have heard of hikers carrying everything from mandolins to Halloween masks between Georgia and Maine, and sometimes it's the small things that can make or break a trip. It's important to ascertain what you want out of your trail experience when considering what to bring with you.

GOOD HIKERS ARE SMART SHOPPERS

Whether you are starting your collection from scratch or merely upgrading, selecting gear can be a daunting task. Every year, numerous magazines and web sites dedicate time and space to reviewing the latest gear. Though these reviews should not be all that you consider in your decisions, they can be helpful.

HELPFUL RESOURCES FOR SELECTING GEAR

- Backpacker.com's Gear Guide (called "Gearfinder," www.gearfinder.com) lists the major equipment categories and allows you to navigate through different gear selections based on your specific hiking needs.
- Many AT hikers provide a link to their personal gear inventory and reviews on trailjournals.com (www.trailjournals.com).
- BackPackGearTest.org provides useful equipment reviews from experienced hikers. These links lists weight, durability, and other information about various brands and models of backpacking equipment.
- GORP.com (http://gorp.away.com/gorp/gear/main.htm) provides well-organized links to *Outside Magazine*'s annual gear guides.
- The Outdoor Gear Guide provided by Trailspace (www.trailspace.com) gives gear lists accompanied by reader reviews, price information, and dealers.
- *Outside Magazine*'s Annual Buyer's Guide in print provides a definitive list of the latest and greatest gear.

It's essential to do your research before buying gear. Talk to hikers in person or online who have already completed long-distance hikes, and listen to their advice. When I went on one of my major gear-buying expeditions at the local outfitters, I took no less than five thru-hiker friends with me for consultation. The soundest advice for purchasing gear is to listen to experience. If something works well for many other hikers, chances are it's a good piece of equipment and may meet your needs as well. Use common sense when you shop. Look for signs of quality such as well-working zippers, flat and straight seam stitching, and overall good design. It's important to be an informed consumer and to take the advice of the sales staff with a grain of salt.

> **A**great way to test gear without making a major financial commitment is to borrow or rent gear. There are major outfitters across the United States that provide equipment rental services. Two of these are REI (www.rei.com/stores/rentals.html) and Lower Gear (www.lowergear.com).

Buy your gear at a reputable outfitter that provides exchanges or replacements when needed, proper fitting, and advice. Typically, manufacturers are more than glad to replace gear and provide support for their customers to avoid having the business's reputation damaged through bad word of mouth. At festivals such as Trail Days in Damascus, Virginia, manufacturers provide booths catering to hikers' gear needs. Festivals serve as a great opportunity to seek upgrades and repairs. Though you shouldn't always expect it to be the case, long-distance hikers (especially thru-hikers) sometimes get better customer service than other users of outdoor equipment. This is because a happy long-distance hiker can provide hundreds of miles of good public relations for a company.

Hiking gear is expensive because it's generally carefully constructed and caters to a niche market. The high cost of gear includes laboratory and field testing as well as the use of pricey exotic fabrics. You can save some cash by buying last year's model when it goes on sale. This usually adds up to a significant savings at the cost of a difference in product color, zipper placement, or a few ounces of weight. EBay (www.ebay.com) and used gear sites such as GearTrade (www.geartrade.com) are good places to save money on gear purchases. Be aware that when you buy from these sites, you typically forfeit the manufacturer and outfitter warranties and may acquire gear with wear and defects.

After purchasing your equipment, become familiar with it. Take it on shorter hikes before you commit to using it on a long-distance trip. Sleep in your bag on a cold night, pitch your tent in the dark, and cook a few meals on your stove. After hiking your first hundred miles, take the time to sort through your pack. Discard any gear you haven't used and don't foresee using in the near future.

THE PACK

Your pack is the most complex (and potentially the most expensive) piece of equipment you'll carry on the trail. It's the piece of gear that has constant contact with your body and gets the most wear and tear. A poorly chosen pack can cause soreness, blisters, and chafing, while a high-quality pack can make a large difference in load-carrying and overall comfort.

Essentially, a pack is a rugged bag supported by a complex suspension system. The suspension system is composed of all of the parts of the pack that play a role in transferring the weight of the pack to your body. These include the hip belt, shoulder straps, sternum strap, load-lifter straps, and compression straps. Most packs provide structural support in the form of stays or a framesheet. Stays are stiff pieces of material made from aluminum, carbon fiber, Evazote, polycarbonate, thermoplastic, Durin, titanium, polyethylene, or other materials that help to transfer the weight of the pack's load. Stays can come in a variety of configurations, such as an X-shape that criss-crosses across the back or a V-shape. Some packs feature removable stays, which allow you to cut down on weight when you're carrying a lighter load. A framesheet, a lightweight sheet of plastic that acts in place of stays, is newer to pack design. The stays or framesheet run parallel and close to the back along the entire length of the pack.

One of the most important parts of the suspension system is the hip belt. A well-fitted hip belt provides load stability and takes up to 90 percent of your pack's load weight, transferring weight to your center of gravity. A hip belt should have good padding and be stabilized with stitching or webbing so that it doesn't twist during use. It should fit correctly, offering the fullest flared area of padding where it rests on the hipbone. Unless you're going ultralight and plan on carrying a total weight of less than twenty pounds, your pack should have a hip belt feature.

Though they support some of the pack's weight, shoulder straps primarily act to stabilize the pack and help it to move with the body. They should be well padded and fit so that the strap begins its flared shape level with your armpit. The sternum strap runs across the chest and also helps to stabilize the pack and keep the shoulder straps from shifting. Diagonal compression straps and load-lifter straps help to steady the load and hold it closer to the body, keeping the contents of your pack in check. Side stabilizers and side tension straps keep the pack from swaying and are necessary in packs where the hip belt is attached directly to the lumbar pad.

Along with the basic features of the suspension system, packs come equipped with a variety of bells and whistles to enhance performance. The lid, or "brain unit," a larger zippered pocket attached to the top of the pack, is a standard feature on many traditional packs. The lid provides a great place to store smaller pieces of gear where they are easy to access. Lids are generally "floating," meaning that they can be adjusted to fit the height of the pack, no matter what volume load you carry. Some lids are versatile and can be converted to a hip pack for day hiking or used as a carry-on while traveling to and from the trail. Certain packs have lids with padding to allow them to be converted into hip packs, but, while this may be a useful feature for some backpackers, chances are you won't have much need for it during a long hike and it merely adds additional weight. Some packs include a side zipper for easy access. These zippers are convenient but add weight and another element of the pack that may fail during your hike. Packs intended for hiking in alpine regions include ice axe loops. These are loops of webbing on the bottom of the pack used to hang ice axes. While ice axes aren't typically needed on the AT, these loops provide convenient tie-down points for gear. Keep in mind that the more features a pack has, the more it is likely to weigh, and every additional zipper and piece of material is another piece of the pack that could fail.

> Over the past few years, I've used a number of lightweight internal frame packs featuring framesheets in lieu of stays. My pack of choice is the Granite Gear Nimbus Ozone. Though this pack's plush suspension was overkill for my lightweight needs (it's able to carry up to forty pounds and I typically carried twenty-five to thirty pounds with full resupply and water), it weighs in at a scant three pounds and has an amazing fit. I also enjoyed the stripped-down simplicity of the pack's design and supplemented its lack of a lid with a Marmot Dry Rib (a small zippered bag that attaches to the hip belt) where I stored my headlamp, snacks, and other odds and ends.

Choosing a Pack

The pack is the foundation piece of all of your gear. It's the piece of gear that has the longest amount of contact with your body throughout the day and is the item most praised or complained about by hikers. Decide what sort of hiking style suits you most and select a pack that best matches it. When purchasing a pack, you may want to assemble all of your other gear and take it to the outfitter with you to test what size and design works best. If you are planning on purchasing your pack before your other gear, you can allow the pack to dictate the rest of your gear inventory. It's a good idea to get your pack from a reputable company, since this is a piece of gear with which you do not want to experiment. Make sure the pack has a good warranty (preferably lifetime) and the manufacturer has a reputation for providing good customer service.

The two types of basic pack designs feature either an internal or external frame. Though still used by some backpackers, external frame packs were popular from the 1950s to the 1970s. This style of pack has a framework that is external to the bag, suspending it above the back. An internal frame pack, on the other hand, has a support system built inside the pack that helps to carry the load close to the body. The external frame design enables one to carry heavier loads more comfortably and, unlike the internal frame, offers ample ventilation. With internally placed stays and framesheets, internal frame packs move with a hiker's body, an important feature over rugged terrain such as that found on the AT. Though the internal frame design does have minor drawbacks such as its lack of ventilation, it's currently the predominant design on the market and sports the latest innovations and the greatest variety of design options.

Your pack should be no more than 10 percent of your total gear weight. For example, use a pack weighing in at two and one-half pounds if you carry a twenty-five-pound load. Your fully loaded pack should weigh no more than a third of your total body weight. It's silly to carry more pack weight than you need to because, unlike other items, pack weight can never be significantly reduced. Most packs are in the two- to six-pound weight range. Arc'Teryx's Bora 80 for men, a six-pound-twelve-ounce pack (that's almost seven pounds *without* any gear in it) is at the heavy end of the spectrum, while Granite Gear's Vapor Trail (a favorite on the AT) weighs in at a mere two pounds.

A long-distance hiker may carry a pack with a capacity of anywhere from less than 2,000 to over 4,500 cubic inches. However, the

Packs specifically designed for women's bodies are available. A woman's pack is not merely a smaller version of a man's; it has a hip belt designed to fit the contour of a woman's hips and shoulder straps positioned to accommodate narrower shoulders. Gregory (www.gregorypacks.com), Marmot (formerly Dana Designs, www.danadesign.com), Osprey (www.ospreypacks.com), Arc'Teryx (www.arcteryx.com), and The North Face (www.thenorthface.com) are among the companies currently manufacturing women's packs. Larger outfitters such as REI and Eastern Mountain Sports have also developed their own lines of female-friendly designs.

norm is a pack in the range of 3,000 to 3,500 cubic inches, a number that seems to be decreasing over the years due to the increasingly smaller and lighter gear introduced to the market. Allow yourself just enough pack capacity for cold weather gear and resupply items. Having an expedition-sized pack with a large load-carrying capacity isn't necessary on the AT as there are many resupply points. AT hikers usually carry anywhere from twenty to forty pounds of gear and consumable items in their packs. Make sure your pack is designed to carry as much weight as you plan on carrying—no less and no more. If the pack is designed to carry small amounts of weight and you overload it, you risk stressing the pack's structure and your back. When it comes to pack weight, some hikers make do with less (lightweight and ultralight backpackers) and some with much more (generally macho men, masochists, and Sherpa-types).

When considering a pack, think about how you'll use the space and what sort of features you may need. You may want external pockets to organize and allow easy access to smaller pieces of equipment. Side pockets should be high and snug, made of mesh or sporting grommets to provide drainage. Packs on the market designed for alpinists don't provide the types of pockets AT hikers use (generally, pockets in alpine packs are low cut and loose). If you select a pack with pockets on the hip belt, make sure they are placed so they won't get in the way of arm movement or belt adjustment.

Hydration-compatible packs have become fairly standard. A hydration-compatible pack provides some sort of internal vapor barrier pocket that holds the water bladder, allowing the drink tube to run through an exit hole at the top of the pack. The hydration option is not for everyone and some hikers prefer to use bottles stored in side pockets so that they can keep tabs on how much water they consume. However you opt to carry your water, it's essential that you have easy access to it and don't have to stop and remove your pack each time you want to drink.

Your pack is one of your largest gear investments. Plan on spending anywhere from $100 to $300 or even more. When selecting a pack, put weight in it and walk around at the outfitter. A good outfitter will provide sand bags for you to use when test-driving packs. You may also bring your own gear to the outfitter to test out pack fit and volume. After you get your pack home, wear it while walking around the neighborhood to get a better sense of how it performs when you're in motion. Only take the pack out on the trail after you're fully confident in it so that it stays clean and is easier to return if it doesn't end up working out for you.

Fitting Your Pack

Typically, manufacturers offer multiple size options for a product. This size indicates the length of the back from the seventh cervical vertebra to the top of the iliac crest (from the base of the neck to the point on the back that rests on the same plane as the hipbones). A person's overall height does not necessarily dictate if she or he has a long or short back, so it's important to take a measurement of the back as a part of the fitting. Your measurement will fall into one of these frame-size categories: small (around 17½ inches and smaller), medium (around 18 to 19½ inches), and large (around 20 inches and up).

After determining your measurement, try on a pack and fine-tune it to your contours. Place the pack on with all of the straps loosened. Tighten the hip belt first, making sure it rests evenly over your hipbones. The webbing should be adjustable enough to allow for weight loss or gain and a variety of clothing layers. Make sure not to tighten the hip belt too much since over a period of time this can lead to problems, such as bruising on your hips or even kidney damage. If you have to tighten the belt excessively for the pack to be stable, it's a sign that the pack design is wrong for your body type. Lean slightly forward and tighten the shoulder straps next. For an internal frame pack, there should be no gaps in the contact between the shoulder straps and your body. Next, tighten the load-lifter straps until you've achieved an angle of forty to fifty degrees between their attachment point to the shoulder straps and the pack's body. If you choose to use it, attach the sternum strap so that it rests comfortably below your collarbone but doesn't inhibit your breathing. The part of the pack in contact with your back should have adequate padding and provide some sort of ventilation through mesh or a contoured gap around the spinal region. It's also important that enough padding rests over the shoulder blades to protect them, and that the hip belt and shoulder straps are well-padded. Finally, check that buckles and connections are placed where they won't rub or chafe. With weight in the pack, walk around the store for a while using the incline ramp, doing squats, and generally testing your comfort and range of motion.

Some hikers feel that it's important to bend the stays in your internal frame pack for maximum fit (some manufacturers recommend this as well), while others feel that stays naturally bend to the contour of your back after a day or so of use. If you do opt to have your stays bent, leave the task to an expert, such as an outfitter employee experienced with fitting packs. Some hip belts and shoulder straps may be adjusted with

Velcro under the pack's padding to optimally fit your shape. Usually these two components of the pack can be shortened or lengthened and can drastically alter the fit of the pack. When having your pack fitted at the outfitter, make sure the salesperson demonstrates all of the pack's features used to make adjustments. Some packs may require tools (often a screwdriver) for adjustment; if this is the case with yours, carry a multi-tool on the trail with you to make adjustments.

Packing Your Pack

Most packs are top-loading, meaning items can be stuffed into them from the opening at the top. There are also packs that have zippered back, bottom, or side openings, and some offer separate zippered compartments for accessing gear. How you use the space in your pack is critical to the pack's performance. Place the heaviest items slightly higher than your center of gravity and evenly distribute weight on each side of the pack to avoid stressing your back. Load everything in the pack before tightening any of the compression straps, and zip the side and bottom zippers before loading to reduce stress on them. To protect your back from discomfort (and also to protect your pack from additional wear or damage), don't carry sharp objects on the inside of your pack.

A standard pack offers a number of different zones, or spaces, for storing gear. If your pack provides a mesh pocket or bucket, use this area to stash wet items such as rain gear, pack towels, or a rain fly. Compression sacks, which squish contents such as clothing or sleeping bags down to a smaller size, are a great way to maximize space in your pack. Use external pockets or the lid for storing items to which you'll require frequent access, such as maps and snacks. It's a good idea to store rain gear at the top of your pack so that you don't have to rummage around for it in a storm, and store fuel in an external pocket or at the bottom of your pack to defray damage that may occur if it spills.

Putting on Your Pack

Putting on your pack may appear to be an intuitive act, but it takes some technique to avoid placing undue strain on your body. Before putting on your pack, make sure that all of the straps except for the load compression ones are loosened, and tighten them only once the pack is on your back. Lift the pack by its haul loop to your thigh (the haul loop is the handle strap at the top of the pack between the shoulder straps). You may also use large rocks or a picnic table as a place to rest your pack and back into it. As is the rule with all heavy lifting, lift the pack with your legs and not your back. While the pack is resting on your thigh, put your arm through the shoulder strap and hoist the pack onto your back. Once on your back, clasp the hip belt buckles, then tighten. Follow by leaning slightly forward and tightening the shoulder straps. Lastly, the sternum strap, load-lifter straps, and side tension straps

> While hiking, it's a good idea to periodically readjust all of the pack straps according to terrain and as a response to muscle fatigue. Though this seems like a time-consuming process, it can be done in a matter of seconds and becomes an automatic activity for many hikers. A pack feels more comfortable when it is fine-tuned throughout the day. While walking, experiment with adjustments on your pack to optimize comfort.

can be adjusted (and readjusted once under way). When you hike, try to reduce the amount of times you need to remove and put on your pack since this activity places uneven stress on your body.

Caring for Your Pack

Packs undergo more wear and tear than any other piece of equipment. Though ruggedly made, they require special care to ensure their longevity. Periodically inspect your pack for tears, unraveled seams, missing parts, cracked buckles, or damaged zippers. By doing this, you can catch potentially disastrous damage and have it repaired before it causes major headaches. Try to keep your pack as clean as possible. Shake off all loose debris and keep ice and mud out of zipper and buckle areas. Silicone can be used on some types of zippers to keep them functioning smoothly. Periodically use a dry brush (such as an old toothbrush) to remove dried mud, and wipe out the inside with a damp cloth or sponge. When necessary, wash your pack with warm water, using a mild soap such as Nikwax's Tech Wash. Never wash your pack in a washing machine. Instead, use a bathtub or outdoor garden hose to do the job. It may be a good idea to use an antibacterial soap such as Dow Scrubbing Bubbles on parts of the pack that have direct contact with your body (such as the hip belt, shoulder straps, and back padding). Apply soap to these areas, let it sit for ten minutes, then rinse well. If you have severe odor problems with your shoulder straps or other padded parts, liberally apply Febreze antimicrobial spray during stays in town. Never soak the entire pack in water for a prolonged period of time, since this may cause the waterproof areas to delaminate. As with any other piece of equipment, check the manufacturer's care instructions, and if you're not

MAJOR PACK MANUFACTURERS

Dana Design: www.danadesign.com

EMS: www.ems.com

GoLite: www.golite.com

Granite Gear: www.granitegear.com

Gregory: www.gregorypacks.com

Jansport: www.jansport.com

Kelty: www.kelty.com

Lowe Alpine: www.lowealpine.com

MountainSmith: www.mountainsmith.com

The North Face: www.thenorthface.com

Osprey: www.ospreypacks.com

REI: www.rei.com

Ultralight Adventure Equipment, popularly known as ULA: www.ula-equipment.com

certain about a cleaning product, use it in a test spot where it won't affect the pack's physical or aesthetic integrity.

Packs aren't waterproof; they're water-*resistant* and require a separate rain cover or waterproof pack liner to keep contents dry in wet weather. The rain cover you use for your pack should fit snugly but allow for fluctuation in the load size. An overly large cover will flap in the wind and let rain in, while a too small cover won't provide adequate protection. A variety of sizes and shapes of rain cover are available so you will be able to find one to fit your pack. Silnylon is the most popular pack cover and liner material since it's lightweight and durable. In lieu of a waterproof liner, some hikers use a sturdy but inexpensive heavy-duty plastic trash bag.

SLEEPING BAGS AND PADS

A sleeping bag is one of the most essential pieces of equipment you'll carry on the AT. Despite relatively low elevations, you may encounter temperatures ranging from the single digits to over a hundred degrees. As well as having to function in a large range of temperatures, your sleeping bag also needs to withstand moisture in the form of perspiration, humidity, and precipitation. A sleeping bag is a necessary piece of gear in all but the hottest weather. It is considered to be a major safety item, protecting you from hypothermia.

Sleeping bags come in a variety of shapes, sizes, styles, and materials. The price range of a sleeping bag runs from $150 to over $500, with synthetic-filled bags generally costing less than down-filled ones. From super-heavy expedition bags made of down to ultralight summer bags filled with PrimaLoft, there's a bag on the market for every hiking condition. The difficulty comes with successfully choosing one or two bags that can fulfill your needs for your long-distance hike. Light bags that can be carried during summer in Virginia are not safe to use during summer in New Hampshire's White Mountains. Depending on the length and regional location of your hike, you may need to increase your sleeping bag inventory.

The basic technology behind sleeping bags has changed dramatically in the past few decades. The most major change is the increased performance of synthetic insulation. Though down is still the most

One of the primary characteristics of a bag is its loft. Loft indicates the volume of insulation and determines how much insulating air is trapped in the bag. Typically, more loft equals more insulating power. In down bags, the loft is determined by the *fill power*, the volume filled by one ounce of down (bags between 500+ and 750+ fill are adequate for a variety of conditions on the AT).

packable and lightweight material for its temperature rating, some newer synthetics are comparable. High-tech materials such as nylon taffeta and ripstop polyester are commonly used as shell materials. Unlike cotton, these shell materials are relatively water-, stain-, and tear-resistant. Some manufacturers go so far as to completely cover their bags with a waterproof material (though these are not fully waterproof and have issues with condensation).

Essentially, a sleeping bag is no more than an insulated body-sized tube. However, there are a number of crucial variables at play when selecting an appropriate bag. These include the size (width and height), weight, temperature rating, stuff size, insulation and construction type, and specialized features such as a draft tube (also known as a draft collar—a line of padding that rests behind the zipper to keep a draft from entering the bag at the neck).

All sleeping bags require some sort of stitching to keep the insulation from shifting or bunching. This is especially true for down bags, which require fairly elaborate systems of baffles to keep the down from shifting. A synthetic bag is typically through-stitched, while a down bag may have a box-wall construction, with internal walls holding the insulation in place. Box-wall construction may feature V-shaped, angled, or parallel walls sandwiched between the layers of the shell. Well-made sleeping bags have a sophisticated distribution of insulation, offering more in the foot area, for example. There are also "bottomless" bags, which have no insulation on the bottom, as well as bags that distribute most of the insulation on the top side of the bag. While these bags save weight, they are not good options for those who sleep on their sides or who are active sleepers.

Choosing a Bag

Insulation is the feature that sleeping bag manufacturers and consumers focus on most, and there is an intimidating variety of insulation options on the market. Insulation determines temperature rating, loft, weight, volume when packed, resistance to moisture, and construction (for example, a down bag has a different internal structure than a synthetic bag). The two main types of insulating materials are natural down and synthetic fiber, and there are a number of arguments on either side as to why one type is better than the other. A few designs on the market combine both types of insulation to create bags that provide, in theory, the best of both worlds.

> Popular manufacturers of quality down bags include Feathered Friends (www.feathered-friends.com), Western Mountaineering (www.westernmountaineering.com), and Marmot (www.marmot.com).

Down is a traditional form of insulation and has been successfully used in sleeping bags for many decades. Down is the soft fluff found on geese and is ideally harvested from birds raised for insulation rather than food. The major benefits of down are its weight and volume to warmth ratio and its ability to retain loft and insulating properties much longer than synthetic insulation. These features make down popular in lightweight and ultralight backpacking circles. However, down has its drawbacks. The initial cost of a down bag is significantly higher than that of a synthetic bag (the cost of a down bag averages $200 to $300 and up). I use the term "initial cost" because a down bag tends to last longer than a synthetic one and, ultimately, the prices of both types of bag are comparable in the long run. Down may pose an ethical issue for hikers who dislike the idea of using animal products. The other pitfall of down is its inability to perform well in the damp conditions that plague the AT. When damp, down fails to retain its insulating properties as well as synthetics. Also, down takes a long time to dry, so a hiker using a down bag needs to take additional precautions when using his or her bag. Many AT hikers swear by down, however, and wouldn't think of using anything else because it is warm, lightweight, and comfortable.

Synthetic insulation is more popularly used on the AT than down. Though generally heavier and bulkier, synthetics are highly functional in damp environments, drying quickly and retaining their insulating properties. Sleeping bags with synthetic insulation are significantly less expensive (a large key to their popularity). Due to their general popularity, a large number of manufacturers make these types of bags. Synthetics are also non-allergenic and are your only insulation option if you have an allergic reaction to down. Synthetics are relatively easy to care for and can be machine-washed. They are also less prone to odors and mildew than down.

There are two basic styles of sleeping bags: the classic rectangular shape and the mummy bag, which features a tapered shape and a hood. The mummy is the choice for most hikers, though there are still a few out there who use a rectangular bag, especially in warmer weather. The mummy bag has the obvious advantage of preventing heat from escaping the head and neck area, where a majority of the body's cooling takes place. One of the disadvantages of this style of bag is the lack of free space because of its tapered shape. A mummy bag's frugal use of space and materials contributes to its overall better temperature rating, weight, and packability. Roomy, rectangular bags are too bulky for backpacking, but there are a few designs that provide a compromise between a rectangular bag's roominess and the packability, weight, and warmth of a mummy bag. These are called semi-rectangular or tapered bags and are manufactured by companies such as Big Agnes and Slumberjack. A few manufacturers (such as Montbell) produce stretchable mummy bags with elasticized stitching, giving hikers the best of both rectangular and mummy worlds.

Your bag should be well-fitted to your body, ideally narrower at the feet and wide enough for your girth around the shoulders and hips. An overly tight bag causes pressure on the insulation, reducing the insulating layer of air, and an overly large bag allows for drafts and creates pockets of cold air. There are a variety of bag sizes, and you should make an effort to shop around to find one that best fits you. Along with bag sizes determined by gender, there are extra-long bags, regular men's sizes, and a few bags that include extra shoulder and hip girth for larger hikers. Try out a

The type of sleeping bag I use depends on the season. I utilize the lightweight and packable characteristics of down during the drier, cooler fall and winter seasons. Lightweight down helps to offset the weight and bulk resulting from the bag's higher rating. Since humidity and precipitation tend to be less of an issue during fall and winter, keeping my down bag dry is less of a chore than it would be during the damp summer season. During the wet spring and summer seasons, I use a synthetic bag that is better able to deal with moisture issues. I use a bag insulated with PrimaLoft, which closely resembles the characteristics of down but dries quickly and has excellent insulating properties when damp.

bag's fit in the store by climbing into it and striking some of your favorite sleeping positions.

A standard sleeping bag falls short of adequately accommodating most women for a variety of reasons, namely size. There's no sense for an average-sized woman (or shorter than average man) to carry the extra bulk of a bag constructed for a six-foot man. A sleeping bag specifically designed for a woman has less length and more insulation in the foot and hip regions. The bag should be designed for a better overall female-friendly fit, with a proportionately wider hip area and smaller shoulder space. For a long time it was thought that women "slept colder," requiring more insulation than a man to stay comfortable. In fact, many women were sleeping in ill-fitting sleeping bags that allowed drafts, reducing the insulating properties of the bag. A woman does not necessarily sleep colder, but she does have different insulation needs (especially in the extremities, since women's circulation is slower in the hands and feet).

When shopping for a sleeping bag, pay attention to the additional bells and whistles as well as the overall quality. All mummy bags used in the cold weather should have drawstrings on the hood to keep out drafts. This feature makes a huge difference on below-freezing nights. Some bags offer a differential draw cord that allows you to adjust various parts of the bag opening. Sleeping bags with a foot box feature, where the foot section of the bag is shaped to allow enough room for the foot without compressing the insulation when you stretch out, are essential in cold weather. Some bags offer expander panels that make the bag roomier and cooler when needed. If you're planning on using the same bag for your entire hike due to budgeting or other reasons, this versatility may be a welcome factor. Zipper configuration can vary greatly from bag to bag. Some bags offer a zipper that extends below the feet to offer more ventilation, while other bags have a zipper that runs only three-fourths of the length of the bag to cut down on weight. When choosing a bag, think about the bag's usability; extra draw cords, zippers, pockets, and other features add weight but may make your bag a more functional piece of equipment.

Temperature Rating

The temperature rating of a sleeping bag indicates the coldest temperature at which the sleeping bag functions adequately. For example, a twenty-degree bag may be relatively comfortable down to twenty degrees. Sleeping bags act as an insulator and help to maintain a warm body at its comfortable temperature. Temperature ratings are usually vague and are determined by manufacturers. Obviously, manufacturers have an obliga-tion to keep these numbers as accurate as possible to promote customer satisfaction. However, twenty-degree bags from various manufacturers may perform differently. The outdoor gear industry attempted to develop an ASTM standard (American Standards for Testing and Measurements) for sleeping bags but abandoned the project when it proved to be futile. The inconsistency in temperature rating has much to do with the design of the bag, the insulation materials used, and other factors such as fit. When shopping for a bag, use the temperature rating as a general guideline but rely on word of mouth and gear reviews for a more accurate depiction of the bag's performance.

So what is an ideal temperature rating to use on the AT? A variety of fac-tors need to be taken into account when deciding this. You need a bag that keeps you warm on the coldest nights but one that is also light and small enough to carry comfortably. Many hikers opt to use multiple bags: a twenty-degree bag for the cold season and a forty-degree bag to use in warmer weather. Northbound thru-hikers switch from cold- to warm-weather gear after passing Mount Rogers, hanging onto cold-weather gear before that

point in order to avoid a surprise at-tack of chilly weather. Southbound thru-hikers shed warm gear after passing through the Whites. Both groups of hikers switch back to cold-weather gear later in the season.

A strategy of using a sleeping bag that is specifically suited to the seasonal temperatures ensures that you are always relatively comfort-able and never have to carry addi-

> Typically, AT hikers will use a twenty-degree bag for spring and fall hiking and a forty-degree bag for the summer months. For more severe winter weather, bags rated as low as zero degrees may be necessary, depending on what section of the trail you're hiking. The bag rating you choose will vary according to factors such as what part of the AT you're on and your personal warmth and weight preferences.

tional gear weight. Some hikers forgo using a bag in the summer and, instead, use a fleece blanket. However, it's not unusual for hikers to be sur-prised by the tenacity of winter, and some find themselves caught in foul weather with an inadequate summer bag. Exercise caution when switch-ing out seasonal gear. After all, it's better to be caught in a bag that's too warm than to be left in a snowstorm with a forty-degree bag.

Caring for Your Sleeping Bag

As a long-distance hiker, it's impossible to avoid abusing your sleeping bag. But with proper care, a bag can last for years.

A long-distance hiker isn't likely to wash his or her bag too many times while on the trail. One thorough washing is adequate for the average dirty thru-hiker. A sleeping bag stays relatively clean with regular airing out and wiping down. If you do need to wash your sleeping bag, use mild soap and water and never dry-clean it. Follow the manufacturer's instructions for cleaning the bag, and, if you're able to, take the bag to a professional cleaner who's experienced in caring for outdoor gear.

So when should you wash your bag? A bag may lose its insulating properties when it becomes really dirty. Perspiration, skin oils, and dirt work their way into a bag's shell and compromise the insulation materials. If you notice a reduction in your bag's insulation abilities, highly visible dirt, or a strong odor, it's time to consider washing your bag.

When you wash your bag, use a front-loading, high-capacity washing machine on the gentle cycle with cool water (this type of commercial machine is easily found in laundromats along the AT). The drums found in top-loading machines have parts that can snag and damage a bag so avoid using these machines. Before loading your bag into the washing machine, zip shut all of the zippers, fasten the Velcro enclosures, and make sure the draw cords are at their loosest setting to allow the

> The first rule of washing your sleeping bag is to avoid doing so unless *absolutely* necessary. Washing lowers the temperature rating and causes more damage than day-to-day use. This is especially true for synthetic bags. Wiping down the bag's shell with a damp cloth and spot cleaning with mild soap can be a good substitute for a full washing.

folds of the fabric to expand. In lieu of using a washing machine, handwashing in a bathtub is also effective (though it may not get the bag as clean as machine-washing). When washing your bag in a bathtub, make sure to rinse well to get all of the soap out of the insulation.

Use a mild soap formulated for technical gear such as Nikwax's Tech Wash or Downwash (www.nikwax-usa.com). It is especially important to use soap specifically created for use on down when washing your down bag, since regular soaps can strip the natural oils and leave the bag with a much lower temperature rating. Never use bleach or fabric softener on your bag. Instead, lightly spot treat and scrub particularly dirty areas with mild soap and rinse well.

Dry a down sleeping bag in a machine and a synthetic on a line (when line-drying, keep in mind that UV rays are damaging to shell materials). If you have a down bag, tumble it dry on low in a machine with a couple of tennis balls to help break up and fluff the insulation. For both down and synthetic bags, you may need to manipulate the insulation with your hands during the drying process to ensure that it's evenly distributed. Make sure that the machine you use is roomy enough to allow air to circulate around the bag. Use the lowest heat setting and periodically check the bag's drying progress to keep the shell from scorching or melting. When handling a wet bag, be careful to support all of its weight, as the shell and interior baffles are prone to tearing under this sort of stress. When line-drying, make sure that there is fresh air circulating. Line-drying inside without fresh air will slow the drying process and encourage the growth of mildew.

Sleeping Bag Liners

A sleeping bag liner is a great investment for extending your sleeping bag's life and usefulness. A liner is a sheath made of fabric that fits inside your bag, lining and protecting it. It helps to keep the bag cleaner, making it last longer, and it increases the temperature rating. Sleeping bag liners are lightweight, easy to care for, and pack well. They come in a variety of materials. Fleece is a bulky material but works well for cold weather. Silk, the most popular liner material, is lightweight and can add almost ten degrees to your bag's rating (check out Jag Bags' line of products for silk liners: www.jagbags.co.nz). Other liner materials include Coolmax, nylon, and cotton (cotton is not recommended because of its inability to wick moisture or dry quickly). When purchasing a bag liner, make sure it fits your bag well and doesn't restrict your movement inside the bag. Along with sleeping bag liners, wearing clothing in your bag goes far to keeping your bag clean and ensuring a long life. Like the liner, your clothing acts as a barrier between dirt and body oils and the bag.

Storage

Store your sleeping bag in a large breathable sack when not in use. This helps the bag to retain its loft and prevents mildew and mold growth. Supposedly, it is fine to store down partially compressed, but I wouldn't recommend it unless you're really short on space. Most manufacturers provide a storage bag. If this is not the case with your bag, use a large cotton or mesh laundry bag. Never store your bag in a waterproof container such as a Rubbermaid tub, as this can promote mildew growth (this is especially true for down bags, which naturally contain a significant amount of moisture and need to breathe). Store your bag in a cool, dry place such as a closet in your home (not the attic, garage, or basement), and make

To pack your bag in its stuff sack, place the bag in the sack, foot end first, and rotate the bag as you stuff it, distributing its bulk evenly.

sure the bag is completely aired out and dry before putting it in storage. When unpacking your bag from its stuff sack, give it a few shakes to help fluff up the insulation.

On the trail, you have the option of using different types of stuff sacks. The standard stuff sack is made of some sort of nylon (silnylon is a popular water-resistant stuff sack material). A compression sack is another option for a sleeping bag. Compression sacks are stuff sacks with a system for further compressing a load once it has been packed (in most cases, a compression sack operates with a set of nylon straps and buckles or a length of cord). Down is an especially compressible insulation material, and down bags work well even after being compressed. Using a compression sack goes far in saving valuable space in your pack. During your hike, remove your bag from its stuff/compression sack and air it out and fluff it whenever you get the chance (such as on zero days or during long rest breaks). Most bags have a sewn-in loop that you can use to suspend the bag from a tree branch or hook at a shelter.

On the trail, you may encounter small problems with your bag. Zippers are a common cause for concern. If your bag gets a zipper jam, don't pull on the zipper. Instead, gently pull the shell material away from the teeth of the zipper. If your bag's zipper is so damaged that it can't be used, duct tape, safety pins, and other means may be used to temporarily seal it up until you are able to get to a town and have it repaired. To care for the zippers, keep them clean and use them carefully. Don't jerk or yank them. If your bag gets a tear in the shell, you can do a quick field repair on it with duct tape or a self-adhesive patch from your repair kit. It's a good idea to carry some sort of patch kit or sewing kit to deal with small sleeping bag emergencies, since this piece of equipment is your first line of defense against the cold.

It's essential to keep you bag as dry as possible. This holds true for both down and synthetic bags, since no bag is able to retain all of its insulating properties when wet. Using pack covers, bag liners, and silnylon stuff sacks goes far in ensuring that your bag and other belongings stay dry on rainy days. Nothing is more miserable than hiking all day in the rain and then having to sleep in a wet bag. Along with rain and humidity, perspiration from your body plays a large role in making your bag damp. After exiting your bag in the morning, turn your bag inside out and allow it to air while you do morning camp chores. This allows the warm, moist air from perspiration to evaporate.

Some AT hikers (predominantly those in the ultralight set) prefer to use quilts that are especially designed for backpacking. These quilts are filled with insulation and may provide straps that attach the quilt to your sleeping pad. Though not as warm as a closed sleeping bag, these quilts offer room to move around and may be the only option for those who feel claustrophobic in a traditional bag. Much like bottomless

SLEEPING BAG MANUFACTURERS
Agnes: www.bigagnes.com
Columbia: www.columbia.com
EMS: www.ems.com
Kelty: www.kelty.com
Marmot: www.marmot.com
Montbell: www.montbell.com
Mountain Hardwear: www.mountainhardwear.com
The North Face: www.thenorthface.com
REI: www.rei.com
Sierra Designs: www.sierradesigns.com

sleeping bags, quilts lack the additional weight of insulation, baffle, and shell material on the underside. If too small, quilts can have gaps that allow air to enter, so it's important to find a quilt large enough to move with you while you sleep. You should look for a quilt that has multiple straps to hold it under you to keep it from shifting off of you while you sleep. A quilt can be worn around camp in addition to a jacket on a cold day. Quilts are a good piece of equipment to have if you intend to use a hammock. In a hammock, the insulation on the lower half of a traditional sleeping bag can be compressed to the point of being useless, and a quilt provides a more functional alternative. Some makers of hiking quilts are Fanatic Fringe (www.fanaticfringe.com), Jacks 'R' Better (www.jacksrbetter.com), and Nunatak (www.nunatakusa.com).

Sleeping Pads and Pillows

Sleeping pads are the essential non-essential backpacking item, and most hikers on the AT carry one. A sleeping pad plays a variety of roles: it keeps you warm by adding a layer of insulation between you and the ground, it protects your hips and shoulders from tough shelter floors and hard earth, and it can even serve as a temporary couch during daily breaks.

There are two basic types of sleeping pad—closed-cell foam and self-inflating open-cell foam. A closed-cell pad consists of a layer of textured material and requires no inflation. These pads are lightweight and long-lasting but don't offer as much comfort as a self-inflating pad. "Self-inflating" is a bit of a misnomer since these types of pads require a few quick puffs of air to fully inflate. The layer of air trapped in these pads provides excellent protection from cold surfaces. When choosing a pad, you have options such as length (pads generally come in regular, three-fourths, women's, and extra-long sizes) and a variety of thicknesses. A popular manufacturer of sleeping pads is Cascade Designs, makers of the Therm-A-Rest series (www.thermarest.com).

It's convenient to keep your closed-cell sleeping pad strapped to the outside of your pack so that you can access it for seating when you take midday breaks. I don't, however, recommend keeping your inflatable on the outside of your pack since it can be damaged by sticks and other objects with which it comes into contact. When storing your sleeping pad, leave it unrolled (under a bed or in a closet), deflated, and away from heat and dampness. Keep DEET and other chemicals away from your sleeping pad as they can damage the coating on it. And always keep your pad away from stove fuel and flames, and out of direct sunlight. Some manufacturers offer repair kits for self-inflating mattresses. To spot a difficult-to-find air leak, inflate the pad and submerge it in water (such as a creek, pond, or bathtub), watching to see where the bubbles come from, which will indicate the leak point.

One of the great luxuries of the trail that very few long-distance hikers indulge in is that of a pillow. There are a number of backpacker-friendly pillows on the market, both inflatable and filled with highly packable fill. Many hikers, however, opt to take no pillow at all, instead using a stuff sack loosely stuffed with clothing on which to rest their heads. A few manufacturers have developed soft fleece sacks (some with a thin padded side) that can be used for this purpose, offering the comfort of a pillow without the obligation of carrying extra bulk in your pack. Sleeping with a pillow is good for the health of your back, but creative multi-use alternatives can easily substitute for this piece of gear.

PORTABLE SHELTERS

For some hikers, a tent is nothing more than a luxury item. For others, it's perceived as a necessity for safety. Tents have been in use for thousands of years by all sorts of travelers, from nomadic herdsmen to the military. The essential design consisting of a canopy supported by poles has not altered much over the years, but the days of canvas and wood are gone and new technical materials have greatly reduced the weight of tents and improved their function. Tents provide protection against small animals, bugs, rain, wind, and the cold. They also provide privacy, a way to sleep away from crowded shelters, and freedom to camp whenever you see fit. However, tents aren't the only option for a portable shelter. Some hikers carry no tent and rely on bivouac sacks, tarps, or hammocks instead. A few hikers carry no shelter at all and rely solely on the shelters constructed along the trail, though this can be an uncomfortable, inconvenient, and even downright dangerous way to hike.

The typical contemporary tent is a predominantly mesh structure with a rainproof fly supported by aluminum, carbon fiber, or fiberglass poles. The rain fly, a secondary layer covering the core of the tent to protect it from moisture, is usually made of polyurethane or nylon impregnated with silicone and attaches to the base of the tent with clips or ties. There are many variations of this basic setup, and some recently designed tents include radical structural or material innovation.

Design Options

There are as many tent designs as there are backpacking styles. The basic shapes of tents include domes, ridgeline, geodesic or semi-geodesic, hoops, tee-pees, and tunnels. The shape of the tent dictates its performance in weather, ease of set-up, and usable space. Typically, backpacker tents are hoop-structured because of this design's ability to provide ample floor space while saving weight on poles and fabric.

Manufacturers assign an occupancy number to their tent designs. This number is intended to indicate how many people are able to sleep in the tent. Many long-distance hikers use a one-man tent in the interest of saving weight, but it's not that uncommon to see a single hiker enjoying the spaciousness of a two-person tent. Twenty square feet is adequate for a single hiker, and the floor space of most one-person tents falls in this range.

Freestanding tents are supported by a system of poles, while other tents require staking out to hold the poles and fabric upright. Freestanding tents are easier to set up and take down and can be pitched in areas where you cannot drive stakes into the ground (such as tenting platforms or rocky soil), but they typically weigh more because of the additional length of poles. Most lightweight tents are not freestanding. (The Big Agnes Seedhouse UL is one of the exceptions to this rule—though it may be argued that this tent is not a truly freestanding tent because it requires some staking out to fully utilize its floor space.) When you use a freestanding tent, it's still important to stake out the corners to keep it safe from wind damage (I

If you opt to hike with a partner and share gear, using a two-person tent is a great way to reduce your combined packs' weight by evenly distributing a single tent's weight between two packs.

once watched in horror as my freestanding tent tumbled across a field in a large wind gust).

Three-season tents are meant for spring, summer, and fall use, while four-season tents (sometimes given the misnomer of "all season") are designed for camping in harsh winter weather. During the standard AT hiking season (March through October), four-season tents are unnecessary. Though they won't be as warm or secure as their four-season counterparts, most three-season tents can hold their own in a moderate snow shower.

Double-walled tents are composed of two layers: the inner canopy of the tent and the rain fly. Single-walled tents are composed of a waterproof canopy only. There are pros and cons to each type of tent. The additional materials used in double-walled tents add to the tents' weight and, for that reason, single-walled tents are favored by some lightweight backpackers. Single-walled tents have some serious condensation problems, though, and tend to dry more slowly than double-walled tents. Condensation is the bane of single-walled tent users and can be severe enough to defeat the purpose of using a tent by leaving a hiker damp. Double-walled tents breathe easily and provide a much more comfortable environment in damp conditions.

Tent construction has come a long way since its canvas and wood days. Contemporary tents are made out of lightweight high-tech synthetic materials. Silnylon, nylon, and polyethylene are used for the rain fly and the tent's body. In three-season tents, lightweight mesh may compose a good portion of the body of the tent. Tent poles and stakes are made of steel, aluminum, fiberglass, or carbon fiber. All are strong and functional, and their differences primarily lay in their weight, with carbon fiber being the lightest and most expensive.

Choosing a Tent

Choosing a tent is a lot like shopping for a house (minus the emphasis on location, of course). You need to decide how much space you want, what layout you like, and how much money to invest in it. A standard one-person backpacking tent costs around $150 to $250. When buying a tent, get in it and stretch out to see how you use the space. If you feel inclined to, bring your gear and see how the tent's space accommodates everything. Ask yourself questions such as how often you plan on tenting versus staying in a shelter or in town. It doesn't make a lot of sense to invest heavily in a tent if you rarely use it. On the other hand, you want to ensure that whatever tent you own is up to the task of keeping you warm, dry, and comfortable. Look for a tent made by a reputable manufacturer that is well-constructed and receives good reviews from field testers. As with other gear, never buy your tent at an army and navy surplus store or at a large general chain retail store. These places generally have inferior products and aren't going to be willing or able to provide you with the sort of customer support you may need while on the trail. Look for tents specifically designed for backpackers or other lightweight travelers such as cyclists (companies such as Velo manufacture cycling tents that adapt well to the AT environment).

The average solo backpacking tent weighs two to four pounds, and a two-person tent weighs four to six pounds. Since poles add weight to tents, choose a design that doesn't incorporate an excessive number of poles in its structure. When looking at tent weight, take the entire packed weight into account in order to err on the side of caution. Companies often use the "trail weight" of a tent as a glorified marketing tool, but this weight is not usually an accurate depiction of what you'll actually be carrying on your back.

When shopping for tents, you may notice three different weight options listed in the specifications. These are the *trail weight, packed weight,* and *fast-pack weight.* Packed weight refers to the weight of the tent along with its stuff sack, stakes, rain fly, and other components, while the trail weight accounts only for the body of the tent, its poles, and stakes. The fast-pack weight is the weight of the footprint, poles, and fly used in the fast-pack setup, an option offered by some manufacturers.

There's a surprising amount of variation in floor space use, which is largely determined by the tent's overall design. Consider how you'll use the space in your tent. Will the tent have enough foot room, good shoulder width, space for gear and moving around? Make sure there's enough room around the perimeter of the interior of the tent so that your sleeping bag won't be touching the sides, which would allow condensation to dampen it. Headroom is an important factor to take into account for overall usable space. There are many solo tents that allow for about thirty-six inches of headroom at the highest point, and this is adequate for sitting up, changing clothes, reading and writing, and other activities you'll want to do when the weather outside is nasty. More room equals more weight, but it may be worth it if you have to spend an extended amount of time inside your tent.

Many solo lightweight tents pack in the ten-by-twenty-inch or smaller range. It's a good idea to split up the components of your tent and distribute them throughout your pack. Many hikers carry the fly (which is often damp) in an outside pocket while leaving the tent's body in their pack. Manufacturers provide space in their stuff sacks for all of the tent's components, making the sack larger than what you may need. Consider downsizing to a smaller, lighter stuff sack to better utilize your pack's space.

There are a few basic things to look for in good tent design. Something as simple as shape can have a large impact on a tent's performance. Make sure that the tent you choose has an aerodynamic form to help shed wind and driving rain. The rain fly should provide an overhanging area, known as the vestibule. This is an important intermediate space between the elements and the inside of your tent, and provides a convenient place to cook in poor weather or serves as a storage space for muddy gear. The fly should be cut to provide a combination of ventilation and protection from the elements, and your tent should have an adequate amount of bug mesh for ventilation. The floor of your tent should be fairly rugged—not so thick as to add useless weight, but able to keep out moisture and prevent punctures from sticks and rocks. There should be no seams on the floor of the tent as this provides an easy entry for water. A floor with a "bucket design" helps to keep seams off of the ground and away from water and reduces stress on the seams connecting the floor to the rest of the tent.

There are many useful bells and whistles available with current tent designs. Look for a tent that's easy to set up (especially in less than ideal conditions). A well-designed tent has ample headroom, a vestibule for storing gear, an easy way to attach the tent body to the poles, and an adequate number of stake-out points. Clips are an easier method of connecting poles, but sleeves sewn into the tent body weigh less and provide better stability during poor weather. Reflective zippers or fabric strips are nice to have when searching for your tent in the dark on trips from the privy. A gear loft, a mesh hammock used for storage, is an optional accessory for those wanting more order at the expense of a small amount of additional weight.

Tent color may not seem like a big deal, but you want to spend months living in a shelter that is aesthetically pleasing to you. Keep in mind that a light-colored tent creates a bright interior environment. Sierra Designs offers an "optic white canopy" that is essentially a light-colored tent roof that makes the interior as bright as possible while offering protection from direct sunlight. Many hikers prefer to use muted colored tents (such as moss or tan colors) since these tents blend into their surrounding environment. Some people even feel that brightly colored tents create visual pollution in the backcountry, while others feel that tents should be brightly colored for high visibility and safety.

Elements such as extra clips, zippers, pockets, and doors may add weight but are a necessary luxury for some hikers. And some hikers opt to remove pockets and other miscellaneous items from a tent to reduce weight and simplify their hiking experience. One of the newer features offered by some tent manufacturers is a fast-pack option. The fast-pack option allows a hiker to only use the poles, ground cloth, and rain fly for a stripped-down shelter. This is a great way to cut down on weight in non-buggy conditions. When using the fast-pack configuration, your tent's body can be mailed ahead, sparing you hundreds of miles of carrying its extra weight and bulk.

Setting Up Your Tent

Before you take your tent on any sort of backcountry trip (especially a long-distance hike), set it up a few times at home to familiarize yourself with it and determine its ease of use. It's better to discover a broken or missing part in your backyard than during a hike in the woods in poor weather conditions. Ideally, you should test your tent in a variety of weather conditions before committing to hiking long distances with it.

Pitching a tent may appear to be an intuitive act (especially if you're a seasoned backpacker), but sometimes there's a specific method of setting it up to avoid undue stresses on the poles or fabric. Always follow the manufacturer's instructions to avoid damaging your tent. Pitch your tent on smooth ground away from sharp sticks, stones, and other damaging debris, and always pitch it with the fabric pulled taut as this helps to shed water and wind. Don't pitch your tent where there may be flooding or excessive water runoff, and avoid setting up under "widow-makers"— dead tree limbs that can fall down on you. A correctly set up tent should have no ripples or wrinkles in the fabric, whereas a loosely, incorrectly pitched tent flaps in the wind, causing wear and tear on the fabric and poles. As you become more familiar with your tent, you'll develop a system for pitching it and packing it that becomes second nature.

To pitch a tent (particularly a freestanding one), you'll need guy lines and stakes, which usually come with the tent purchase. There are a few different types of tent stakes, but you'll most likely only need standard stakes on the AT (snow stakes are usually unnecessary unless you plan on doing intense winter camping). Stakes are usually made of aluminum or, a lighter alternative, titanium. Guy lines, typically supplied with the tent,

During the night, a person perspires and exhales about a cup of fluid. This builds up on the tent walls and results in condensation when the inside of the tent is warmer than the outside. On cold nights, fight the urge to completely close up your tent. Leave ventilation points open to make the tent a drier, more comfortable environment. In a single-walled tent, condensation is more prevalent than in a double-walled tent but can be reduced by leaving the door opened a bit to provide a flow of air.

can be supplemented with parachute cord for extra stability in windy weather, or reflective cord to help with nighttime visibility. Store your stakes in a small, brightly colored stuff sack to keep them from getting lost.

Footprints

The necessity of a footprint is up for debate in the hiking community. A footprint is a fitted piece of waterproof material that is slightly smaller than the perimeter of your tent. It provides protection against abrasion and helps to keep water from penetrating the floor of the tent. Some hikers are opposed to using a footprint because of its additional weight and bulk to carry around. Footprints typically cost $25 to $35. Most contemporary tents are usually made with sufficiently rugged bottoms to keep moisture out and are relatively unaffected by normal wear and tear. However, without question, a footprint extends the life of your tent, keeps it cleaner, and goes to great lengths in keeping it drier.

A footprint shouldn't extend beyond the walls of the tent because, if it does, it funnels the runoff from your rain fly under the floor, defeating its purpose. This is the reason why a fitted footprint rather than a normal ground cloth is useful. When using a footprint provided by the manufacturer, make sure the correct side of the footprint is touching the ground (for many, there is a shiny side and a matte-finished side). A footprint can be a high-tech, fitted liner that goes under your tent or a basic lightweight trimmed tarp made out of plastic or Tyvek. In a pinch, a space blanket can be used, reflective side up, to make a footprint that keeps the tent's interior warmer. Store your footprint in a separate bag to contain the dirt and moisture it collects.

Tent Care

A tent is, pound for pound, an incredibly rugged piece of equipment, but there are precautions that you need to take with it in order to extend its life. Avoid prolonged and unnecessary exposure to UV light as this damages the materials and waterproof coatings. Keep all things really dirty, smelly, and damp out of your tent, and put them in the vestibule instead. Don't ever cook or have any sort of open flame in your tent. Though tents are generally made of flame-retardant materials, they are not fireproof and are not designed to vent the potentially toxic smoke created by stoves and lanterns. Another good reason to not cook in your tent is to minimize the food smells lingering near your camp. These smells are quick to permeate the tent's fabric, possibly attracting hungry critters. Make sure your tent's manufacturer can provide replacement parts and repairs for your tent during your hike. Many reputable manufacturers carry a supply of spare parts and accessories for tents that are no longer on the market.

Before taking your tent out on the trail, you need to seal its seams. This is something that needs to be done for every tent on the market, regardless of the manufacturer or tent design. Even if seams are taped, it's a good idea to seal them to make them fully waterproof. It doesn't need to rain for moisture to penetrate your tent's seams. Dew and other moisture can seep in through the seams to make a tent noticeably damp.

Seal your tent's seams using a product recommended specifically for that use (some manufacturers give their own product recommendations for the job). Seam sealant is made of polyurethane- or silicone-based material. Clean your tent's seams before applying sealant to ensure a good bond, and use sealant in a well-ventilated area. Seal the fly and the seams close to the ground on the tent's body. Sealant should go on the inside of the seam (on the underside of the rain fly, for example) unless the product or manufacturer recommends otherwise. Allow the sealant to cure fully in a well-ventilated space before packing up or using the tent. Reapply sealant periodically while on the trail to keep your tent waterproof.

Keep your tent as clean as possible to avoid mildew, jammed zippers, fabric deterioration, and other problems. Allow your tent to dry, shake out debris before packing it, and never use harsh detergents or chemicals on it (such as laundry soap or cooking fuel). When dirty, wash your rain fly, tent body, stakes, and poles in warm water with mild soap, and allow them to fully dry before storing. Wash in a bathtub or on the lawn with a hose but never in a washing machine. Be careful lifting your tent when it's wet as its extra weight adds strain to the seams, making them more likely to tear.

Mildew is caused by fungus spores and is characterized by a musty smell and small, cross-shaped dark spots. It damages waterproofing by causing delamination

Popular seam sealants are McNett's SilNet, Seam Grip, and Seam Sure (www.mcnett.com), Grangers LP85 Seam Sealant, Seam Grip Seam Sealer, and REI Seam Lock.

and fabric deterioration. There is no way to fix mildew damage once it has occurred, so use preventative measures to avoid it. Air out your tent as often as possible (a freestanding tent may be flipped over on its side to allow the bottom to dry out), and try to keep it as dry and clean as possible.

A homemade anti-mildew solution can be made from one cup of salt, one cup of lemon juice, and one gallon of hot water. Saturate affected areas of the tent with this solution and allow the tent to sit in the sun to dry.

In its early stages, mildew can be successfully treated. There are a number of mildew remedies available on the market, one of them being McNett's MiraZyme. Another option for killing mildew is to place your tent in a waterproof bag and place it in the freezer for a day or two to kill the spores. Be careful when treating and rinsing your tent as the mildew may have damaged the fabric. After treating a tent for mildew, it may be necessary to re-treat the fabric with a waterproofing agent such as McNett's Tent Sure or Kenyon Recoat 3.

Field Repairs

Despite all of the good care you lavish on it, the wear and tear of a long-distance hike can eventually take its toll on your tent. Usually small repairs can be made in the field to keep the tent functional. For delamination of the waterproof coating, apply a waterproofing substance to the fabric to rejuvenate it. Duct tape is great to use for repairs on holes in the fabric, tears, and broken zippers and poles. Some manufacturers supply a short sleeve to join halves of broken poles (the sleeve slips over the pole at the broken point, reinforcing it and making the pole whole again). In a pinch, two small hose clamps (easily found in most hardware stores) can be used to attach a homemade sleeve of flashing to the pole. Cover the clamps with duct tape to keep the sharp edges from tearing the tent's fabric. Carry an extra stake with you in case you break or lose one. A spare stake is a simple lightweight item that can save you a lot of grief. You may also want to carry a small square of ripstop repair tape or taffeta repair tape in your bounce box or mail drop box.

For long-term storage, loosely fold your tent and store it on a shelf, or keep it in a roomy storage sack that allows for good air flow. Never store your tent in its stuff sack as this inhibits the circulation of air and creates stresses in the fabric and waterproof coating. Make sure your tent is completely dry before storing it. Tent poles should be stored fully assembled to reduce the strain on the internal shock cording. When you pack your tent into its stuff sack, randomly stuff it in instead of rolling or folding it. Rolling and folding cause repetitive creasing of the same areas of fabric and may lead to wear and delamination. Purchase a slippery stuff sack made of Cordura or silnylon for your tent; this makes packing the tent easier and reduces wear and tear on it. Pack your tent poles in a place where they won't get damaged while you hike. Make sure their weight is evenly distributed and that they won't puncture your water bag or tear stuff sacks.

TENT MANUFACTURERS

Bibler/Black Diamond: www.bdel.com

Big Agnes: www.bigagnes.com

Coleman: www.coleman.com

Eureka: www.eurekatent.com

Kelty: www.kelty.com

Mountain Hardware: www.mountainhardwear.com

MSR (Mountain Safety Research): www.msrcorp.com

The North Face: www.thenorthface.com

Sierra Designs: www.sierradesigns.com

Hammocks

A hammock is a lightweight and surprisingly comfortable alternative to a conventional tent. There is a cult-like following of hammock users on the AT who swear by this type of shelter. Many of them are ultralight or lightweight backpackers (the Hennessy Hyperlight A-Sym weighs in at a mere one pound eight ounces). Hammocks intended for backpacking are very different from those used in a backyard setting. A backpacking hammock is specially designed to endure the wear and tear of the backcountry, and it incorporates special features such as bug netting and a tarp shelter. Backpacking hammocks also feature a special shape that allows for comfortable sleep even for those with back problems.

When using a hammock, your only restriction on where you can sleep for the night relies on your ability to find two appropriately spaced strong trees. Rocky, boggy, and other undesirable ground conditions are easily dealt with since the hammock is hung well above them. Hammocks make it easy to stealth camp and are great to use in crowded campsites. Using a hammock is a boon in some weather situations, as it can be pitched out of the way of cold exposed areas where others are forced

I joined the steadily growing cult of hammock hangers a few years ago when I purchased a Hennessy hammock. I enjoy being off the ground and having the flexibility of camping in places where a tent would never work. The weight, comfort, and ease of use fit well into my hiking style, and I even use it comfortably in colder temperatures.

Tents and hammock at Jarrard Gap, Georgia

to tent. Hammocks are a very low impact way to camp because vegetation doesn't get trampled and small critters can move freely below you as you sleep.

A significant drawback to hammock camping is staying warm in cold weather. A hammock, while great to sleep in during balmy seasons, can be uncomfortable once the temperature dips below forty or fifty degrees. This is because air is able to circulate freely around your body, and the loft of your sleeping bag compresses against the bottom of the hammock, greatly reducing its insulating properties. There are several strategies to combat this problem, such as using a sleeping bag with a higher rating or keeping a closed-cell sleeping pad or reflective emergency blanket in your hammock to increase insulation. A hammock can be made more waterproof and retains heat better after an application of a DWR (durable water-repellent) spray. In warmer weather, this coating may be removed through repeated washing, restoring the fabric's ability to breathe. Some companies, such as Jacks 'R' Better (www.jacksrbetter.com), specialize in cold weather hammock gear, and there are under-quilts and other specialized accessories on the market designed to keep hammock hangers warm in bad weather.

In brutally cold weather, you may want to use your hammock as a tarp or opt to sleep in a shelter. Some hikers use a tent in cold weather and switch out to a hammock in warmer seasons, including it in a bounce box with their warm-weather gear. Since

> **MANUFACTURERS OF HAMMOCKS**
> Clark Jungle Hammock: www.junglehammock.com
> Crazy Creek: www.crazycreek.com
> Hennessy Hammocks: www.hennessyhammock.com
> Speer Hammocks, Inc.: www.speerhammocks.com

hammocks function a lot like tarp tents, it's not much of a stretch to set one up on the ground using trekking poles or other supports. Along with doubling as a tarp tent system, many hammocks are easy enough to set up that a hiker can throw it up for a place to take short breaks or naps. And, since it hangs above the ground and stays relatively clean and dry, there's never the need to store a wet, muddy shelter in your pack.

Tarps and Tarp Tents

Tarps and tarp tents have experienced a large surge in popularity thanks to the ultralight hiking movement. Tarps are very versatile and can be set up almost anywhere using a combination of trekking poles, downed trees, rocks, or other anchor points. Tarps are designed to leave a hiker more open to the elements, and this style of shelter offers no protection from insects and harsh weather. Backpacking tarps are composed of a high-tech material suited for the outdoors. It's not a good idea to use a tarp bought at a hardware store because of its bulk and fragility. A

> **MANUFACTURERS OF TARPS AND TARP TENTS**
> GoLite: www.golite.com
> Integral Designs: www.integraldesigns.com
> MacCat Tarps: www.outdoorequipmentsupplier.com
> Six Moon Designs: www.sixmoondesigns.com
> Tarptent: www.tarptent.com

tarp tent is a hybrid of a simple tarp setup and conventional tent design, and it is more enclosed than a basic tarp, providing more protection from insects, driving rain, and wind. Tarps and tarp tents are ideal because they are lightweight, inexpensive, and can be homemade.

Bivouac Sacks

A bivy sack (short for bivouac sack) is a waterproof bag used to sleep in. Originally designed as emergency shelter for mountaineers, bivy sacks are used by hikers and other outdoor athletes short on space. A bivy sack is a nylon (or other waterproof material such as Gore-Tex) cover for the sleeping bag. Some bivy designs incorporate mesh screens and hoops over the head area to allow for a more open feeling. An average bivy weighs one and one-half to two and one-half pounds, noticeably lighter than a tent.

One large advantage of the bivy is that it can be set up just about anywhere due to its small footprint. Many hikers are leery of bivy sacks because of their reputation for causing claustrophobia and being condensation-ridden. With the explosion of tarp tents on the market, bivies are losing popularity on the AT. Bivy shelters, a more spacious version of the bivy sack, were developed in response to the reputation of bivy sacks' claustrophobic feel. These shelters are essentially very simplistic hybrids between tents and bivy sacks. Another benefit to their small size is that bivies can be used inside a shelter on really cold nights for additional warmth.

> **MANUFACTURERS OF BIVY SACKS**
> Bibler/Black Diamond: www.bdel.com
> Integral Designs: www.integraldesigns.com
> Outdoor Research: www.outdoorresearch.com

BACKPACKING STOVES

For many hikers, a stove is a necessary safety and comfort. Because it's practically impossible to cook over a fire every night, a stove offers an easy and environmentally friendly way to heat up meals and drinks. On cold nights, a warm meal can equal the difference between physical comfort and misery, and a hot drink in the middle of a cold, rainy day can give you the warmth and energy to make it to the evening's destination. But not every hiker opts to carry a stove. Some, wishing to save weight in their packs, choose to eat cold foods along the way and only enjoy hot meals in town.

There is a backpacking stove to fit every hiker's style. Essentially, a stove is a system composed of a burner and a fuel source. Choose a stove based on the amount of cooking you plan on doing, the weight you wish to carry, the type of fuel you'll be able to obtain, and the amount of time you'll want to spend cooking. Along with considering the price of your stove, you need to think about its fuel efficiency and the cost and availability of fuel on the trail. When considering a stove's weight, take the total weight of fuel and necessary cooking accessories into account. Select a stove specifically made for backpacking, as a car camping stove is too heavy and bulky to carry.

It's important to purchase a stove from a manufacturer who can supply you with replacement parts and a good warranty. Talk to other hikers and read gear reviews to find out which stoves have a high failure rate or are difficult to use. As with most gear, the more simplistic the design, the lower the failure rate and the easier it is to use. Some stoves require a lot of assembly and maintenance to operate, and some do not. When choosing a stove, ask yourself if it is easy to set up, light, and cook with. Can you adjust the power of the flame to cook a variety of foods? Are you able to cook for multiple people if you plan on hiking and sharing gear with others? Make sure the stove is stable and won't tip over easily when cooking on less than perfectly even surfaces or in windy conditions. Along with losing your dinner, a stove that spills can attract animals to your campsite.

Take into consideration the amount of noise a stove makes when in use. This is important if you're an early riser and stay in shelters with other hikers (and wish to remain friends with those hikers). I can't adequately express how annoying it is to be woken early in the morning by the jet engine sound of someone firing up a stove.

Stove Ratings

The most common stove performance standards used by manufacturers, outfitters, and reviewers are *boil time* and *burn time*. Boil time refers to the amount of time it takes a stove to boil a liter of water at sea level, and burn time indicates the amount of time a stove burns when provided with a standard unit of fuel such as a canister or ounce of liquid fuel. For stoves that use multiple types of fuels, boil and burn times are listed for each type of fuel. Less popular methods of rating stoves are BTU (British Thermal Unit) output or listing the liters boiled per 100 g of fuel. These are very accurate measurements, but, for pragmatic backpackers, are just not as helpful as the boil/burn data.

Types of Stoves

Stoves come in a variety of shapes, sizes, and price ranges. The beverage-can stove is free to make and weighs less than half an ounce, while the multi-fuel Brunton Optimus Nova stove weighs in at almost a pound and costs $140. Styles of stoves are categorized by the types of fuel they burn: solid fuel, pressured gas, liquid fuel, wood, or a combination of fuel types. There are numerous options for backpacking stove fuel. Isobutane, white gas, kerosene, unleaded auto fuel, butane, Stoddard solvent, denatured alcohol, aviation fuel, naptha, mineral spirits, Trioxane, and Esbit tablets are among those fuels used in backpacking stoves.

Liquid fuel stoves operate with a number of different types of fuel such as denatured alcohol or white gas and are some of the most popularly used stoves on the trail. Stoves using this type of fuel operate either with a fuel container attached to a pump (as with the Whisperlite) or by adding fuel directly to the stove (for beverage-can style stoves). Liquid fuel weighs more than other fuel types, but weight can be pared down with frequent fuel resupply. It's relatively easy to find fuel for these stoves at most AT resupply stops. Some popular types of liquid fuel stoves are Brasslight (www.brasslite.com), beverage-can stoves, and MSR's Whisperlite (www.msrcorp.com).

Pressurized gas stoves (typically propane, butane, and isobutane) are the most efficient stoves in terms of cooking time. But, because of the fairly complex design of these stoves, they can be high maintenance. The jets and fuel lines on pressurized gas stoves require frequent cleaning, and these types of stoves have a much higher failure rate than others. Such stoves are somewhat bulky and can take up a lot of pack space because of the size of the fuel canisters. However, stoves such as the MSR Pocket Rocket Stove currently provide smaller canisters, which take up less pack space and offer exceptional cooking performance.

A major drawback to using pressurized gas is the need to pack out emptied fuel canisters. Empty canisters need to be dealt with in an ecologically responsible manner. This entails refilling, recycling, or disposing of them properly. These canisters are considered to be hazardous waste because they are capable of exploding even when empty. Contact your local outfitter or waste management provider to see how they should be dealt with. Some canister types may be refilled. For those canisters that cannot be refilled there is usually an indication written on the canister to that effect.

Solid fuel stoves are typically lightweight and simplistic. They are slow-cooking and somewhat old-fashioned. A solid fuel stove is com-

I use a beverage-can stove fueled with denatured alcohol. This stove weighs less than half an ounce, is small enough to tuck inside my cooking pot, and was free. Denatured alcohol is easily found in a number of places along the AT such as outfitters, large department stores, and hardware stores. It burns clean and is environmentally friendly because it's not derived from petroleum. Its wide availability made it my choice for stove fuel to use when hiking the AT. HEET, an antifreeze product for fuel lines that can be purchased at gas stations and auto repair shops, can be substituted for denatured alcohol (use the type in the yellow bottle that contains methyl alcohol). HEET burns less efficiently than denatured alcohol and, fortunately, I only had to resort to using HEET a couple times on the AT. Like many long-distance hikers, I carried my denatured alcohol in a clean, empty soda bottle, which I changed out every so often to prevent it from disintegrating.

posed of a holder for the fuel and some sort of frame for the pot to sit on. Fuel for these stoves may be completely solid (such as Esbit or Trioxane tablets), gel, or Sterno-can form. Because of their simple design, these stoves can be easily made at home. The nice thing about solid fuel is that there aren't postal restrictions on it so it can be sent through the mail. Fuel pellets can also be used to start campfires when it's rainy or if tinder isn't available.

A specialized form of solid fuel stove, the wood-burning stove, uses dried twigs and bark for fuel. In theory, wood-burning stoves are great because you have all of the fuel you need for free. You can hike lighter with this type of stove because there is no need to carry fuel and there are no toxic petroleum products with which to deal. These stoves can be made at home or purchased inexpensively. However, these stoves are somewhat bulky, are not very efficient, and are seldom used by long-distance hikers. Fuel for a wood-burning stove needs to be dry in order to burn, and finding such is not always an easy task on a rainy trail such as the AT. There are a number of wood stove designs available, such as the Stratus Trailstove (www.trailstove.com).

There are stoves capable of using a variety of fuel types, such as the Primus MultiFuel, MSR Whisperlight Internationale, and the MSR Dragonfly (advertised as being able to "burn just about everything but Yak butter"). Multi-fuel stoves take a number of solid and gas combinations such as white gas, auto fuel, kerosene, Stoddard solvent, denatured alcohol, aviation fuel, or naptha. Stoves not meant for a variety of fuels may be altered to take different types of fuel with different adapters and new fittings provided by the manufacturer.

When traveling to and from the trail, make sure you are able to carry your needed fuel supply with you. Most transportation providers, especially airlines, prohibit combust-

> For safety reasons, it's critical to follow the manufacturer's recommendations for usable fuels. Failure to follow manufacturer's directions can result in a serious stove malfunction or even personal injury.

ible materials. If you're unable to carry your fuel with you, make sure there's an outfitter, hostel, or other resource available to replenish your supply once you get to your destination. Check with your local post office or online at www.usps.com for fuel shipping restrictions that may apply to you. A great resource for researching fuel capabilities and characteristics can be found at the "On the Venturing Trail" web site (home.earth link.net/~barbmurray/cooking.htm).

Stove Maintenance

It's important to care for your stove during your hike. Your stove's manufacturer can provide you with basic maintenance information, replacement parts, and maintenance kits. Maintenance kits contain lubricants, tools, and other accessories required to keep your stove in working order. A stove that is well-maintained is more reliable and safer to use. Components such as O-rings can make or break a stove's usefulness, so it's important to keep all of a stove's smaller parts in working order. You may want to carry your stove in a bag to keep the burners from being damaged. Many hikers carry a small stove inside of a cooking pot to keep it from being squashed inside the pack. If you choose to do this, store the stove in some sort of waterproof barrier to keep residual food away from it. A plastic baggie works well for this and can be replaced when torn or soiled.

Stove Accessories

To increase the efficiency of your stove, use a windscreen. This is a heavy piece of foil that sits around your stove and pot while cooking to provide protection from wind and keep heat from escaping. The windscreen acts as a heat reflector and insulates your pot, allowing for faster cooking times. Windscreens are often left at shelters or in hiker boxes (boxes left at hostels, outfitters, and other places that act as a repository for unwanted gear and food) so it's sometimes easy to find replacements and upgrades along the trail. You may choose to use a heat reflector as well. Heat reflectors are composed of metal that sits under the stove and reflects the heat upward, speeding up cooking time and protecting the surface on which the stove rests. Some stoves require a pot stand, a metal framework that holds your pot above the flame of the stove. Pot stands can be purchased or easily made out of coat hanger wire.

Remember to carry a lighter or matches for lighting your stove. You can have lots of fuel and food, but if you're unable to light the stove, you'll go hungry or have to eat a cold, nasty meal. Butane lighters won't function below freezing temperatures so, when hiking during

STOVE MANUFACTURERS

AntiGravityGear (manufacturer of beverage-can stove): www.antigravitygear.com

Brasslight: www.brasslite.com

Brunton: www.brunton.com

Jetboil: www.jetboil.com

MSR: www.msrcorp.com

Optimus: www.optimus.se

Snow Peak: www.snowpeak.com

Vargo: www.vargooutdoors.com

colder months, carry matches. You may get butane lighters to work in cold weather by stashing them in an internal clothing pocket where your body heat can keep them above thirty-two degrees Fahrenheit. Keep your lighters and matches protected from moisture in a sealed plastic bag. Sometimes it's impossible to keep things dry, so some hikers choose to carry waterproof matches to deal with the damp weather.

HEADLAMPS

Essential for night hiking, setting up camp in the dark, and evening privy visits, a headlamp is vital for the AT. A headlamp is a lightweight light source attached to a headband that automatically trains its beam on whatever you are looking at. Flashlights aren't popularly used on the trail because they are heavy and bulky and don't leave your hands free to do tasks.

There are two major types of headlamps: those with LED (light-emitting diodes) light sources and those that utilize miniature incandescent bulbs. LED lights are the most commonly used type of headlamp light source. LED lights weigh less, use less battery power, shine brighter, and have longer-lasting bulbs. Incandescent lamps are outdated technology and tend to break easily, weigh more, and use significantly more battery power than LED lights.

Headlamps cost anywhere from $30 to $80 and can come with a variety of features. Choose your headlamp based on the approximate battery usage and lifespan, its various lighting settings, and the strength of the beam. Headlamps run on standard AA or AAA batteries housed in the lamp's body or stored externally on the back of the headband. Batteries are easily found at resupply locations, but remember to carry spares. Choose a headlamp with recessed switches that can't accidentally turn on in your pack and drain the batteries. Keep in mind that a lamp with low battery power burns significantly less brightly than one with fresh batteries. Some lamps have an indicator or warning light to let you know when the battery power is low. When you see that you're running low on battery power, put an extra set of batteries in your pocket or other easily accessible place so you don't have to fumble around in the dark for them when your light goes out.

Some headlamps offer multiple settings: a bright, unfocused light

> It's important to have easy access to your headlamp. Carry it in your pack in a place where it's easy to locate. When dusk nears, wear it around your neck so it's readily available when you need it. In camp, store it in a mesh pocket in your tent or next to you in the shelter in case you need to use it in the middle of the night.

HEADLAMP MANUFACTURERS

Black Diamond: www.bdel.com

Petzl: en.petzl.com

Princeton Tec: www.princetontec.com

for night hiking, a narrow beam for doing camp chores, a diffused low light for playing cards or reading, and an emergency flashing setting. On the maximum strength setting, the beam of a headlamp may illuminate from fifteen to sixty meters, with thirty-five meters being the norm for most lamps. When sitting with other hikers at night, a headlamp with multiple settings allows you to turn your lamp down to its lowest setting to avoid blinding everyone. The lower settings are useful for prolonging the life of the batteries while giving you enough light to stumble to the privy and back. Some lamps also offer a white or red diffuser. The red diffuser helps you to retain your night vision while using your headlamp, while the white diffuser softens the beam.

TREKKING POLES

Trekking poles, also known as hiking poles, mountaineering poles, and sissy sticks, have become a common gear item on the AT. Because of the trail's rough terrain, the additional stability and shock-absorbing powers of trekking poles is a welcome thing. A lot of weight and impact are removed from the knees and other leg joints when using trekking poles. Trekking poles aid in balance, are useful in fording streams, and can be used to probe and explore questionable surfaces such as standing water or ice. Trekking poles can assume multiple responsibilities such as serving as tarp tent poles, laundry line props, and even weapons of self-defense against aggressive dogs. Also, when used properly, trekking poles help to maintain upper-body fitness, which is ordinarily prone to disintegrating during long-distance hikes.

Expect to pay between $60 and $150 for a pair of poles. Good quality trekking poles are adjustable and can be telescoped to packable size and adjusted to optimize a custom hiking length. The shaft can be composed of aluminum or, in better quality lightweight poles, carbon fiber or titanium. Make sure the joints on telescoping poles are easy to adjust and can hold the pole at its set length while you hike. Poles should have a reliable device for adjusting and locking sections together. Some poles have a flip-lock that's easy to use and adjust, while others feature a twist-lock, which is more difficult to tighten and may be impossible to adjust if not made out of an anti-slip material.

There are some options you need to pay attention to such as grip design. Grips are the ergonomically designed handle covers at the tops of the poles. It's important that the grip fit the shape of your hand. Grips can be made out of hard rubber, syn-

> Some hikers use a staff, a single pole that functions similarly to trekking poles. Staffs are easier to carry over obstacles such as stiles and boulders, but may provide less stability and give the body an uneven workout.

thetic or genuine cork, soft rubber, or plastic. Synthetic cork is a great material for grips because it stands up to a lot of wear and tear and doesn't generally create blisters. Grips can be set atop the poles in a number of ways. There are straight grips (which are aligned with the pole) and forward-angled grips (the grip is set from the pole at a gentle angle intended to decrease wrist strain). The type of grip you select is dictated by your personal hiking style and ergonomic needs. When buying gear, try a number of grips to determine which shape and material feels best in your hands.

The poles' tips are the pointed metal bottoms that provide traction. You should be able to replace the tips on the ends of your poles in case they break or wear down, or if you want to use a specialized tip for a specific ground condition. The standard tips for good quality poles are made of carbide or steel (carbide is preferable) and have a "chiseled" shape to them. A chiseled tip has a notched surface and is capable of dealing with a variety of terrain. Another type of tip is made of rubber, which is great for walking on the AT's stretches of granite. However, the standard chiseled tip is adequate for all of the surfaces you'll encounter on the AT.

Baskets are the small rubber or plastic hoops at the bottoms of your poles, situated close to the tip. They should screw on, lock, or attach to the pole in a manner that makes them changeable. Baskets keep the poles from sinking into snow, mud, leaf debris, or other soft surfaces. This ability to keep the poles from sinking is called *float* and is important for properly utilizing the poles and protecting the trail surface. According to the conditions you'll be hiking in, you can choose to use a basket specifically designed for that surface. Many AT hikers just use small summer baskets that are about an inch in diameter and don't have any perforations in them. Larger, perforated baskets are for use in the snow, while unperforated baskets are better for muddy conditions.

Some trekking pole designs have additional features such as a built-in compass or the ability to double as a camera monopod. Poles may have a shock-absorbing feature built into their shaft, which functions similarly to shock absorbers found in the forks of mountain bikes. In theory, this

In order to experience the full benefit of your trekking poles, you need to adjust them correctly to your height and hiking style. A good starting point for adjusting the height of the poles is to have them long enough so that your elbow forms a ninety-degree angle when your hand is on the grip. Poles can be lengthened for descending and shortened for ascending. Some hikers will place duct tape around their poles to act as a second hand grip for ascents. Along with creating a second hand grip area, this makes the tape easily accessible.

system helps to reduce impact and wear and tear on the arms. Few hikers on the AT use poles with this feature as they are expensive, weigh more, are loud (the shocks make a squeaky sound when they get worn and dirty), and break more easily than regular poles. Anti-shock poles are useful on descents but can actually make ascents more difficult. If you choose to use anti-shock poles, select a pair that allows you to turn the shock-absorption feature on and off. You don't necessarily have to purchase traditional trekking poles. To save money, you can use ski poles found at a thrift store.

Security loops are the loops that go around your wrists. Typically, they are tightened enough so that your wrist bears some of the weight and your hands are held snug against the grips. The wrists should naturally flick the poles forward with each stride, leaving you free from having to carry the full weight of the pole. Some hikers prefer not to use security loops for a variety of reasons. Without the loops on, it's easier to stow the poles or use them intermittently over terrain where poles aren't needed all of the time. Your outfitter can show you how to correctly adjust and safely use the loops on your poles.

Trekking poles don't require too much maintenance. If you like, you can carry an extra tip and a set of expanders (the plastic gaskets that keep the pole's sections in place) in your mail drop or bounce box. Replace tips, expanders, and other parts as needed. After getting wet, poles should be taken apart and allowed to dry thoroughly. Before hiking every day, you should double-check that the locks are securely tightened on each pole joint. These tend to loosen after miles of hiking, causing the unpleasant surprise of collapsing poles.

TREKKING POLE MANUFACTURERS

Black Diamond: www.bdel.com
Komperdell: www.komperdell.com
Leki: www.leki.com

TRAIL TECHNOLOGY

One look at all of the high-tech gear currently on the market shows that hikers love modern technology and that taking a long-distance hike on the AT doesn't have to entail going totally primitive. There are pros and cons to taking gadgets such as cell phones and MP3 players on the trail with you. The trail's conditions are far from ideal for sensitive electronic devices, and the extreme heat, cold,

> I couldn't imagine hiking without trekking poles because they reduce the stress on my back and knees and have saved me from taking bad spills numerous times. Currently, I use Komperdell's Alpinist Trekking Poles sold through EMS. The synthetic cork grips are comfortable, and the telescoping joints are strong and reliable.

and wet weather tends to destroy devices. Also, using these devices may pose ideological problems for hikers wanting to have a pure "wilderness experience."

There are a number of options for hikers interested in staying connected on the trail. Internet access found at libraries and internet cafes is spaced many days apart, and for hikers communicating with loved ones or those keeping online trail journals, PocketMail is a good alternative (www.pocketmail.com). PocketMail is a small inexpensive keyboard device that weighs a little over eight ounces (including the AA batteries required to power it). It allows you to type your e-mail entries, save them, and then send them by holding the device's transmitter up to a cellular or pay phone receiver. PocketMail is able to compose, send, and receive e-mails but doesn't act as a web browser. PocketMail is one of the favored electronic gadgets on the AT and other long trails, and the company acknowledges its hiker customer base.

Durable music storage devices provide hikers with hours of music to hike to or to enjoy at the shelter at the end of the day. MP3 players are essentially external storage devices designed to hold compressed music files. Along with storing music, Apple iPod products (www.apple.com/ipod) also play videos and include an organizer among other options. Some MP3 devices can store other compressed files such as audio books and movies. Before buying one of these devices or choosing to carry the one you already own on the trail, consider the warranty of the item (will the company replace it if you drop it in a creek?) and, most importantly, the device's power source. Rechargeable devices are great in an environment filled with electrical outlets but are an issue when you aren't staying in town on a regular basis. Choose a device that runs off batteries, which are easily found at resupply points. Walking with music can be an asset while tackling a big-mileage day or it can be a liability when stumbling deaf upon a rattlesnake. Use your headphones sensibly and always be aware of your surroundings while you hike.

Many hikers carry cameras with them on the trail. There's been a big switch from film to digital media, offering hikers better image-making capabilities without the cost of carrying more weight. Some digital cameras even include video and sound options. Digital is cheaper and faster than film and allows you to edit and easily post images to the web. When choosing a digital camera, look for a camera that runs a long time on its batteries. Keep in mind that most digital cameras require lithium batteries or special rechargeable batteries provided by the manufacturer, making resupply difficult. The megapixel number refers to the amount of information (i.e., resolution), in pixels, recorded over the space of the photograph. This number can be very vague and misleading and the industry tends to abuse it. But, generally, a camera with a larger megapixel number is a better camera (the quality standard on the market is around five megapixels or higher).

Look for a camera with a zoom lens and user-friendly features. Purchase a large storage card so you can shoot many miles worth of trail experiences without having to delete images. Camera cards can usually be downloaded and disks burned with the images at photofinishers, chain drugstores, or department stores. Not all self-serve downloading kiosks will accept cards larger than one gigabyte. Cards can also be mailed home to review and edit at a later date. It's always a good idea to take some notes about what images are on the card.

Film is more expensive to use than digital, but has characteristics that can't be replicated in digital form, such as tonality and archival stability. Carry your film in a waterproof container and keep it away from extreme heat, cold, and moisture. You may choose to have disposable point-and-shoot cameras mailed to you. Test a few models out before hitting the trail and pick the one that consistently takes the best images. A number of companies sell disposable cameras in bulk (usually for weddings and other events), which can help you save money in the long run.

Cell phones are both hated and loved on the trail. Certain cell phone users can be loud and obnoxious and can rob hikers of a wilderness experience. But cell phones may

If you choose to use a film camera as opposed to digital, there are many good lightweight point-and-shoots available. A few hikers choose to carry more complex SLR (single lens reflex) cameras to create better quality images, but these cameras are heavy and more delicate than their point-and-shoot counterparts.

serve as a vital umbilical cord to loved ones. Cell phones work in many parts of the AT, and highly populated and higher elevation areas frequently offer good reception. Most often, a hiker carries a cell phone (turned off) in his or her pack and opts to use it in town where there's reception and the phone can be charged. Pay phones are becoming more and more scarce, and the few pay phones towns offer may be vandalized or have a large queue of hikers waiting to use them. In areas with reception, cell phones can be a safety blanket, a way to contact civilization in case of an emergency. Unfortunately, the ability to call for help is sometimes abused by hikers. If you carry a cell phone, use it in a way that is respectful to other hikers. This includes leaving the ringers and alarms off and using general common sense and courtesy in how and when you use it.

For techno-geek hikers, there is a whole world of devices that can be taken to the trail. This includes GPS (Global Positioning System) units, altimeters (to determine elevation), barometers (to help anticipate weather patterns), and watches that include altimeters, barometers, or GPS units. Using a watch can be useful when trying to get to town on time for post office hours or in determining the amount of daylight you have left to get to a shelter (especially in spring and fall when the days are shorter and daylight is at a premium). Most waterproof or water-resistant watches do the trick of correctly telling time whether they cost $10 or $200.

Be sure to always have an adequate supply of batteries for your devices. Opt to carry lithium batteries for those devices requiring extra power, such as digital cameras. Though more expensive, lithium batteries are long-lasting, meaning you can carry a smaller supply of them in your pack. Some hikers opt to use rechargeable batteries on the trail, picking up fresh batteries at every mail drop and sending the used batteries back to their support crew at home for recharging. In cold weather, keep batteries and electronic devices warm. Batteries tend to drain easily in chilly temperatures, and carrying them in your pocket will extend their life substantially. Remove the batteries from your devices when storing them long-term, as the batteries can cause corrosion and damage.

MISCELLANEOUS GEAR

Along with the main articles of gear such as tents and stoves, a lot of incidentals can fill your pack and make your trip more enjoyable. The most popular way to store and organize things is by keeping them in stuff sacks, small drawstring bags made of materials such as silnylon or Cordura. Some stuff sacks have a compression feature that allows you to squash the contents of the sack. Use different colored stuff sacks to color-code your belongings so you can find them easily, and use sacks that are just large enough to carry their contents. A tight stuff sack may tear under stress and can make packing a misery. On the other hand, an overly large stuff sack allows its contents to rattle around and adds unnecessary weight. Freezer bags are great for further organization and protection for food, clothing, maps, and journals. A standard stuff sack is water-resistant but not fully waterproof, so it's a good idea to use freezer bags for items such as electronics, maps, and journals. Multi-tools are useful for gear repairs and other tasks. A good multi-tool has scissors, tweezers, screwdrivers, a knife, and, of course, a bottle opener. (I use the Leatherman Micra, which is ultralight yet serves all of my needs with half the weight of other multi-tools. Information on Leatherman tools may be found at www.leatherman.com). Lastly, you may want to carry a small pack thermometer. These are tiny thermometers that clip onto your pack and give you somewhat accurate temperature readings.

PACKING LIST

On the next page is a sample gear list compiled to meet the needs of a typical long-distance hiker. Before hiking, print out a copy of a gear list tailored to meet your specific needs. This list may be modified for weekend versus longer term hikes, and it's a good idea to make modifications to the list as you gain more experience on the trail during shorter training hikes. Make notes about how much fuel, water, and other supplies you used during a trip in order to better prepare yourself for resupply and future packing.

MAKING, REPAIRING, AND MODIFYING GEAR

Necessity is the mother of invention, and one of the joys of the AT is the creativity that abounds. Hikers have to be innovative when it comes to getting water, hitching rides to town, and finding ways to be comfortable in all sorts of conditions. One of the most interesting manifestations of this creativity can be seen in homemade gear. Elegant and simplistic, this gear is not only low-cost and functional, it also bears the authorship of its maker. Most homemade and modified gear I've seen on the trail belongs to ultralight backpackers because their needs are highly specific and are not always well-catered to by manufacturers. A number of specialized backpacking gear manufacturers, such as GoLight and Moonbow, have arisen from the work of innovative hikers who modified and built their own gear.

SAMPLE GEAR LIST

The Big Three
- Pack (including pack cover or liner)
- Portable shelter (including footprint, stakes, guy lines, etc.)
- Sleeping bag, sleeping pad, bag liner

Clothing
- Base layer (Capilene shirt, running tights, etc.)
- Middle layer (fleeces, etc.)
- Outer layer (wind shell, down vest, etc.)
- Rain gear
- Socks and sock liners
- Hats, gloves, bandanas
- Hiking shoes
- Footbeds or orthotics
- Camp shoes
- Gaiters

Cooking
- Stove
- Windscreen
- Cooking pot and utensil(s)
- Fuel and fuel container
- Matches and lighter
- Food
- Bear-bag cord
- Water treatment

Health and Hygiene
- Toothbrush
- Toothpaste
- Baby wipes
- First-aid kit
- Toilet paper
- Vitamins and prescription medications
- Hygiene products (for women)
- Antibacterial hand gel
- Sunblock
- Insect repellent

Safety and Utility
- Multi-tool or knife
- Headlamp
- Guidebook and maps
- Trekking poles
- Hydration system

Miscellanea
- Camera
- Radio or MP3 player
- Watch
- Cellular phone
- Calling card
- Batteries
- Freezer bags
- Stuff sacks and compression sacks
- Photo ID
- Debit or credit cards, cash, and/or checks
- Contact information
- Notebook
- Pens and pencils

Many different pieces of equipment can be homemade, including tents, packs, sleeping bags, and clothing. There are a lot of useful resources available for hikers interested in making their own gear:

- One of the better resources for homemade gear instructions can be found on the Lightweight Backpacker web page (www.backpacking.net/makegear.html). The information on this site mainly focuses on creating money-saving lightweight gear such as stoves, shelters, and packs (use the navigator bar on the left to look up instructions for making various pieces of gear).
- The TrailQuest web site has a section devoted to "Alternative Gear," which features frugal alternatives (many of which are homemade or modified) to expensive gear (www.trailquest.net/TQaltgear.html).
- Mark Verber's Recommended Outdoor Gear web site features a section on homemade gear (www.verber.com/mark/outdoors/gear/homemake/index.html). This site includes information on Henry Shire's infamous tarp tent design, directions on how to make your own G4 pack, and hammock designs.

By far, the most popular piece of homemade gear is the venerable beverage-can stove. It weighs in at less than half an ounce and is an inexpensive alternative to a store-bought stove. Made from a single recycled can, a beverage-can stove requires no special skills or tools to build and is very durable and reliable. Backpacking.net offers very concise instructions for making a standard beverage-can stove (www. backpacking.net/makegear/stove).

Other stove designs available for do-it-yourself backpackers include the wood-burning stove, Trangias, and more. "Wings: The Homemade Stove Archive" (http://wings.interfree.it/html/main.html) is one of the more useful backpacking stove resources on the web. It includes detailed directions for a number of stoves. The Zen backpacking stove page (http://zenstoves.net/LinksGeneral-DIY.htm) is just as comprehensive.

Windscreens can be easily made from various types of sheet metal or heavy-duty aluminum foil (the foil screens usually won't stand up to much bending and folding but are good in a pinch), and you can make reflectors using the same materials. Hikers interested in shaving down ounces may opt to replace denatured alcohol fuel bottles with smaller recycled heavy-duty plastic bottles (never do this for designs that connect the fuel bottle directly to the stove). Clean hydrogen peroxide and rubbing alcohol bottles make good choices for sturdy, corrosion-resistant fuel storage containers, and a sports-bottle cap can be used for easy access.

Tyvek, a waterproof plastic construction sheeting designed by DuPont Industries, is great for do-it-yourself projects. This material is breathable, offers protection against rain and snow, and doesn't break down when exposed to UV light. Tyvek can be used for ground cloths and tarp tents. Typically, this material is sold in huge rolls, but some independent retailers buy large rolls and cut them down for resale. AntiGravityGear (www.antigravitygear.com) sells Tyvek by the foot, and you can also sometimes find it on eBay in small amounts.

If you don't feel up to the task of making gear from scratch, you can always modify the gear you have to make it better suit your needs. Ultralight fanatics often do this by cutting off excess straps, pockets, and other unnecessary elements of gear. Or you may want to add to your gear by sewing on reflective strips or mesh pockets. Keep in mind that when you modify your gear like this, you may negate any product warranty that covers the item. Something simple that all hikers should do is write their name, telephone number, and e-mail address in permanent ink on their major pieces of gear (especially the pack). Though writing your name on your pack has a hokey summer camp feel to it, this makes it easier to track or return lost or stolen items.

FIELD REPAIR KIT

No matter how well you care for it, gear does break down. If you experience gear failure, contact the manufacturer first. Usually, companies have a customer service or warranty department that can assist you with repairs or replacements. If the manufacturer of your gear is unable or unwilling to assist you, go to an outfitter. Sometimes an outfitter can give you replacement gear immediately and work out the time-consuming details with the manufacturer later. Or they may be able to make repairs or replacements for a modest fee.

It's a good idea to have a small repair kit in your bounce box or mail drop. It's not necessary to carry a huge inventory of repair materials and tools with you as resupply is usually close by, but I recommend carrying a few essentials in your pack such as duct tape and sewing needles. You can purchase premade repair kits from companies such as McNett, or design a kit of your own.

Admittedly, gear is fun and fascinating stuff. If you are really enamored with gear and would like to share your gear experiences and opinions, you can write your own reviews on BackpackGearTest (www.backpackgeartest.org). Don't stress out over your gear too much because, after your first hundred miles or so, you'll probably make some (if not a lot) of changes to what you use. Outfitters near the AT sometimes offer AT hikers discounts and a large variety of upgrades and other gear options. Long-distance hikers are, after all, the cash cow of many outfitters. When choosing your gear, make sure that it will keep you warm and relatively comfortable, and, above all, safe from extreme elements.

ITEMS TO INCLUDE IN YOUR GEAR REPAIR KIT

Air mattress patch kit: These are usually available through the manufacturer or at most well-stocked outfitters.

Duct tape: You should always have duct tape with you since it's great for fixing almost everything. Rather than carrying a whole roll, wrap a few yards of it around your trekking poles or roll some into a small, tight roll and stash it in your pack.

DWR (durable water-repellent) spray: Bounce-box a can of waterproofing spray to apply to your rain fly and rain gear.

Ripstop nylon tape or fabric: This is great stuff for patching tents, sleeping bags, and clothing. This material comes in a number of forms and may have a self-adhesive backing or require the use of a separate adhesive. Cut pieces to a variety of sizes and include them in your repair kit.

Seam sealant: You may have to reseal the seams on your tent at some point during the trip. Always use a new tube of seam sealant for the job. You can buy this at an outfitter en route or pack a tube in your bounce box. Some seam sealant material doubles as glue and can be used to apply patches.

Waterproofing spray: If you use leather boots, you'll need to periodically reapply waterproofing or some sort of dressing.

Sewing kit: A small sewing kit with sturdy needles, thread, dental floss, or fishing line is useful for repairing clothing and gear such as sleeping bags. If you opt to carry a sewing kit with you, make sure to house the needles so they won't puncture items in your pack.

Parachute cord: Carry enough parachute cord for bear-bagging, to use as spare lines for staking out your tent, and for binding things. About forty to fifty feet will do the trick.

Spare parts: It's not necessary, but if you have a piece of equipment with chronic problems or one that is difficult to find spare parts for, you may want to stockpile buckles or other parts and keep them in a bounce box.

MAJOR OUTFITTERS

Altrec.com

www.altrec.com

customerservice@altrec.com

"Live Help" customer service available Mon. through Fri. 6 A.M. to 6 P.M. (PDT)

800-369-3949

Altrec.com

Customer Service

135 Lake Street South #1000

Kirkland, WA 98033

Backcountry Gear Limited

www.backcountrygear.com

800-953-5499

541-485-4007

bcgeartech@backcountrygear.com

Fax: 541-683-1609

Backcountry Gear Limited

1855 West 2nd Avenue

Eugene, OR 97402

Campmor

www.campmor.com

To access customer service e-mail:

www.campmor.com/webapp/wcs/stores/servlet/campmor/ask_cs.jsp

800-525-4784

201-335-9064

Hours: Mon. through Fri. 8:30 A.M. to 9:30 P.M., Sat. 8:30 A.M. to 6:00 P.M.

Campmor

400 Corporate Drive

P.O. Box 680

Mahwah, NJ 07430

EMS

www.ems.com

customerservice@ems.com

800-463-6367

Hours: Mon. through Fri. 8 A.M. to 9 P.M., Sat. 9 A.M. to 6 P.M., Sun. 10 A.M. to 6 P.M. (EST)

(Store locator on home page)

Moontrail (formerly Backcountry Equipment)

www.backcountry-equipment.com

800-569-8411

888-779-5075

210-682-9881

Hours: Mon. through Fri. 8 A.M. to 6 P.M., Sat. noon to 4 P.M. (CDT)

Backcountry Equipment

5407 Bandera Road #117

San Antonio, TX 78238

Moosejaw

www.moosejaw.com

877-MOOSEJAW (877-666-7352)

Store hours: Mon. through Thurs. 7 A.M. to 10 P.M., Fri. 7 A.M. to 7 P.M., Sun. 10 A.M. to 5 P.M.

Customer service e-mail contact: www.moosejaw.info/customers/MJEmail.aspx

Store locator: www.moosejaw.com/moosejaw/dept.asp?s_id=0&dept_id=5

Mountain Gear

www.mgear.com

info@Mgear.com

"Live Help" customer service

800-829-2009

509-326-8180

509-444-3341

Fax: 509-325-3030

Mountain Gear

North 730 Hamilton

Spokane, WA 99202

Northern Mountain Supply

www.northernmountain.com

mtn@northernmountain.com

800-878-3583

707-445-1711

Hours: Mon. through Fri. 8:30 A.M. to 7:00 P.M., Sat. 9:30 A.M. to 7:00 P.M., Sun. 10:00 A.M. to 5:00 P.M. (PDT)

Northern Mountain Supply, Inc.

125 West Fifth Street

Eureka, CA 95501

REI

www.rei.com
"Live Help" customer service
800-426-4840
253-891-2500
Fax: 253-891-2523
Hours: Mon. through Sun. 4 A.M. to 11 P.M. (PDT)
Store locator: www.rei.com/stores/index.jsp
REI
Sumner, WA 98352-0001

Travel Country Outdoors

travelcountry.com
info@travelcountry.com
800-643-3629
407-831-0777
Fax: 407-831-4204
Travel Country Outdoors
1101 East Altamonte Drive
Altamonte Springs, FL 32701

6

Trail Couture

When you have worn out your shoes, the strength of the shoe leather has passed into the fiber of your body.
—Ralph Waldo Emerson

Summer solstice is the longest day of the year, and it's an AT tradition to hike at least a little bit of your daily mileage naked on that day. The rest of the hiking calendar, however, calls for the high-tech protection of various garments. Gone are the days of wearing bulky wool clothing and gargantuan leather boots. Instead, these have been replaced with an elegant array of high-tech lightweight garments. The AT is not a house of high fashion by any stretch of the imagination, and most long-distance hikers wear the same dirty and stinky clothing day in and day out. But what you wear can have a large impact on your comfort and safety on the trail.

STRETCHY, WICKING, HIGH-TECH FABRICS

Backpacking garments are a showcase of high-tech fabrics. There are few exceptions to the synthetic-only trend in backpacking clothing, namely the occasional wool or silk hat or socks. Aside from wool, down, and silk, you won't really find any natural materials on the market. This is for a good reason—synthetics have the ability to wick away moisture, retain their shape, and dry quickly. When you think of synthetics, an image of your dad's bowling league shirt or something equally tacky probably comes to mind. However, synthetics are modern, lightweight, and resilient, and they retain their insulating properties in a variety of conditions.

> Avoid wearing cotton and cotton blends. While cotton is comfortable off the trail, it's difficult to dry, weighs a lot when moisture-logged, is bulky, and loses its shape when exposed to the elements.

The list of available synthetic materials gets longer and more complex by the year as companies develop innovative ways to deal with the needs of technical clothing. Materials may be used together in blends to utilize the properties of each individual fiber

MATERIALS USED IN BACKPACKING GARMENTS

Acrylic: Acrylic is a synthetic that is practical for all types of technical clothing. It is available in specialized forms, such as Wickspun or Duraspun (known for its wicking properties) or in blends with wool or other synthetics.

Fleece: Fleece comes in a variety of pile thicknesses and performance capabilities (such as its windproof form). It has good insulating properties, is soft to the touch, wicks moisture, and is durable and quick-drying. Fleece can be made of polyester, nylon, polypro, or acrylic. Fleece should be closefitting to insulate properly.

Nylon: Nylon can be used for shirts and pants and is a mainstay of many articles of rain gear when coated or impregnated with waterproofing materials. Silnylon is a form of nylon impregnated with silicon, and Supplex nylon is nylon coated with a Teflon-based waterproofer.

Polyester: Polyester is one of the most commonly found backpacking materials. It repels water and is lightweight, but has a low wicking ability (unless treated) and therefore makes for a poor base layer material. Capilene, a trademarked type of polyester manufactured by Patagonia, has superb wicking abilities and is ideally used for base layers.

Polypropylene: Also known as polypro, this material tends to retain odor, as is the case with most synthetics. It is inexpensive, lightweight, and good at wicking moisture. Polypro needs to be cleaned regularly to preserve its wicking capabilities.

Silk: This is a natural and expensive fiber that is absorbent and feels good against bare skin. It requires special care and takes a long time to dry. Silk is most commonly used for sock liners.

Wool: Wool is a natural fiber that wicks moisture and can become very damp before it loses its insulating properties, making it a nice material for socks. It's also durable and naturally odorresistant, but it may cause an allergic reaction when worn next to bare skin. Wool doesn't burn or melt as easily as synthetics, but it is bulky and heavy in some forms (there are newer types of light wool that compare in weight and bulk to synthetics).

type, as seen in many wool-blend socks. Quite often an existing material can be slightly altered by a company to make a new trademarked material.

BASICS OF LAYERING: INNER, OUTER, AND BASE LAYERS

Layering maximizes the clothing you carry by cutting down on weight while giving you the versatility to meet the demands of a variety of weather and temperature conditions. Generally, temperature control is easier when you have a number of options to deal with as opposed to a single heavy jacket or lightweight shirt. By adding or removing layers, you can fine-tune your own temperature as you hike throughout the day. A single day of weather on the AT can include temperature variances of forty

When hiking through multiple seasons, opt to carry season-specific clothing. Mail unnecessary garments home or bounce them ahead to a post office. It's a good idea to always have a rain jacket and a spare set of dry clothes with you, regardless of the time of year. Winter jackets, thermal underwear, gloves, hats, and other warm clothing can be shipped ahead when walking through the area between Mount Rogers, Virginia, and Glencliff (or Hanover), New Hampshire, during the summer months. In spring and fall, it's advisable to have warm things because cold temperatures may occur at elevation in all sections of the AT. Warmer clothing may be necessary in the summer while hiking in areas of higher elevation, especially in the north. This especially holds true for the White Mountains, where snow can fall any month of the year.

During warm seasons, I wear a hiking skirt paired with a synthetic tank top, lightweight wool-blend crew socks, and well-ventilated hiking shoes with short gaiters. I protect myself from the sun with a visor or bandanna and carry a rain jacket for hiking in precipitation and staying warm on chilly evenings. When cooler weather arrives, I add more layers to my existing wardrobe such as Capilene tops and tights, heavy wool socks, waterproof hiking shoes and gaiters, a windproof fleece, and rain pants. I supplement these items with wind- and waterproof gloves, a fleece hat, and, for very cold weather, a balaclava and down vest. And I always carry a set of camp shoes with me no matter what season it is.

degrees or more, making versatility important. Layering makes the most of clothing's warmth by capturing insulating air between layers. It also allows you to avoid perspiring, which damages the insulating properties of your garments with dampness.

When referring to layers in technical clothing, there are three basic levels to which to pay attention. The *base layer* is the layer that goes next to your skin. This layer should wick moisture away from the skin, keeping it as dry and irritation-free as possible. The rule of thumb is, the lighter the weight of the fabric, the faster it wicks away moisture. Staying dry is particularly significant in cooler weather, when dampness can interfere with the insulating properties of clothing. The base layer should be composed of a quick-drying synthetic material such as Capilene.

The *middle layer* is a general insulating layer. High-pile breathable materials with good insulating properties, such as fleece or wool-blends, are good to use for this layer. Do not use a non-breathable material such as Windbloc or Windstopper fleece for your middle layer since it will cause moisture to build up.

The *outer layer* is possibly the most significant layer you'll carry on the AT. Outer layers include heavier wind shells, rain gear, and weather-resistant coats and vests. Many hikers don't carry an insulating outer layer with them during the summer months. So what should you use as your outer layer? This depends largely on your style of hiking and budget. The average hiker will carry a water-resistant insulated jacket with full-length sleeves in cold weather or a rain suit in warmer temperatures. Many lightweight and ultralight backpackers opt out of carrying a heavier jacket and may instead bring a down vest or even rely on a sleeping bag for warmth when not hiking.

JACKETS, SHELLS, AND VESTS

A jacket is a good option for hiking in the AT's colder seasonal temperatures and for hikers with a generally low tolerance for the cold. Choosing a down jacket can be tricky since, unlike sleeping bags, down jackets aren't rated according to their ideal temperature range. Fill power is listed on better down products and a higher fill number indicates a warmer coat. Down can also be fairly expensive but, for many, it is a worthwhile investment.

Down is highly packable and lightweight considering its insulating abilities, but you need to keep in mind that its capacities are severely compromised when exposed to moisture. Unlike a sleeping bag, a jacket is exposed to more weather and perspiration, both enemies of down. Never sweat inside your down jacket and avoid hiking in it, using it only when in camp. If down seems too high-maintenance for you, you may opt to use a jacket with a synthetic fill such as PrimaLoft or Polarguard. While these jackets aren't as lightweight and won't pack as small as their down counterparts, they are a lot more resilient when exposed to moisture and afford a higher level of insulation when damp. Synthetic insulation is often incorporated in shell-type technical jackets, allowing for waterproofing, windproofing, and warmth in one package.

In cold weather, have your jacket easily accessible so that you can throw it on at camp and during breaks before your body temperature drops. On all but the coldest days during the regular hiking season, a jacket is only necessary in camp since body heat does an adequate job of making you comfortable while you hike (I've comfortably hiked in twenty-degree weather wearing a shell over a long-sleeved tech shirt).

To save on weight, use a vest in lieu of a jacket. Vests keep the trunk of your body comfortable and spare you the excess bulk and weight of sleeve material. Many

> Try to keep your jacket as clean as possible because, like a sleeping bag, multiple launderings can destroy its loft and insulating abilities.

hikers use a windproof or waterproof shell along with layers of tech materials to stay dry and warm. Shells are lightweight, breathable, movable jackets that are good for keeping you comfortable on moderately cool days. There are different types of shells: general ones for cool and dry weather, wind shells, and rain shells. A wind shell can be used in warmer weather to protect you from the rapid cooling that can occur from the effect of wind chill.

Being aware of where your body tends to lose heat helps with selecting an intelligent wardrobe for your long-distance hike. Your torso is the most important part of your body to keep warm because your vital organs are housed there. Heat also escapes from the head and neck, making hats, neck gaiters, and balaclavas essential. This is why you will see many AT hikers in the snow wearing jackets, hats, and shorts.

A coat can be a lifesaving piece of gear (literally) and can add much-needed warmth in an underrated sleeping bag on cold nights. Look for a coat that fits well and gives you a good range of motion while keeping warm air trapped inside. For coats and vests with pockets, make sure the pockets are accessible even when your pack is on and cinched up. Look for a coat with Velcro sleeve enclosures to keep water and wind away. Features such as small pockets, for headlamps and maps, and zipper-vented underarms are options found in most quality coats and, though they add weight to the item, are invaluable. Avoid coats, vests, and shells with an excess of bells and whistles, especially those things adding unnecessary weight or those that may cause discomfort if worn with a pack.

HATS, GLOVES, AND MISCELLANEOUS CLOTHING

Typically, long-distance hikers try to carry as few things as possible but often hats, gloves, and other odds and ends end up in the pack. Some hikers take their minimalism so far as to use extra socks for mittens and a spare shirt as a turban-like hat. Decide what you deem necessary and pack accordingly.

A lot of heat escapes from the body via your head (this is why we grow copious amounts of hair there), and a fleece or wool-blend cap helps to maintain a comfortable body temperature in frigid conditions. Ideally, your hat should be water-resistant and dry easily. A balaclava, a garment that looks like a hat and scarf combined, is great for keeping heat from escaping through the carotid artery, an area of heavy blood circulation lying near the skin's surface. A balaclava may be used alone or in tandem with a hat in severely cold temperatures.

Use some sort of sun hat to protect your face. This is especially important for the winter, spring, and late fall months when there isn't a lot of vegetation on the trees to block out the sun. A ball cap, visor, or fisherman's style hat can be used over a fleece hat or alone to provide protection from the sun. A brimmed cap, when worn under a waterproof rain jacket hood, also helps to keep precipitation off the face. A bandana makes a nice makeshift head covering and can be used in the summer to cool the head by periodically dipping it in a cold stream or in the winter for warmth by layering it with a fleece or wool hat.

In all but the coldest weather, you can get away without wearing gloves or mittens. Most hikers find that the blood flow caused by constant physical activity keeps the hands warm enough. For camp chores requiring manual dexterity, gloves are sometimes a necessary accessory. Make sure you are able to use your fingers to work zippers, open your pack, and do other essential functions while wearing your gloves or mittens. Some hikers use mittens with retractable finger coverings for easy access. If you use trekking poles, you may want to wear gloves with a reinforced grip

Vista near the New York/New Jersey state line

area to prevent wear. Gloves designed for use with ski poles are cut differently than regular gloves and are ideal for use with trekking poles. Glove liners are a lightweight alternative to wearing gloves. Liners are intended to be worn under gloves for an added layer of protection against the elements, but are adequate on their own for more mild weather protection. As with hats, fleece or wool-blends are good fabric options. The material should be water-resistant and wind-stopping.

Hiking in skirts and kilts is becoming more popular for both male and female hikers. These garments are excellent alternatives to shorts and pants because they offer a great range of motion and ventilation. They also make privy breaks quick and easy. Companies such as Mountain Hardware (www.mountainhardwear.com), Royal Robbins (www.royalrobbins.com), and Sport Kilt (www.sportkilt.com) offer versions of backpacking kilts and skirts in high-tech fabrics and designs.

Protective clothing sporting insect-repelling and sun-blocking capabilities is fairly new to the market. Typically made of tightly woven high-tech cloth, sun-blocking fabric filters out more sun than standard cloth and helps protect skin from dangerous UV rays. Many sun-blocking garments advertise having a UV protection rating similar to that found in sunblock lotions. Insect-repelling clothing features a chemical repellent impregnated in the fabric that helps to ward off a wide array of pests, including mosquitoes and ticks. This sort of clothing claims to relieve the need to use harmful repellent chemicals, a good thing for those with chemical sensitivities. Buzz Off, a popular manufacturer of this sort of apparel, has a line of clothing that contains a built-in repellent that lasts for up to twenty-five launderings (www.buzzoffoutdoorwear.com).

TOWN CLOTHES

Many long-distance hikers carry a set of clean clothes to wear while getting hitches and doing chores and resupply in town. It's nice to have even a spare shirt to wear after taking a shower, since nothing is more demoralizing than showering and then having to put back on grimy clothing or a rain suit. Town clothes need be nothing more than a spare tech shirt and maybe a pair of shorts that you don't wear too often on the trail. Some hikers pack lightweight non-hiking shirts and some female hikers carry wrinkly cotton peasant skirts. You can mail a bounce box with a set of town clothes ahead to towns that you plan on spending multiple days in. The nice thing about bounce-boxing town clothes is that it keeps clothes dry and clean and spares you the work of having to carry them on your back.

A number of hostels on the trail provide hikers with a fun, eclectic collection of town clothes to wear after showering and on zero days (these include Hawaiian shirts, frumpy house dresses, and denim from the 1980s).

NO PAIN RAIN GEAR

There's a popular saying that states, "If you want to get to Maine, you have to hike in the rain." The Appalachians experience a lot of precipitation throughout the year, particularly in the springtime. At best, rain is a hassle, but in the worst case scenario a wet hiker is in danger of hypothermia. The body uses moisture to combat overheating, which is why your body sweats when it's hot. Rainwater has the same effect as sweat, rapidly cooling the body off, especially in freezing temperatures. For this reason, it's important to keep your body and clothing dry. Regardless of the season, a rain jacket is an essential piece of clothing to carry.

There are a number of options for rain gear. You may use a rain shell coupled with waterproof pants or a single large poncho that acts as a rain suit and pack cover combined (one popular super poncho is the Packa, available at www.thepacka.com). Many hikers only use rain pants in colder weather, mailing them ahead during the summer. Frogg Toggs (www.froggtoggs.com) are a nice compromise for the hiker concerned with weight as they offer full coverage at a low weight. Some ultralight hikers opt to use umbrellas in lieu of rain gear. Though umbrellas weigh less, they aren't very effective in windy weather and are inadequate for blocking out blowing rain and cold temperatures.

Materials used in manufacturing rain gear are made up of water-resistant, chemical-impregnated, or coated synthetic fabrics. There are two basic functional types of materials: breathable and non-breathable. Gore-Tex is a good example of a high-end breathable waterproof fabric. This fabric has a finely permeated membrane that allows air out but won't let water seep in. Rain gear made from non-breathable material holds in more of your body heat and perspiration, creating an environment inside the clothing that rivals the dampness of what's outside. Generally, breathable materials cost significantly more that non-breathable ones. And all rain gear causes at least some sweating and dampness, regardless of its cost.

Pockets in waterproof jackets should be easily accessible while you hike with your pack on (this usually means that they are up higher and placed closer to the front zipper than in regular jackets). Ideally, jackets should have zippered underarm vents to control perspiration and allow a flow of air. Another nice feature is a stiff bill on the hood to keep rain and debris out of your eyes. The hood should be able to be tucked away in a pocket when not in use.

Store your rain gear in an external pocket or at the top of your pack so it's easy to get to in a hurry as few experiences are more demoralizing than getting soaked while rummaging around your pack for your rain gear. Whenever the weather looks menacing, I strap my rain jacket to the outside of my pack so I can get to it within seconds. A mesh outer pocket is a good place to store wet rain gear for easy access and drying.

Because of waterproof chemical coatings, rain gear is more difficult to take care of than other garments. Don't wash your rain gear in a standard washing machine, particularly not in a top-loading one with a drum that may tear the jacket. Instead, rinse rain gear out in a bathtub or with a hose to get the major filth and grime off. Always consult the garment label for washing instructions. Materials that are coated rather than impregnated with waterproofing may lose their effectiveness as the coating wears off. Revitalize rain gear with DWR spray, available at most outfitters. This is the same spray used for other waterproof and water-resistant items such as tent flies. Make sure the DWR coating is flexible, won't damage the material, and won't peel off when the fabric moves. Always do a test patch before applying coating to the entire garment.

THE TRUTH ABOUT HIKER UNDERWEAR

Not many people give a thought to backpacking underwear until out on the trail. Truth be told, traditional underwear isn't found too often on the AT. Instead, there's a motley assortment of breathable tech undergarments. Some hikers wear spandex shorts in lieu of underwear since they are fairly breathable, reduce chafing, and provide support. If you opt to wear underwear, keep in mind that you'll want to change it frequently, meaning you'll have to carry a number of clean pairs with you in your pack. Since most underwear is in close contact with the body, there are a lot of opportunities for unsavory bacteria to grow in it. As an alternative, many hikers go "commando," letting the fresh air ventilate their nether regions while keeping the pack weight down.

Women, especially, need to consider their underwear options, as health issues can easily arise from the wrong decisions. For women prone to yeast infections, cotton is the first choice off the trail. However, on the trail, cotton is about the worst thing a person can wear. Ladies with recurring problems should consider wearing special breathable and wicking underwear or doing without.

DAMAGE CONTROL: GARMENT CARE

Caring for technical garments is fairly straightforward: wash in regular cycle on warm and tumble dry low. When selecting clothing for your long-distance hike, read the labels to see what sort of care the items require. Avoid clothing with special needs, as this can turn into a major hassle on the trail. Go for the wash-and-dry stuff that can be handled at any ordinary trail town laundromat.

Synthetics tend to retain odor, even those treated with antimicrobial agents. After being on the trail for a while, it may take a few washings to get clothing fully clean. Many a desperate hiker has replaced a shirt because of its stench. When using the town laundromat, opt for a front-loading machine as opposed to the top-loading type with the drum mounted at the bottom. Front-loaders are easier on fabrics and won't snag or tear zippers and seams. Be careful not to dry synthetics (especially nylon) at an overly high temperature as this can cause the material to melt.

Between town stays, rinse your clothing out to rid it of salt deposits from sweat. These deposits can act as a skin irritant, especially in socks, shirts, and waistbands. And dirt eventually disintegrates fabric, decreasing its lifespan significantly. Rinse clothing at least two hundred feet from water sources. If you choose to wash clothing on the trail with soap, use a biodegradable soap and rinse well. Clothing can be hung from your pack to dry while you hike, or you can use your bear-bag line as an improvised laundry line at camp. I have a sturdy Velcro loop on my pack for the purpose of hanging clothing to dry while I hike on sunny days. Carry large freezer bags in which to store dirty socks and other articles of clothing to cut down on odor in your pack.

Down and some wool garments require special care. There are soaps manufactured specifically for cleaning these materials, and you'll want to pay special attention to manufacturer labels for washing instructions. Most wool-blend socks can be washed normally and tumbled dry at a moderate temperature. When down garments require laundering, you may want to take them to a professional. Ask for cleaner recommendations at the local outfitters before entrusting your garments to a laundromat's care.

Keep your clothes dry by storing them in a silnylon bag or a freezer bag. I recommend putting at least one shirt and a pair of socks in a large freezer bag to ensure dry clothing no matter the weather conditions. It's essential to have something dry to change into at the end of a long, wet day for psychological as well as physical comfort. Place slightly damp clothing inside your sleeping bag to dry with your body heat. Don't, however, put soaking clothes in your bag with you. Along with failing to dry the clothing, this will soak your bag, damaging its insulating properties.

FOOTWEAR: A LOVE/HATE RELATIONSHIP

Aching feet are the number one physical complaint for hikers. Choosing proper footwear takes both know-how and a little experimentation. Try out various kinds of footwear on day and weekend hikes. Newer synthetic hiking shoes and boots don't require the same break-in period that old-fashioned leather boots do, allowing you to switch footwear fairly easily.

There are many types of footwear on the trail: traditional heavy boots, medium-weight boots, lightweight boots, hiking shoes, trail runners, running shoes, and hiking sandals. Footwear can be made of a variety of materials such as leather, nylon mesh, polyester, and synthetic leather. Choose your footwear based on the type of hiking you do. Mileage, pack weight, and specific foot needs dictate what will work best for you. Someone with a twelve-pound pack can hike with lightweight trail runners, while a hiker with a heavy pack probably needs the full support of a boot. Since gear has become lighter over the years, more hikers are switching from the old leather behemoths of yesteryear to lighter models.

There's an art to shopping for hiking shoes and boots. Go shopping at the end of the day, when feet are at their largest. The difference between tired, swollen feet and fresh feet can account for an entire shoe size; and it's better to err on the side of having a bit too much room, as too little room can restrict circulation and cause toenail damage, among other problems. When shopping, bring along your footbeds, orthotics, sock liners, outer socks, and whatever else you put in your shoes. Many brands of hiking footwear offer both men's and women's designs. Women and men generally have different ergonomic needs when it comes to comfort because of variations in stride and hip width. Men generally need a larger toe box and more shoe width. Try on both men's and women's models as you may find a better fit through cross-dressing. Choose a shoe that's a bit larger (a half or full size) than what you typically wear in street shoes, and make sure that your toes have adequate room in the toe box area.

Perhaps the most important aspect of a shoe is its heel, as it pro-

If you choose to hike in leather shoes or boots, you need to break them in before you begin a long hike. Start by wearing them around the house and on short walks before proceeding to day and weekend hikes. While this process isn't necessary with lightweight synthetic footwear, it's important to observe this breaking-in period for heavier leather shoes and boots.

vides a majority of the shoe's stability. Make sure your heel fits well and doesn't have room to shift around, which could cause instability or blisters. Shoes come equipped with a *heel counter,* the stiff, reinforced part of the heel that provides support for the foot and ankle. Some hikers claim that a low-cut shoe with a good heel counter can provide more ankle support than a tall boot. It can also be argued that a lighter hiking shoe gives you a better "feel" of the terrain underneath you and, as a result, offers more stability and balance.

Footwear should provide ankle support, arch support, and good cushioning. The soles should be puncture-resistant (to prevent stone bruises and other injuries to the foot) and should be constructed of a resilient and grippy material such

> If you have an existing foot condition such as bunions or pronation, you'll need to pay special attention to your footwear and may want to enlist the advice of a podiatrist when selecting shoes.

as Vibram. Soles should also have good, deep tread that can deal with a variety of terrains from bare granite to mud and ice. Look for lateral stiffness (stiffness from one side of the foot to the other), but avoid footwear that is stiff from the toe to heel.

The toe box should provide adequate room for your toes without letting them move around too much, which could generate blisters, ruin support, and damage toenails. Find the proper fit that allows room for socks and normal foot swelling. Footwear should have some sort of sewn-in tongue or scree collar—the part of the shoe's or boot's structure that keeps small debris and dirt out of the shoe.

When trying out new shoes, walk around, squat, roll your ankles, and stand on your toes, trying to mimic the large variety of movements your foot may experience while hiking. Make use of the incline board, a ramp that many good outfitters provide that imitates the feel of walking up and down hills. When trying on shoes, put on both shoes because most people have different-sized feet. Select the size that accommodates your larger foot. Keep in mind that leather boots and shoes will stretch in width but not in length, so buy a pair that is adequately long enough for your foot. After using your shoes or boots on a number of shorter hikes, make note of the wear and tear on your socks. Uneven wear or holes may indicate improperly fitted footwear.

Shoes and boots have many features. There are a variety of lacing styles from which to choose. Make sure that the lacing helps the shoe to fit better and doesn't apply too much pressure across the bridge of your foot.

Look for strong, straight stitching when buying shoes, and try to choose a shoe design with as few seams as possible.

Waterproofing is another feature advertised by many shoemakers. The insides of all shoes and boots eventually get wet and uncomfortable when subjected to the damp conditions on the AT. Though they may keep your feet drier a little bit longer, waterproof footwear takes much longer to dry out and weighs a good deal more than its breathable mesh counterparts. However, if you're hiking during the cold season, you'll want to avoid breathable shoes that leave feet more exposed to the elements.

Footwear can cost anywhere from a meager $50 to well over $200, and it's best not to skimp or make do with the bargain choice (though some hikers have happily done many miles in inexpensive work boots found at major retail shops, and the infamous Grandma Gatewood wore Keds). Custom-made boots are an option for hikers with special needs and disposable income. A number of manufacturers construct custom-made boots and give you the option of taking your own measurements at home and sending them to the factory. Each company has its own fitting procedures and, ideally, you should be measured in person by a trained salesperson. A couple of the larger manufacturers are Limmer Boots (limmerboot.com) and Esatto (www.esatto.biz). Regardless of whether you buy shoes ready-to-wear or if you have them custom-made, you should look for signs of durability and good craftsmanship.

In 2005, I met a southbound hiker who'd initially bought sandals to spite a know-it-all salesperson at an outfitter. Eventually, she fell in love with hiking in sandals and had used them successfully for hundreds of miles. Sandals are relatively new to the world of long-distance hiking. Hiking sandals differ greatly from regular street wear and even from most other sport sandals, providing extra support and ruggedness. There are a number of different manufacturers of hiking sandals, Keen (www.keen footwear.com) and Chaco (www.chacousa.com) being the two major names on the market. Keens offer a sturdy rubber toe guard while Chacos have excellent arch support (enough support, in fact, to render them uncomfortable for some people with low arches). Sandals are great because they're lightweight and breathable, and they eliminate the need to carry a pair of camp shoes. Fording and slogging through puddles is made more convenient when wearing sandals, and they dry quickly. On the down side, they leave your feet vulnerable to sunburn, bug and snakebites, cuts, and other problems.

You may need to buy multiple pairs of shoes throughout the course of your long hike as footwear periodically wears out and needs to be replaced. Occasionally, someone with very rugged boots is able to make an entire thru-hike without changing footwear. But wearing the same footwear for thousands of miles is generally not a good idea since, as the shoe breaks down, it provides less support for your foot even if the sole is intact and the stitching is holding up. The general rule of thumb is to change out shoes at least every five hundred miles and heavier boots every thousand miles. After a period of time, the cushioning compresses and internal structural damage occurs in the shoes, offering the foot less protection. Whatever you do, don't buy multiple pairs of shoes before you start your long hike. Feet can change radically during the course of a hike, rendering your spare pairs uncomfortable and useless. A hiker's foot may grow anywhere from a half to a full size larger during the course of a long-distance hike. It's easy enough to get shoes replaced on the trail through local outfitters, ordering over the phone, or shopping online.

I've experimented with many types of footwear ranging from traditional leather boots to hiking sandals and lightweight trail runners. Through trial and error, I found my ideal shoe, the Moab, manufactured by Merrell. I've been wearing the Moab and its predecessors off and on for some time with great success. Oddly enough, the men's version of the shoes fits me best, giving me ample toe room and ergonomic support. I replace the factory insoles with Shock Doctor insoles and, if my feet are feeling especially tender, I use a thin gel heel insert (bought at a drug store) under the Shock Doctors for additional impact resistance.

At the end of a long day, it's nice to have something comfortable to slip your feet into. Camp shoes are the AT equivalent to bedroom slippers and are essentially lightweight shoes you can wear around camp. Hikers hang Crocs (www.crocs.com), Waldies (www.waldies.net), flip-flops, or plastic shower shoes from their packs to wear while in camp. It's really important to have dry feet, and it's nice to be able to change out of boots and shoes that you've been wearing all day. Camp shoes also give your footwear time to air out and dry. Yes, there's the option of going barefoot at camp, but this is less than desirable in cooler weather and subjects your feet to injuries and infections.

Footbeds and Orthotics
Hiking shoes and boots come from the factory with cushioned and formed, fitted linings placed in the bottom. These linings are adequate for occa-

sional use, but many hikers opt to switch out the factory lining with a footbed purchased separately. A footbed is an insole-type lining created to make the shoe more stable and impact-resistant. You don't need to have existing foot problems to benefit from the use of footbeds. In fact, footbeds help prevent many problems before they start. There are a number of different brands of footbeds on the market. One of the most popularly used is Superfeet (www.superfeet.com). Superfeet insoles are manufactured for a variety of activities, but the green ones are specially suited for hikers. Other brands of footbeds are Sole Custom (www.your-sole.com) and Shock Doctor (www.shockdoc.com). Sole footbeds are a more recent innovation. They can be custom-fit to your feet by heating in the oven and then shaping them to conform to your feet while they are warm and malleable. Bunheads, a company that caters primarily to dancers, has developed a line of jelly foot cushions that are useful to hikers (www.bunheads.com).

If you have a preexisting foot problem such as supination, you may want to wear prescription orthotics in your shoes. Much like footbeds, orthotics help to stabilize the foot inside the shoe, but they also help to ergonomically compensate for deficiencies with foot conformation. For example, if your foot tends to roll to the outside of the heel when you take a step, an orthotic helps to offset this imbalance. A podiatrist can determine what sort of orthotic you need and can create a custom-made set to specifically meet the needs of your feet. Orthotics are usually made of a heavy-duty molded plastic and take time to get used to because they can feel rigid. Some hikers feel that orthotics increase the impact of the foot on the ground by negating the springy resilience of the foot's arch. Whether or not this is true, many hikers with foot, knee, hip, and back problems have seen great results after using them.

Footwear Care

A long-distance hiker's shoes take a beating. They are subject to delaminating soles, ripped stitching or material, disintegrated cushioning, and other problems. Though you will likely have to replace your shoes on the trail, there are some tips to coaxing a few extra miles out of them. With the advent of synthetic shoes taking over the previously leather-boot-dominated market, footwear care has become a relatively simple thing. Leather boots last much longer than synthetic hiking shoes and boots on the market today. However, there is a trade-off since traditional boots require a good bit of care to stay in top shape.

Generally, it's good to try to keep your footwear free of debris, inside and out. Debris on the inside causes foot discomfort and can shorten the lifespan of the shoe. If your shoes or boots get particularly dirty, you may want to wash them off with a garden hose or in a sink. Instead of washing the inside, wipe it out with a damp cloth instead. As with other equipment, keep your footwear out of direct sunlight when you're not wearing it as UV rays can rapidly break down the materials.

If you opt to wear leather footwear, you need to periodically waterproof and treat the leather. Seal the seams and waterproof your boots before wearing them, since dirt makes it more difficult for the chemical treatments to adhere. Stitching should be treated before waxing. Products for treating leather can be found at any major outfitter or footwear store in a variety of forms, such as waxes or sprays. Waterproofing needs to be repeatedly applied because it tends to wear off over time. Since wax impairs leather's ability to breath, the amount of wax you apply to your boots dictates how breathable they are. In cold weather, apply more wax; in warmer temperatures, apply less.

Every hiker dreads putting on wet shoes at the beginning of the day. Though this is unavoidable, there are ways to speed up the drying process while causing the least amount of damage. At the end of each day, remove inserts or footbeds, loosen the laces, and pull the tongue out to help air the shoe out. This helps to cut down odor and keeps the shoe drier and in better condition. If your shoe is really wet and you want to dry it out thoroughly during a town stay, you can stuff it with paper towels or newspapers and place it near a heater or fan. Never set shoes directly on top of a heater, in front of a fire, or in the dryer at the laundromat, as rapid drying and heat may cause major damage, such as delamination of the soles. Always dry footwear slowly (this is especially true for leather). If you have leather footwear, be sure to let the material dry thoroughly before applying dressing or waterproofing.

Frequently, days away from an outfitter, a hiker's shoes or boots give up the ghost. A quick way to fix shoes is with duct tape. A little tape can go a long way in holding the soles on and keeping debris out until you get a replacement. In town, Shoo Goo and other heavy-duty shoe adhesives are useful for reattaching delaminated soles (this is a relatively common problem and, oftentimes, a shoe can be worn for many miles more after having the sole reattached). Contact cement is also a good product to use for a quick fix in a bind. Reattach the sole by cleaning the shoe, applying glue, clamping together with duct tape or packing tape, and leaving overnight. In theory, more significant repairs are only worthwhile on expensive medium- to heavy-weight leather boots. Generally, lightweight trail shoes die too quickly to bother with extensive repairs or resoling. If you have an expensive pair of boots with problems, you may want to take them to a shoe repair shop at a trail town in lieu of replacing them. Cobblers can make worn boots like new through resoling and repairing stitching.

SOCKS

Hikers require a special type of sock to deal with the wear and tear of daily high-mileage use. Some hikers wear a combination of two socks: a wool-blend outer sock with a synthetic or silk sock liner. Ideally, hiking socks should be composed of a wool-blend. Wool retains its density and insulating properties when wet, and doesn't hold odors as much as synthetic materials. Wool fiber is blended with acrylic, spandex, and other materials to provide elasticity and shape. If you have an allergy to wool, you may be able to remedy the situation by wearing thicker sock liners and making sure your skin isn't exposed to the wool material. If not, there are socks with lower wool content such as Isowool (50 percent merino wool and 50 percent polypropylene blend) or fully synthetic socks.

Sock liners serve a number of functions. They help wick moisture away from the foot, and they protect against chafing and blistering by reducing friction between the shoe and foot. Sock liners can be made of a variety of materials: silk, nylon, polypropylene, Thermax, Coolmax, or Orlon. Silk is good for cold-weather use and polypropylene is used in warmer temperatures. While many hikers use sock liners, some elect not to and others (mainly those using sandals) hike without any socks at all.

While socks are somewhat bulky and can take up a bit of pack space, they are some of the most essential pieces of clothing you'll carry. A lot of hikers tend to reuse their wool outer socks a number of times before washing them and wear a clean pair of liners as often as possible (liners are cheaper, take up less pack weight, and can be easily washed by hand and air-dried). Particularly in hot weather when you're sweating a lot, change your sock liners often

There are waterproof outer socks made of neoprene and Gore-Tex. These socks have been used by hikers with mixed reviews. If conditions are really wet, you can wear plastic bags sandwiched between your liners and socks. Plastic bags can also help to keep feet warm on chilly days.

to allow them to dry and air out. Rotate between two pairs, hanging one on your pack to dry while you hike while wearing the other. Always make sure to have at least one pair of relatively clean and dry socks on hand. Hikers usually carry two to three pairs of socks, including the pair on their feet.

> One of the most popular brands of wool socks on the AT is SmartWool (www.smartwool.com). I met a hiker who had traveled some 1,500 miles in a single pair of SmartWools before he finally got a small hole in one. Other reputable brands of wool socks are Darn Tough (www.darntough.com) and Dahlgren (www.dahlgrenfootwear.com).

When selecting socks to use, you should try them on, the same way you would try on shoes or boots. Socks should have a snug (but not overly tight) fit to prevent blisters and chafing. Make sure that socks don't fit tightly enough to impair circulation as this plays a key role in keeping feet warm and healthy. The socks you use should be thick enough to absorb impact, fitted to the foot, and well-constructed. Socks shouldn't have any prominent exposed seams, as these may cause abrasions and sores on the foot.

GAITERS

Gaiters are a type of legging worn between the ankle and knee to keep feet and legs safe from debris. Gaiters have many benefits: they keep legs protected, muscles warm, your pants dry, and pebbles and dirt out of shoes and boots. They also protect against tick and snake bites as well as poison ivy. They come in various sizes, weights, and styles for a variety of outdoor conditions. Six- to eight-inch gaiters are adequate for general use, including hiking in light snow cover, and are the most popular choice for AT hikers. There are longer types of gaiters that come to right below the knee, which are good for deeper snow, hiking on poorly groomed trail, or bushwhacking, and some hikers prefer to use these types of gaiters for the protection they afford.

There are a few different types of closures for gaiters. Velcro closures keep out moisture and are easy to put on but may be difficult to use when covered in mud or snow. Zippers are harder to use and may get stuck with debris, and snaps are sturdy but difficult to open and close. The heel strap, the part that holds the gaiter snug to the bottom of your shoe, is the first part of a gaiter to fail. Look for gaiters that have replaceable heel straps instead of ones with permanent straps so that you can switch them out when they break.

Most all of your time spent on the trail will be in the same set of shorts and dirty shirt. Occasionally, on really cold days, you may opt for the classic AT look of layering shorts over long johns, or don a hat. Some hikers, including the guys, choose to wear skirts or kilts (showing that the trail truly is a liberated place). Regardless of what styles of technical clothing and footwear you choose to wear, take care of your garments, keep them relatively dry and clean, and they will serve you well.

7

Eating and Drinking

Hunger makes you restless. You dream about food—not just any food, but perfect food, the best food, magical meals, famous and awe-inspiring, the one piece of meat, the exact taste of buttery corn, tomatoes so ripe they split and sweeten the air, beans so crisp they snap between the teeth, gravy like mother's milk singing to your bloodstream.

—Dorothy Allison, *Bastard Out of Carolina*

Spend any amount of time with a group of long-distance hikers and, invariably, the conversation turns to the topic of food and drink: what to eat in town, how to cook on the trail, which spring has the sweetest and coldest water. An average human burns about 2,000 to 2,500 calories per day, whereas a hiker requires anywhere from 4,000 all the way up to 6,000 calories a day to fuel the body. Water is also a concern as hikers require many liters of water every day. While the AT is a notoriously wet trail in terms of weather, finding water is an acquired skill and can be a challenge. No wonder hikers are so consumed (pun intended) by thoughts of food and drink.

WATER, WATER, EVERYWHERE

The average sedentary adult needs to consume two liters of water per day to sustain a healthy level of hydration. Multiply that figure two or more times and that's how much a sweating hiker needs. Now add to that the fact that hikers aren't able to stroll over to a faucet and turn on the tap to get clean, fresh water. A hiker needs to locate, collect, filter or treat, and store every drop of water he or she drinks.

Drinking is more crucial to a hiker's well-being than eating. A well-hydrated body is less prone to fatigue and injury. A large percentage of the human body is composed of water, and drinking plays a vital role in replenishing fluids and electrolytes that enable the body to function. While you hike, it's important to drink often. Never wait until you're thirsty to drink, as the body begins the process of dehydration well before you feel thirst.

Water sources can be found in numerous locations on the AT, and they are listed in the major trail guides, maps, and data books. Drought and typical late summer weather conditions can bring about a scarcity of water and some states, such as Pennsylvania and New York, are drier than others. As a long-distance hiker, you'll get your water from backcountry sources such as streams, ponds, and springs, and developed sources like pumps, spigots, and faucets. Most shelters and campsites have some form of water source on site or relatively close by.

FIGHTING THE WAR ON *GIARDIA:* WATER TREATMENT

To treat or not to treat is a question commonly asked by hikers. Remember, though the U.S. is a developed country, contaminated water may be encountered anywhere, and all it takes is a small amount of contaminated animal or human fecal matter to ruin a water supply. While new hikers are overzealous about water treatment, many tend to get lackadaisical after hiking hundreds of miles.

Why is it even necessary to treat water? There are many commonly occurring microscopic organisms that find their way into water sources. These organisms, such as *Giardia lamblia* and *Cryptosporidium,* can cause serious health issues if allowed to take up residence in the human digestive tract. What results can be something as minor as a stomachache or as significant as an illness that drives a hiker off the trail with weakness, nausea, and diarrhea.

Ideally, a hiker should always treat or filter water from backcountry sources, but I have yet to meet many long-distance hikers who treat 100 percent of the time. Some hikers manage to hike hundreds of miles without ever treating water and never experience negative repercussions, while others treat

Though the physical appearance of water won't give you any indication of its quality, there are some basic rules about what you should consider as a safe water source. Collect water from moving sources such as flowing streams or springs, and avoid stagnant pools, lakes, or ponds. Select a water source high in elevation and close to the earth. Mountain springs are ideal water sources (a spring is water flowing directly from underground). If you see a water source near farmland or housing, skip it and go elsewhere. Avoid sources with signs of animals such as beaver dams, scat, carcasses, or tracks. And keep in mind that water is especially susceptible to contamination after heavy rainfall, particularly in lower elevations.

and still get mysterious intestinal ailments. Skipping the step of treating your water is like playing a game of Russian roulette, and you stand the chance of getting unpleasantly ill if you drink untreated water.

There are times during a hike when you have to collect water from a less than desirable source. When this occurs, definitely use some form of chemical treatment or filtration method. It's a good idea to treat seemingly reliable sources as well, even water drawn from springs and hand pumps. Often, pumps and other developed sources of water are tested for harmful bacteria populations on a regular basis, but there's always a lingering chance of contamination.

Shelter registers are a good place to keep tabs on the status of developed water, directions to alternate water sources, and other vital water information. Trail maintainers and hikers leave news on the water situation in shelter registers, but keep in mind that a positive recommendation on a water source may count for very little. It takes a week or two before signs of bacterial or viral infection make an appearance and, by that time, affected hikers have moved well past the location where the contaminated water was collected, leaving you out of the informational loop. When in doubt, filter or treat your water. Yes, it takes a few extra minutes, but it may save you countless zero days and a lot of physical discomfort.

There are many ways to render water safe to drink. The three basic methods are chemical treatment, mechanical filtering, and purification. Chemical treatment, which is popular among AT hikers, renders the bacteria harmless through chemical means. The filtering method utilizes a mechanical device to clean harmful materials out of water, and purification is filtering with an added chemical step.

Chemical Treatments

The most well-known chemical treatments are chlorine dioxide (such as KlearWater or Aquamira brands) and iodine. Chemical treatments are added to water in drop or tablet form. The water is shaken to mix in the chemical and then left to stand while the chemical takes effect. Chemical treatments require a certain period of time for activation. Depending on the brand of treatment used, you may have to wait anywhere from twenty-five minutes to a number of hours until the water can be safely consumed.

In the early 1900s, *chlorine dioxide* was first used as a large-scale water treatment method at a spa in Belgium. It effectively kills microorganisms through oxidation, and it became a mainstream method

> Because of its low weight, inexpensive price tag, and ease of use, I prefer to use Aquamira water treatment drops. I don't mind the time it takes to activate the solution and treat water, and I like not having to deal with the mechanical breakdowns and maintenance issues associated with water filters. Aquamira is easily found along the trail at most outfitters, and the bottles of solution last a relatively long time.

for water treatment in the 1950s. Chlorine dioxide is currently used in a large number of public water supply treatment facilities. It is a relatively stable material in liquid form (how it is packaged for backpacking use) when stored in proper conditions. Chlorine dioxide is very soluble in water and is more effective in colder temperatures than other chemicals. It is also believed to be more effective than iodine, particularly on organisms such as *Cryptosporidium, Cyclospora,* and *Toxoplasma,* and cuts through the slime that coats and protects bacteria.

Iodine is a well-known method for treating water. It comes in a few different forms: tablet, crystal, and tincture (solution). Tablets are most familiar to backpackers and the easiest to use. Though iodine has long been a trusted method of treating water, it is believed to not be as effective as chlorine dioxide in killing certain types of parasitic bacteria. Many hikers, however, place a lot of faith in this chemical—an attitude based on hearsay and habit rather than scientific evidence.

The potential health risks of repeated exposure to iodine are not fully known, but it is suspected that it may have an adverse effect on the body, particularly the thyroid gland. You may want to choose an alternative treatment method if you have a thyroid condition or a family history of thyroid problems. Some individuals may display a hypersensitivity to iodine (such as that found in fish or iodized table salt), and pregnant women should avoid ingesting iodine. Because of the potential health issues related to iodine, some hikers carry it only as an emergency backup method of water treatment.

Aside from chlorine dioxide and iodine, there are a number of other options for chemical water treatment. *Aerobic oxygen* (also known as stabilized oxygen or aerobic O_2) is a stabilized liquid form of oxygen that has been in use for years by disaster relief programs and international travelers. Ounce for ounce, aerobic oxygen is extremely efficient and cost-effective. One ounce of it makes fifty-five gallons of water safe for five years. This treatment utilizes oxygen to kill off harmful bacteria without destroying the naturally beneficial bacterial flora that populates the human digestive tract.

Chlorine, found in common household bleach, kills microorganisms and is utilized in some commercially marketed treatment products. Though not as effective against a wide range of organisms such as *Giardia* cysts, household bleach is easy to find, inexpensive, and can be used in a pinch. A few hikers even opt to use it as a primary treatment method. Use plain

When using chemicals, a general rule of thumb is, the colder the water, the stronger and longer a chemical treatment is needed. The same holds true for treating cloudy water. Follow the manufacturer's recommendations for chemical storage, keeping chemicals out of extreme heat and humidity. Never use a chemical that has expired, and keep treatment products away from eyes, skin, and gear.

bleach (without added dyes or fragrances) for treatment at the amount of eight drops per gallon in cool water, allowing water to sit for thirty minutes before drinking. Scentless water should never be consumed because the presence of a chlorine smell indicates that the water contains an effective level of solution (don't use too much as this has adverse health effects). Hikers who opt to carry bleach usually store it in a clean recycled eye dropper container, which makes it easy to measure the drops. It's also handy to have bleach to rinse your cooking pot and water containers. This helps to kill off bacteria and keep things smelling fresh and clean.

Halazone used to be a popular water disinfectant marketed to backpackers. Like iodine, this chemical comes in tablet form. Halazone is a chlorine-based chemical and, like other chlorine-based treatment methods, it is slow to disinfect, sometimes unstable, and pH-sensitive. It also leaves a foul taste in treated water and may create toxicity in humans and aquatic life. With the advent of other treatment chemicals, halazone has seen a decrease in popularity.

Filtration Systems
For hikers with chemical sensitivity, a general aversion to chemical treatment, or who want to avoid some of the hassles associated with mixing solutions and waiting for clean water, there are filtration and purification methods. Both processes involve a step of forcing water through a filter membrane in order to strip it of dangerous microorganisms. Purification uses an extra step, passing the water through a material such as iodine resin or carbon to kill any remaining organisms that may be too small to remain trapped in the filter. A standard filter operates with a hand pump that creates suction and forces water through the filtering medium. Filters and purifiers are wonderful because the treated water can be consumed

There are various types of water filters: gravity-fed filters that hang and drain water through the filtered part using gravity's pull, pump filters that require manual pumping to force water through the filter, and bottle-fed filters that force water through the cartridge when the bottle is squeezed.

immediately. Plus, there's no fear of long-term health effects from chemicals. However, filters and purifiers generally weigh about a pound or so and require a commitment to maintenance.

Select a filter based on its weight, pumping speed, the micron size of the filtering apparatus, and the reputation of the manufacturer. Organisms come in various sizes with *Giardia lamblia* weighing in at the top of the scale at 5 to 30 μm, and smaller organisms such as viruses at 0.03 μm. A filter's pore size determines what organisms are blocked by the filter. Ideally, your filter should meet the American National Standards Institute (ANSI/NSF) International Standard #53 (this information is usually provided on the product's packaging or in the product literature). A filter meeting this standard ensures cyst removal and is effective against *Giardia lamblia* and *Cryptosporidium*.

Unlike chemical treatments, filters have the advantage of cutting out the waiting period to safely drink the water. They also help to reduce the unpleasant taste of water from tannic acid or turbid sources. There are some major disadvantages to using a filtering system, such as the weight and bulk, cost, and complexity of use. The initial investment for a quality filter is approximately $75 to $100 (with replacement cartridges costing between $30 and $40 on average), and they typically weigh in at around a pound.

Filters have a tendency to crack, clog, and break down. A filter may even develop cracks unbeknownst to the person using it, allowing all sorts of harmful organisms into the drinking water. A good deal of care is required to use a filter effectively. Intake and output hoses need to be kept well away from one another to avoid contamination, a difficult task in a small pack or when filtering in less than ideal conditions. Wrap plastic bags around the outlet hose and hold in place with rubber bands to keep it from touching and being contaminated by the rest of the unit. Some filters provide an attachment so the output hose can be directly attached to your water bottle or bag, reducing the risk of contamination. When using a filter in cold weather, make sure to empty the water from the filter housing after use so that it doesn't freeze, as this causes small cracks. Dropping a filter, particularly a ceramic one, may create fractures and render it useless.

Filters require regular maintenance, so it's a good idea to learn
how to dismantle and service your
filter before taking it on your long
hike. Dangerous levels of bacteria
and mold can build up in a filter
that's not cared for properly. When
dealing with cloudy, turbid water,

> **WATER FILTER MANUFACTURERS**
> First Need by Generalecology:
>   www.generalecology.com
> Katadyn: www.katadyn.com
> MSR: www.msrcorp.com/filters
> PUR (owned by Katadyn): www.purwaterfilter.com

you need to pre-filter, using a bandana or a paper coffee filter to strain out
particles that could damage the device (a coffee filter or bandana can be
rubber-banded around the intake hose to simplify the process). An alternative method of pre-filtering is to collect water in a container and allow
it to stand long enough for particles to settle to the bottom before filtering.
Watch for signs of clogging and other problems. If the handle becomes difficult to pump, troubleshoot and clean the filter. Regular cleaning and
maintenance extend the life of the device. Keep spare parts, such as replacement cartridges, in your bounce box, and always carry a chemical
backup method for water treatment (such as a small bottle of iodine
tablets) in case your filter fails.

Purification Systems

Water bottle purifiers are relatively new to the market but have gained popularity with long-distance hikers wanting to trim down on weight. A bottle
purifier is an all-in-one unit composed of a bottle housing a purifier leading to a drinking straw. To use, fill the bottle with water, and when you
drink, the suction created by squeezing the bottle and drinking through the
straw forces water through the purifier unit, rendering it safe. Purifier
bottles are fairly lightweight compared with more traditional filters and
are relatively effective against viruses and bacteria. However, the bottles
are limited in their volume capacity and require periodic replacement of
costly purifier cartridges. One popular model of bottle purifier is the
Exstream XR water bottle purifier by Katadyn.

The *MIOX Water Purifier* by
MSR is a newer system for purification. MIOX purifies water by ex-
posing it to mixed oxidants. It does
this by sending an electric current
through salt water in order to create
brine. The brine is then added to a

> Some hikers carry a lightweight multi-gallon
> hanging water bag to fill and hang at shel-
> ters. These bags take up little pack space and
> can provide a group of hikers with fresh water
> with only one trip to the water source.

larger volume of fresh water, rendering it safe to drink. This system runs on batteries and costs about the same as most filtering systems. Though there's no pumping or maintenance required to use this lightweight unit, it does take up to four hours to kill certain types of microorganisms, such as *Cryptosporidium.*

Man-made ultraviolet (UV) light has been used as a water purification method in treatment plants and other facilities since the middle of the twentieth century. Ultraviolet light effectively sterilizes water without chemicals or heat. Hydro Photon's *SteriPen* (http://steripen.com) is a handheld unit that shines UV light into water, making it safe to drink. UV rays don't necessarily kill every organism. Rather, they sterilize them so they can't multiply in your body and cause illness. The SteriPen device weighs less than half a pound including batteries, and is a good option for those who want to travel light but are reluctant to use chemicals.

To use the SteriPen, dip it into a container of water, turn the light on, and stir until the light automatically turns off. This method of water treatment isn't highly effective for cloudy water since the suspended particles obscure UV rays. When treating cloudy water, filter through a bandana or collect the water in a container, allowing the sediment to drop to the bottom before putting it in a bottle and treating it. A benefit of the SteriPen is its ability to work in hot or cold temperatures. The initial purchase price is a bit high but it is a good investment because it doesn't require replacement cartridges or use much battery power. SteriPen has been proven effective against a broad spectrum of organisms, including *Cryptosporidium* and *Giardia lamblia.*

Boiling is an old-fashioned method of water treatment and is very reliable. It effectively kills microorganisms through heat without the use of chemicals. The Center for Disease Control recommends bringing water to a rolling boil and allowing it to boil for one minute. After boiling, allow water to cool in air temperature. This is not an ideal way to treat water during a long hike, however. The amount of fuel needed to boil water is wasteful, and the weight of the fuel is prohibitive. This treatment method is, by far, the most time-consuming and labor-intensive, and I can't imagine a hiker stopping to boil water many times a day. But, in a pinch, it is a reliable backup method of water treatment.

Always carry a little more water than what you need in case you meet up with unreliable water sources or delays. Nothing is more demoralizing than having to walk for miles without a drink because of a dried-up stream or leaky water bottle.

TRANSPORT OPTIONS

A *hydration system,* essentially a water storage bag with an attached drinking tube, allows you to drink frequently while on the move. Some hikers prefer hydration systems while others like water bottles because they're less prone to leaking and allow one to see the status of his or her water supply. Most hikers opt for a hydration bag ranging between two and three liters. Choose a hydration system that is constructed by a reputable manufacturer.

Plain water bottles such as those made by Nalgene (www.nalgene-outdoor.com) are used to carry water as well. You can choose between rigid Lexan bottles or lightweight collapsible plastic bottles such as the ones manufactured by Platypus (www.platypushydration.com). Keep in mind that a water container with a large opening is easier to fill than one with a small opening. This is important when accessing drying streams and dribbling springs. Instead of using a heavy and expensive Lexan bottle such as Nalgene,

> Periodically clean out your water container with hot water and a drop or two of bleach to help keep microorganisms at bay. Allow containers to dry fully, especially before storing for any period of time, and keep the lids off to allow air flow when not filled.

many hikers opt to keep water in recycled wide-mouthed sports drink bottles. These bottles are cheap and sturdy, easy to replace, and weigh very little.

People who don't live in the woods take for granted the abundance of readily available things to drink. Tea, coffee, juice, soda, and other beverages keep hydration tasty but are too heavy to carry on the trail. Water is the most vital thing a hiker consumes and it's important that your water is appealing and inspires you to drink a lot of it. Powdered milk, iced tea mix, and powdered hot chocolate are nice treats to drink at the end of the day and can be carried in your pack for whenever you're in the mood. For hikers who need some caffeine in the morning, instant coffee in powdered or bagged form and teas are easy to make.

Energy drinks, such as powdered Gatorade, E.mer'gen-C, Succeed! Electrolyte caps, and E-Caps Endurolytes are good at helping to restore electrolytes and enhance your vitamin intake. These tablets also help to reduce nausea, cramping, swelling, and blistering when you are sweating a lot. Try to avoid drink mixes high in sugar as they'll ultimately work to dehydrate your body. Some hikers who treat with iodine use some sort of product with citric acid, such as crushed vitamin C tablets or citrus-flavored drink mixes, to help neutralize the taste. Drink powders are also good for masking bad tastes in water that is rusty or high in bitter tannic acid content.

FOOD ON THE AT

Brian Wansink, director of the Cornell University Food and Brand Lab, claims that the average person makes over two hundred decisions about food every day. That's a lot of brain power directed toward food! Food is what long-distance hikers fantasize about during waking hours and is the inspiration to complete the long miles leading into town.

> It's important to get enough calories while hiking. *Bonking,* a term referring to the body's loss of energy due to running out of fuel, can be avoided through proper diet. Eating snacks throughout the day is essential to keeping the body fueled and can keep a hiker from bonking.

An average hiker requires about one and a half to two pounds of food per day while on the trail. This equals many calories, far more than what the average sedentary human requires. A lot of hikers tend to carry too much food during the early stages of their hike, but you eventually learn that it's pretty difficult to starve on the AT. With resupply points typically spaced three to five days apart, and "trail magic" (food left by others to help you out) and random eateries interspersed in-between, there's food everywhere. It's always a good idea, however, to carry an extra meal or two in case you get slowed down or are just extra hungry.

Hikers have two main approaches to getting food: mail drops and re-supplying in towns along the way. Hiking leaves little time or energy for food gathering or hunting, making it impractical to "live off the land" by foraging or hunting for food during your hike. These activities are also rough on the environment. Caching, another method of resupply, is the

> Hikers typically resupply every three to five days while on the trail. Because of the close proximity of towns, general stores, and gas stations near the trail, AT hikers usually don't have to carry more than five days' worth of food at a time. Hiker boxes, trail magic, dollar stores (a great place to save money on resupply), and restaurants along the trail can further reduce the amount of food you need to carry in your pack.

practice of storing food and water in sealed containers at waypoints on the trail. Unlike a long trail such as the Pacific Crest Trail, where towns are far apart, the abundance of towns makes the logistics of resupply on the AT fairly easy, negating the need for caching.

Hikers who mail food to themselves at towns along the trail have a lot of control over their diets and are able to prepare meals at home in advance. If you opt to use mail drops, be sure to include a variety of foods and give yourself an allowance to buy extra food products in town to satiate unforeseen cravings as they arise. Relying on buying food in town may give you freedom, but with that freedom comes some risk. The major guidebooks do a good job of outlining where one can do long-term and short-term resupply, but you never know when a store may be out of stock of a certain item. If you have special dietary needs, you may want to consider relying heavily on mail drops. If you have no special needs, you may prefer the freedom of getting food when and where you decide you need it.

Hiker resupply

Because of its weight, bulk, and tendency to spoil, fresh food is not suitable for backpacking. In its place is an assortment of dried and processed trail-friendly foods. Be sure to eat plenty of fresh produce when in town, and take vitamins to compensate for a lack of complete nutrition

The caloric strain hiking puts on your body kicks your appetite into overdrive. In response to these nutritional demands, many hikers develop strange food cravings, much the same way pregnant women do.

while out on the trail. Occasionally, fresh foods can be packed out of town and eaten on the same day (I heard of one hiker who carried an entire cake up a mountain, and I hiked through the Smokies with a box of cherry tomatoes on my back). After resupply, reduce food weight in your pack by eating your heaviest meals first. Leave a tasty snack in your pack as a pick-me-up for your taste buds days after a town visit.

Use a bag made of a lightweight waterproof material (typically silnylon) for storing your food. Some hikers opt to use a dry sack, a bag with a top that folds over to create a waterproof barrier and handle. Aside from aiding in organizing your pack, a food bag makes it easy to bear-bag and helps to contain spills and odors. In your food bag, you'll want to keep things under further control, using freezer bags to protect food and help keep it fresh. Foods such as peanut butter can be stored in food tubes available at your local outfitter. Instead of using the heavy plastic bottles and containers from the grocery store, recycle small, lightweight packaging. I used an empty plastic spice container with a screwon lid to hold my instant coffee, keeping it dry and lightweight. To reduce weight and clutter, minimize the amount of packaging you take out on the trail with you. Before heading out to the trail, repack all of your food in freezer bags to reduce extra weight and trash generated by packaging.

Spicing Up Your Menu

A long-distance hiker's diet can get pretty tedious after a while. Though there are many varieties of Lipton Sides, the day-to-day grind of eating the same meals over and over can really get to a person. It's important to keep food exciting so that you eat enough to stay nourished. Products such as Butter Buds (a dehydrated butter product), dehydrated milk, and spices go a long way to enhance meals without adding much bulk or weight to your pack. I met a southbounder who poured maple syrup on practically everything he ate in order to make it appetizing. Spices are some of the lightest things in your pack—use them. A little paprika or Mrs. Dash can go a long way.

Put your favorite spices in small plastic baggies or empty pill containers. Don't use film containers to store spices (or vitamins and medications, for that matter) because the container can contaminate them with harmful chemicals. Single-serving condiment packets are great to liven up meals. When in town, snag packets of mustard, mayo, relish, jam, ketchup, honey, BBQ sauce, and salad dressings to add to your meals. You can also find single-serving salt and pepper packets at fast-food restaurants and convenience stores. Many an epicurean backpacker carries a small leak-proof container of olive oil. It's convenient to find a group of like-minded (or like-bellied) hikers with whom to share bottles of spices and oils to avoid waste.

Nutrition ... or Not

Shortly into their hike, long-distance hikers quickly discover that food is energy. Many people subsist day to day on a sub-par diet, but the physical demands of hiking require more. Nutrition is a big challenge on the trail. A hiker has very complex dietary needs yet has to carry almost everything he or she eats in a pack, severely limiting access to foods such as vegetables. It's the old conundrum taken advantage of by dieters who eat celery to lose weight: for hikers, the energy expended carrying the food may be greater than the energy obtained from the food.

On short backpacking trips, it's easy to draw on reserves if you aren't getting adequate nutrition. On a long-distance hike, you need to be very careful about not falling into a state of deficit. Take vitamins and watch your calories to ensure your body is getting what it needs. A good rule of thumb for getting proper nutrition is to have variety in your diet. Eating an assortment of foods is the best way to ensure that you are meeting all of your dietary needs.

Many hikers eat poorly, and I've seen hikers, subsisting on chips, Pop Tarts, and candy bars, who look to be in perfect physical health. Not everyone is able to survive on that sort of diet, and even if they do, it's a poor way to treat your body. True, logging big miles every day is going to help counter the risks of a high fat/high calorie diet, but it won't make you immune to all the side effects of poor eating. Most of us have a good grasp on what is and isn't healthy. Read labels when you pick up food for your resupply. Avoid eating an excess of the obvious suspects such as sugars, harmful fats, and chemical additives. Make intelligent choices such as picking granola bars over candy bars.

Don't start a radically new vitamin regimen on the trail. Some people have adverse reactions to certain vitamins and supplements, so it's good to establish what will work for you before starting a long hike.

Many hikers will take the time to make hot meals while they are in camp (especially on cold or wet days). For many hikers, lunch is eaten cold and resembles a glorified snack rather than a real meal. Nothing beats a cooked meal, but because it involves spending time heating water, using fuel, and cleaning up, not too many hikers opt to cook more than once or twice a day.

The great thing about the body is that, if you listen to it, it usually tells you what it needs. Your cravings, taken with a dose of common sense, will go far in helping you to tailor your menu. The most common craving on the AT is for high-fat foods, and some fats are necessary for good health. Seek sources of unsaturated fats such as nuts, seeds, and olive oil, and avoid harmful saturated fats (found in dairy products, lard, and shortening) and trans-fatty acids (found in processed foods such as margarine and potato chips).

Be aware of your intake of protein, dietary fiber, vitamins, and minerals. Ideally, your diet should consist of 40 to 50 percent energizing carbohydrates (pastas), 30 percent protein (beans and cheeses), and the remainder should be healthy fats. It's important to ingest enough calcium, not provided in most multivitamins, to support wear and tear on your skeletal system. A balanced diet is difficult to achieve with the carbohydrate- and fat-laden smorgasbord of food on the AT. Though nearly impossible, try to keep your consumption of processed foods down to a minimum. And, when possible, use pure seasonings in place of the prepackaged, MSG-laden spice packets. There's no need for salt tablets on the AT because a lot of backpacker foods are high in sodium.

Avoid the cheap thrills of sugar rushes and look for the consistent energies obtained from healthy carbohydrates. Eat many small meals throughout the day. Digestion is a big drain on the body's energy, and it's better to give your digestive system small workloads throughout the day so more energy can be directed toward hiking. Seek a happy balance between total indulgence and healthy eating, and your body will thank you.

THE BACKPACKER'S KITCHEN

Backpacking cookware includes pots, pans, mugs, and other accessories needed to prepare meals. The typical hiker carries a pot, eating utensil(s), and possibly a mug or other container out of which to drink. Pots and mugs can be made from a wide range of materials, such as aluminum, titanium, hard anodized aluminum, stainless steel, and Inoxal and can have non-stick coatings. Titanium is the preferred pot material for ultralight backpackers because of its strength and weight, but aluminum is also suitable.

Some pots require a separate handle that can be clipped on to move it to and from the stove. Most handles are made of two hinged aluminum pieces that clamp onto the pot's edge. Some pots have a built-in handle that folds out, eliminating the need for a separate pot gripper. A one- to one-and-a-half-liter pot is adequate for all of your cooking. Most hikers carry one pot and no additional cookware unless hiking with a partner or group. To cut down on weight, you can easily cook most meals in one pot and use the pot as a serving dish. There are folding and telescoping plastic dishes and mugs on the market, such as Orikaso origami dishes (www.orikaso.com), but there's really no need to bring any additional kettles, pans, or pots—they'll just add a lot of weight to your pack. It's convenient but not necessary to have a mug or drinking container. Your pot can double as a drinking container as well.

Flatware for the trail generally comes in stainless steel, aluminum, and Lexan. You can get an entire set of utensils including a spoon, fork, and knife, but most hikers make do with only a spork (a spoon/fork hybrid). Utensils made of titanium are lightweight and almost impossible to break, and, as far as flatware goes, the titanium spork is the ultimate multipurpose cooking tool. Lexan, though lightweight, is a relatively fragile material for the many abuses of trail cooking, while stainless steel is sturdy and inexpensive but too heavy for those counting ounces.

There are a few tricks to being fuel-efficient with cooking. Allow your pot to blacken on the bottom because the dark color of the pot's bottom absorbs more heat, making the pot more fuel-efficient (there's no need to paint the bottom of your pot with heat-resistant paint as repeated cooking does the trick of blackening it). When cooking, use a windscreen and a reflector to create an oven-like atmosphere that retains a surprising amount of heat. Keep the lid on your pot while cooking to avoid heat loss, and allow dried foods to rehydrate as much as possible before cooking. One of the easiest ways to save fuel is to soak food and then allow water to come to a boil with the food already in it.

Pot cozies are a recent fad embraced by lightweight and ultralight hikers. These devices keep pots warmer longer and allow the cooking process to continue even after your stove has been turned off. There are ready-made cozies for sale, or you may opt to make your own. Cozies can be made out of fleece, recycled potholders, or pipe insulation. There are a few web sites with cozy-making directions (look on www.backpacking.net in the "Make Your Own Gear" section, at Zen Backpacking Stoves: http://zenstoves.net/PotAccessories.htm, or at Brasslight: www.brasslite.com/potCozy.html). Cozies can be purchased online from ultralight specialists such as AntiGravityGear (www.antigravitygear.com).

After food is partially cooked, turn your stove off and allow the food to continue cooking from the residual heat.

JUST ADD WATER: MAKING DEHYDRATED MEALS

For hikers who have special diets or who enjoy cooking and having control over their diets on the trail, dehydrating food at home is a healthy and relatively inexpensive alternative to buying ready-made backpacking meals. Dehydration is the oldest form of food preservation (it's also the cheapest and simplest). Since water makes foods heavy and susceptible to decay, dehydrating converts foods into an ideal preserved state for backpacking.

An electric dehydrator creates a heated space with circulating air that transports moisture out of items of food. Buying an electric food dehydrator is not a large investment (they start at about $30) and, over the course of a multi-month hike, it will pay for itself. Some hikers opt to build their own dehydrator or use a conventional oven. Most dehydrated foods last up to a year if stored correctly (in the freezer, tightly sealed in a bag), but you may wish to invest in a vacuum sealer to store food longer. When dehydrating food for mail drops, clearly label all food. Most fruits and veggies can be dehydrated, as well as sauces and already prepared meals such as chili. Avoid dehydrating food with high moisture content such as lettuce and cucumber. Experiment with dehydrating a variety of foods to see what works for you. There are many books and web sites that offer recipes and tips.

Dehydration is simple but labor-intensive. Slice the food you wish to dry into thin, even strips. Some foods require special pre-dehydration treatment, while others can be optionally marinated or seasoned before being placed in the dehydrator (avoid applying oils or greases to foods prepared for dehydration). Pay special attention to keeping a clean workspace for preparing foods. Place food in the dehydrator in a way that exposes the most surface area to the heated air. Not all foods dry at the same speed, so keep an eye on all the different types of food in your machine. Once food begins drying, do not interrupt the process as this can result in spoilage. Avoid dehydrating foods with strong flavors with other types of foods, as the flavor can taint everything in the dehydrator. For additional preservation, food can be put in the oven at 150 degrees for a few minutes to kill off microorganisms. Allow dried food to cool completely before placing it in bags.

IT'S IN THE BAG: FREEZER-BAG COOKING

Freezer-bag cooking (known as FBC by its fanatic followers) is one of the newer cooking trends on the trail. Embraced by ultralight and lightweight backpackers, this method of cooking involves carrying premade meals in heavy-duty freezer bags and adding heated water directly to the bag of food, eliminating the need for cleanup. A pot or bag cozy is used to house the bag while hot water cooks the food, reducing the amount of fuel you need to carry with you. This way of cooking lessens the amount of weight in your pack (particularly if you're carrying freezer-bagged meals for two or more) by being fuel-efficient and reducing packaging waste. Check out http://freezerbagcooking.com for great recipe ideas and helpful hints on this method of cooking. The AntiGravityGear web site (www.antigravity gear.com) features cozies and other accessories specifically geared toward freezer-bag cooking.

Freezer-bag cooking is a great way to prepare meals in advance if you plan to rely heavily on mail drops. The meals come portioned out and premade, requiring only hot water. If you resupply in town, you can place instant meals such as Lipton side dish packets, puddings, or Stove Top stuffing into bags for waterproof storage and to reduce packaging waste. Powdered milk, salt, spices, and other dry ingredients can be easily added to the bag before hitting the trail. Once on the trail, you can cook multiple things at once because you don't have to rely on a single pot; main courses and dessert can simmer at the same time, getting calories to your body faster.

There are health concerns associated with eating food out of heated plastic containers. When heated, plastics release small amounts of highly dangerous plasticizer substances such as phthalates, acetyltributylcitrate, dioxins, and dioctyl adipate. To keep health risks to a minimum, use bags that are heavy-duty and marketed for microwave use, boiling, or storing warm foods. The actual toxicity of foods cooked in plastic is up for debate, though many feel that there's not much risk in freezer-bag cooking. While research shows that these harmful chemicals are present in plastics, it is unknown what their effect is on someone who eats out of a heated plastic bag once or twice a day for months on end.

Looking for some inexpensive alternatives to freeze-dried meals marketed specifically to backpackers? Here are some examples of backpacker foods found in many grocery stores:

Bacon crumbles—These come dried in bottles for use in salads. Add them to mashed potatoes or soups.

Beans—Beans such as Dal (small lentils found in Indian food) or powdered black beans are great for the trail. You may also carry dried beans and place them in a filled water bottle to hydrate while you hike.

Bouillon—Though usually high in sodium, this is great stuff for flavoring noodles and other dishes or to use in hot water to make broth.

Butter—Butter is all about calories and good taste. Carry it in powdered form (Butter Buds) or use a margarine substitute in a squeeze bottle.

Candy bars—Though not a great source of nutrition, candy gives you a quick pick-me-up between meals.

Cereal—Though it tends to get pulverized pretty quickly, cereal and powdered milk make for a good quick meal.

Cereal bars—These are a more healthful alternative to candy bars and many are a good source of calcium.

Cheese—Hard cheeses such as cheddar or packaged cheese in string form will last a long time on the trail. Softer cheeses may be carried in cooler weather. Carry your cheeses in a freezer bag and avoid touching them with your hands as the bacteria makes them mold faster. You can also use products such as Vermont Cheese Powder or Parmesan in a shaker container for taste.

Couscous—This is a simple and healthy dish that cooks easily and can be used as a filler with meals.

Cream cheese—Surprisingly, cream cheese lasts for a day or two in moderate temperatures.

Cream of rice—Different from cream of wheat, this food has tons of energy-giving complex carbohydrates.

Eggs—In powdered form, eggs are a good way to get protein into your diet.

Energy bars—Bars such as Cliff and Luna are loaded with healthy goodness (though they tend to be dense and heavy).

Flour—Flour can be used as an additive to meals or to make simple flat breads.

Fruit—This comes in dehydrated form such as fruit leather or raisins in gorp (trail mix). Be warned, the sulphides used to treat dried fruit create gas!

Granola—Whether loose or in bar form, this is a healthy, high-energy food.

Grits—Instant prepackaged grits are ideal for trail breakfasts. The cheesy style is readily available in the southern states.

Honey—Honey is instant energy and can be added to bread or crackers for an extra shot of sweetness.

Hot dogs—These have enough chemicals in them to last overnight without refrigeration.

Hummus—The powdered form is lightweight though not as tasty as the fresh-made variety.

Lipton Sides—These packaged meals are some of the most popular premade inexpensive hiker foods on the trail.

Macaroni and cheese—This is a staple of the long-distance backpacker on a budget.

Mashed potatoes—These are easy to carry in the instant powdered form and the Idahoan brand tastes great even when cooked with plain water.

Milk—The powdered form of milk can be used for drinks and to add to recipes.

Nuts and seeds—Nuts and seeds are high in good fats and protein and are packed with energy.

Oatmeal—Instant and prepackaged oatmeal is easy to find at resupply points. Pour hot water straight into packets to cut down on cleanup.

Pasta—Pasta is the basis for many backpacker meals because it's lightweight and full of carbohydrates. Carry spare pasta to add to premade meals to increase portion size.

Peanut butter—This is great on bread or crackers, or by itself. You can also add PB to ramen to create a Thai-inspired flavor.

Pop Tarts—These are a classic high-calorie hiker breakfast or snack.

Potato chips—Chips are tasty and have tons of fat. In fact, they're so greasy that they can be used to start a campfire.

Pudding—Pudding makes a great-tasting dessert, though it's disappointingly low in calories and nutritional value.

Ramen—Ramen is the quintessential cheap backpacking food. Add dried veggies or peanut butter to it for taste and substance.

Rice—Instant rice is a great way to bulk up existing premade meals such as Lipton Sides or to add to dehydrated veggies.

Soup mixes—These are great to eat alone or to add to pastas and rice along with dried veggies for flavor.

Stove Top Stuffing—This weighs next to nothing and is a meal by itself.

Tortellini—Use the packaged dried version along with powdered pasta sauce and olive oil.

Tortilla wraps—These make for a long-lasting, impossible-to-smash bread to go with meals.

THE NO-COOK OPTION

Most backpackers carry some sort of stove, but there is a minority that prefers the simplicity of doing without. For example, in 2005 there was a hiker named Snackman who subsisted solely on snacks and got by without cooking. There are benefits to not dealing with a stove: you don't have to worry about equipment failure or getting fuel when you resupply, and, in theory, it cuts down on weight. Many cold foods are heavier than light-weight dehydrated meals, and some hikers argue that cold and hot foods don't differ from one another too much in terms of pack weight. No-cook foods range from preserved meats to simple powdered meals that can be re-hydrated with cold water. Stoves do have the added benefit of providing warm drinks and foods in cold weather, so you may want to carry one only during the colder seasons on the AT. Even if you're opting to use a stove, it's good to have a supply of ready-to-eat, no-cook foods for quick snack breaks or if you have a situation such as bad weather or stove failure.

COLD FOODS FOR THE AT

Tuna, chicken, or ham in a pouch

Powdered breakfasts such as Carnation® Instant Breakfast

Power Bars, granola bars, and candy bars

Ramen (it actually is very good to eat dry— save the seasoning packet for cooking)

Cereal

Dried fruits

Nuts

Sausages and pepperoni

Hard or flat breads such as pita, bagels, and tortillas

Cheese

Chips and crackers

Spreads such as peanut butter and Nutella

RESOURCES FOR THE BACKPACKING CHEF

Adventure Foods: www.adventurefoods.com

AlpineAire: www.alpineaire.com

Backpacker's Pantry: www.backpackerspantry.com

Fantastic Foods: www.fantasticfoods.com

Harmony House Foods: www.harmonyhousefoods.com

Harvest Foodworks: www.harvestfoodworks.com

Just Tomatoes: www.justtomatoes.com

Mountain House: www.mountainhouse.com

Natural High and Richmoor: www.richmoor.com

Wilderness Dining: www.wildernessdining.com

8
Preparing Your Itinerary

book your trip ...
—Graffiti seen in Wiley Shelter, New York

Logistically, the AT is a straightforward trail to hike due to the prevalence of towns, transportation, and other people. Yet there are as many ways to hike the Appalachian Trail as there are hikers to hike it. For thru-hikers who aspire to hike the entirety of the trail in the course of a calendar year, there are a number of standard options for avoiding bad weather, insects, and crowds. While thru-hikers have more rigid time constraints, other long-distance hikers have more freedom in their planning. Regardless of whether you're going out for six days or six months, you'll need to fine-tune your itinerary according to seasonal weather, resupply needs, and other factors.

GUIDEBOOKS, MAPS, AND OTHER RESOURCES

There are a variety of resources to use when determining the logistical aspects of your long-distance hike. The major guidebooks are *The Thru-Hiker's Handbook* edited by Bob McCaw (known for its former editor, Dan "Wingfoot" Bruce) and the *Appalachian Trail Thru-Hikers' Companion,* compiled by the Appalachian Long Distance Hikers Association (a free online version can be found at www.aldha.org). These books offer data on mileage, shelters, water, resupply, and other useful information for hikers. Regional AT guidebooks are available as well (the ATC regional guides are sold individually or with map sets). The *Appalachian Trail Data Book* is a basic logistical workbook that corresponds with the ATC maps and guidebooks and gives only the most essential trail data.

Maps show road crossings, elevation profiles, water sources, shelter locations, and state lines. Many hikers use maps and include them in their mail drop boxes. Because of the complexity and expense of producing updated map sets, some maps may be out-of-date, containing potentially

A ny combination of maps and guidebooks is useful in figuring out resupply points, mail drops, and meetings with friends and family. Smaller decisions, such as where to tent for the night (there are many well-guarded stealth tent sites in the Whites, for example), are best made based on word-of-mouth, shelter register information, or on a whim.

misleading information. Purchase the most updated map sets and guides that you can. If your resources are out-of-date, speak with ridge-runners, rangers, or other hikers to confirm your information. Most other resources are updated on an annual basis, and, if not, should indicate when the most recent updates occurred. Don't attempt to save money by purchasing outdated materials. In the long run, you'll be glad you spent the money on newer maps and guides.

SOBOS, NOBOS, HOBOS, AND EVERYONE IN-BETWEEN

Section hikers, those who hike the AT in sections, can be found almost any time of year, from winter in the White Mountains to springtime in Georgia. Section hiking is a great way to experience long-distance hiking in multiple-week or month-long chunks. When planning a section, it's a good idea to research weather conditions and potential restrictions on the section you intend to hike. Section hikes can be shorter than a hundred miles or longer than a thousand and may offer more flexibility in terms of planning, allowing hikers to travel each section of the trail during its ideal season.

A common approach to a thru-hike is to travel northbound, starting at Springer Mountain in Georgia and traveling toward Katahdin in Maine. Hikers traveling in this direction are known as *NOBOs*, short for northbounders, while those who travel north to south are known as *SOBOs*. A southbound thru-hike is a good option for the hiker who is less socially inclined, has life obligations that preclude a northbound start (such as finishing up school), or prefers to do things in an atypical fashion.

Northbound thru-hikers typically begin their trip between mid-March and early April, though it's possible to start earlier or later. When selecting a start date for a northbound trip, keep a few factors in mind. Seasonal weather is a concern at high elevations, particularly in New England. Because of severe winter weather, Baxter State Park (the home of Katahdin) closes down for overnight camping in mid-October and doesn't open again until the following spring. If you're a northbound hiker who's running behind schedule, you may be forced to miss out on Katahdin and, worse yet, find yourself caught out in the temperamental New England weather patterns. You don't want to start too early, however, as weather in the south can be challenging during early spring. Even hikers starting in the standard time window from Springer often find themselves caught in snowstorms, particularly in the Smoky Mountains.

Southbounders typically begin their hikes at Katahdin in June. One of the major drawbacks to this start date is the massive bug problem in New England during the summer; black flies have driven many a SOBO hiker to madness. Also, the terrain at the northern end of the AT is demanding and, to the uninitiated, can make for an intimidating start. A southbound trip, however, affords you the luxury of taking your time since winter in Georgia is preferable to winter in Maine.

For those who find themselves running behind schedule, a *flip-flop* hike is a good option for sustaining a thru-hike. Many flip-floppers begin at Springer and hike a large segment of the trail before traveling to Maine to hike back to where they left off. This style of hiking lacks continuity and tends to be less of a social way to hike. Also, the completion of a flip-flop may be anti-climactic, with the hiker stepping out into a road crossing in Pennsylvania or some other nondescript location to finish as opposed to summiting Katahdin or Springer. A popular flip-flop completion point is Harpers Ferry, West Virginia, the psychological halfway point on the trail, which also offers easy access to transportation. A flip-flop hike provides a hiker with a large window of time to complete a hike, as well as a longer period of hiking in moderate weather.

There are many other ways to approach a long hike. Hikers may opt to do a *circuit hike*, in which they complete the trail in two or more large sections, always hiking in the same direction (such as southbound), or a *leapfrog hike*, where a hiker skips large sections and returns to do them at a later time.

TRAVELING TO AND FROM THE TRAIL

The AT guidebooks provide detailed directions on getting to Katahdin and Springer Mountain,

Traveling between sections of the trail can waste time and money, but there is a strong support crew of trail angels willing to offer shuttle services to and from the trail. A good way to get a ride is to post a request on whiteblaze.net, trailjournals.com, or the AT listserv. These resources also provide frequent updates of shuttle service and trail conditions. The average cost of shuttle services is $1.50 per mile. This is an expensive though sometimes necessary alternative to hitchhiking. Providers of shuttle services are available through guidebooks, trail club web sites, and word-of-mouth.

the northern and southern termini of the AT. You may also check out trailplace.com (go to the "Hiker Resources" section) and the Georgia Appalachian Trail Club web site (www.georgia-atclub.org) for travel instructions. For all points between Katahdin and Springer, contact the local trail maintaining organizations for further transportation directions (a listing of clubs and their contact information is provided in the back of this book).

If you're a NOBO thru-hiker planning on staying the night at one of the more popular hiker lodgings such as the Hike Inn (www.hike-inn.com), Hiker Hostel (hikerhostel.com), or Amicalola Lodge (www.gastateparks.org/info/amicalola/), be sure to book a room well in advance of your trip to secure your spot.

When traveling to and from the trail, store your pack in a wire security mesh bag or duffle bag to protect it. If it has a lid, detach it to use as a carry-on for vital things such as prescription medicine, maps, and contact information. Check the weight and size limits of luggage before traveling with your pack to avoid excess baggage charges on airlines (though it is almost impossible to go over these fairly large weight limits). Be aware of restrictions on what you can and can't bring onto airplanes, buses, and trains, and make sure to check with your carrier before traveling for regulations and special notices. Since September 11, restrictions on carry-on and other baggage have become strict and more closely monitored. You cannot travel with filled fuel canisters, so you need to make sure you can get fuel at your destination (solid Esbit tabs are the only travel-friendly fuel).

You may elect to mail your pack ahead and pick it up at the post office once you arrive. Aside from being expensive, this requires some delicate coordination between transportation times and the post office's hours of operation. There's always the chance, too, that your pack with all of its carefully selected and pricey contents may be lost for days . . . or forever. If you choose to mail your pack ahead, insure it and cross your fingers that it makes it to its destination without problems.

CONNECT THE BLAZES: NAVIGATION ON THE AT

Once on the trail, navigation is much like a game of connect-the-dots—all you need to do is follow the blazes. The AT is marked along its whole length with white blazes every hundred yards or so. Blazes are painted rectangles, two inches wide by six inches tall, which appear singly or in pairs. Pairs of blazes indicate a turn on the trail, sometimes with the upper blaze pointing in the direction of the turn. Blazes are typically painted on trees, but may appear on rocks, posts, or even telephone poles. In treeless areas, blazes may be replaced with stone piles called *cairns*.

Other trails intersect the AT and are marked with various colored blazes. Blue blazes indicate side trails that intersect and meet up with the AT. These trails sometimes provide alternate routes for AT hikers, hence the term *blue-blazer* used to describe hikers who wander off the AT in search of better scenery or easier terrain. The trail may sport flags, indicating survey work, or red blazes, which act as stop signs. The AT is also adorned with metal survey markers and signage for shelters, water sources, or other noteworthy places. Following the blazes is relatively easy in most areas, even at night, when the white paint appears luminescent in the glow of a headlamp. Sections of the trail, particularly those near shelters, are marked with reflective pin blazes to aid with night navigation.

Navigating can be tricky in large pastures, on balds (large high-elevation areas in the south that lack trees), in the snow, and wherever vegetation is sparse. If you lose your way, stop and look around or backtrack to the place where you last saw a blaze. Often you can relocate the trail merely by turning around and looking at the blazing behind you. If you feel totally lost, yell; after all, it's the AT and odds are that another hiker is nearby. It's not uncommon to lose the trail accidentally, particularly in areas such as the Whites, so it's important to pay attention to blazes. Some directionally challenged hikers may accidentally backtrack at some point during their hike. This usually occurs after leaving the shelter or taking a long break and may be due to fatigue or the fact that the same patch of woods can look entirely different heading south than it does north.

A GOOD NIGHT'S SLEEP: ACCOMMODATIONS

On the trail, you have the option of staying in the elaborate shelter system. There are over 260 shelters (known as lean-tos in some regions) along the AT. These shelters are primitive structures built of wood or stone and typically have three walls, leaving the shelter exposed to the open air on one side. Shelters fit anywhere from four to twenty-five hikers, with the average shelter having a six- to nine-person capacity.

For people hiking in the south during the spring, shelters may be very crowded because of the large number of thru-hikers and college students on spring break. Popular national parks such as Shenandoah National Park and Great Smoky Mountains National Park are also susceptible to crowding issues in the shelters. Scout troops may also unexpectedly appear, leaving no shelter space for long-distance hikers. Aside from the

AMC (Appalachian Mountain Club) huts in New Hampshire's White Mountains and shelters in the Smokies, shelters operate on a first-come-first-served basis and can fill quickly. Of course, in bad weather, there's always room for one more. No one has any special rights or privileges to using the shelters, and a spot is never guaranteed, which is why you need to be prepared to camp by having a tent, tarp, or other portable shelter with you when you hike. Staying in the shelters is a wonderful way to get to know fellow hikers and can be a spot for socializing at the end of the night (just remember to bring your earplugs if you want to get any sleep).

Lakes of the Clouds Hut in the White Mountains, New Hampshire

There are some exceptions to the backcountry simplicity of AT shelters. There are shelters with interesting designs, such as the Overmountain Shelter, which was converted from an old barn. The privately owned Secret Shelter, an enclosed heated cabin located in New Jersey, is known only to long-distance hikers (meaning it's a safe haven from throngs of scouts and weekend hikers). Partnership Shelter in Virginia sports two stories, a shower, and pizza delivery service (the 501 Shelter in Pennsylvania and the RPH Shelter in New York also offer pizza delivery for hikers). Near Fontana Dam in North Carolina is a shelter known as the "Fontana Hilton." The Hilton is situated relatively close to picnic areas, free showers, and phone service at the Tennessee Valley Authority Visitor Center.

There's a thirty-mile stretch in central New York that is devoid of shelters, but in the midst of it lies the Graymoor Monastery, a friary and substance-abuse treatment facility. There, hikers are welcome to sleep in the picnic pavilion at the ball field and also have access to running water, a cold shower, and food delivery.

Most of the AT shelters are located directly on or within sight of the trail. Some shelters are placed a good distance off of the AT, accessible via blue-blazed trails. Sometimes the round trip distance to these can be well over a mile, and a variety of factors such as daylight, weather, and water sources will affect whether or not you choose to stay that far away from the trail. Most AT hikers prefer not to do the extra miles, though shelters found off of the beaten path are usually great places to get some peace and solitude as they tend to be less crowded.

Camping is restricted on certain parts of the AT, but tent sites are provided near shelters and in many other locations. These restrictions help to lessen the impact of hikers on the land and, for that reason, it's important to follow them closely. Of course, you have the odd night when you need to quit early or the mileage just doesn't add up and you'll want to stealth camp. When camping off of the beaten path, remember not to stay in an overly exposed area as you don't want to be surprised by a nighttime storm.

An online database of Appalachian Trail shelters is provided at www.thebackpacker.com (follow the "Trails and Places" to the "Appalachian Trail Database" link). This resource provides general information, mileage, and reviews for the shelters along the AT and is a great online trip-planning tool.

Be aware of the restrictions placed on campfires. Some states forbid the use of fires at shelters and campsites, and AMC ridge-runners hired to patrol the trail enforce these rules by imposing fines. Some of the sites allowing fires provide a fire ring, Dutch oven, or metal grating to make the fire more enjoyable. Remember to put out fires before you leave camp, and leave your campsite as you found it.

As a long-distance hiker, you'll be spending a night here and there in the domestic tranquillity of a hotel, motel, hostel, or bed and breakfast. When getting a motel in town, hikers usually share a room (on the sly or in plain sight) to defray costs. Hostels are cheaper than motels, more protected than shelters, and may include meals as part of the cost, making them an ideal place to get a good night's sleep. Some of the better known hostels on the AT are The Place in Damascus, Virginia, and Kincora in Hampton, Tennessee. For some fortunate hikers there's the option of stay-

There are many hiker-friendly places to stay on the AT. Hostels and hotels along the trail are listed at http://whiteblaze.net/forum/links/index.php? under the "Hostels and Stays" link. This site provides an overview of many of the popular AT hostels, as well as links to the businesses' web pages.

ing with friends and family who live near the trail. Sometimes locals offer hikers a place to stay as well. One of the strangest alternative places to stay on the AT is in the basement of the town jail in Palmerton, Pennsylvania, which offers a hot shower and bunk beds for long-distance hikers.

A FEW NOTES ON RESTRICTED AREAS

Hiking in certain protected lands requires a permit, reservations, or a combination of the two. This practice helps to control and minimize human impact in popular recreation areas. It also acts as a safety measure, allowing for backcountry hikers to be accounted for in the event of an emergency.

In the Great Smoky Mountains National Park in North Carolina and Tennessee, you need to sign up for a permit, which can be obtained for free at kiosks at either end of the park. When obtaining your permit, supply the ranger with an itinerary of what shelters you'll be staying at (you are not allowed to camp at non-designated areas in the park). Thru-hikers aren't required to make reservations but some other long-distance hikers are. Reservations for the Smokies may be made by visiting www.nps.gov/grsm/ (look under the "Fees and Reservations" link) or by calling the Backcountry Information Office at 865-436-1297.

In Virginia's Shenandoah National Park, hikers may sign up for their required permits at self-serve kiosks near the north and south boundaries on the AT (the northern registration station is on a blue-blazed trail). The permit for this park is free. Thru-hikers and certain long-distance hikers don't need to worry about reservations. For Shenandoah visitors' information, visit www.nps.gov/shen (look under the "Fees and Reservations" link) or call 540-999-3500.

The Green Mountain National Forest in Vermont is another restricted area through which the AT runs. At sites run by the Green Mountain Club (GMC) caretakers, hikers are charged for overnight stays. This fee helps the club to conduct Leave No Trace education on the trail. GMC typically provides caretakers at summits and pond areas that are prone to high use. Further information on this forest may be found by visiting www.greenmountainclub.org, www.fs.fed.us/r9/gmfl/, or by calling 802-747-6700.

Overnight stays are only permitted at designated areas in the White Mountain National Forest. The Appalachian Mountain Club (AMC, a group sometimes referred to as the "Appalachian Money Club" due to their monopoly of fee-based places to sleep in the Whites) provides tent sites and warming lodges for a fee. Reservations are needed to stay in the warming huts, but long-distance hikers are frequently accommodated. Long-distance hikers looking to save money have the option of doing work with the "croo" for room and board at the huts, saving themselves about $80 to $90. Typically, there are one or two spots available at each hut offering work-for-stay positions, and the labor involved isn't that demanding. Camping is allowed within a quarter mile of the huts but is forbidden above tree line. There are both AMC fee-based and stealth tent sites available to hikers away from the huts. Visit www.fs.fed.us/r9/forests/white_mountain/ or call 603-528-8721 for more information.

In Baxter State Park, hikers can register at one of the park gates. Information on Baxter may be found at www.baxterstateparkauthority.com or by calling 207-723-5140. Hikers who climb Katahdin must register with the ranger at Katahdin Stream Campground. There, you are given the option of leaving your pack with the ranger to lighten your load for the big climb. Depending on the season, the times hikers are allowed to climb Katahdin are controlled. Keep in mind that the mountain periodically closes due to inclement weather. It's important to check in with a ranger before starting your ascent to get weather information and let him or her know of your whereabouts. The park closes for camping on October 15 and most sites (including Katahdin Stream and Daicey Pond Campgrounds) reopen on May 15.

Please note that, while hikers can enter parks for free via the AT, cars may be charged fees. Check with the office of the park you plan on hiking in for further information. It's a good idea to call ahead or visit the park's web site to get current information on trail conditions such as severe weather or impassable stream crossings. Park offices are staffed with knowledgeable people who are happy to answer your questions to help ensure you have a safe and enjoyable trip.

DEVELOPING A TIMELINE

Though a long hike seems idyllic and carefree (mostly it is), a long-distance hiker is constantly hiking against time. Baxter State Park closes for overnight camping on October 15 for safety reasons, and it's generally unpleasant or even risky to be caught at high elevations during winter weather, even in the southernmost part of the AT. When planning your hike, it's important to take terrain, local weather conditions, and town distances from the trail into consideration. While you might blow through states such as West Virginia, you need to plan for lower mileage days in New England, particularly in the White Mountains and southern Maine. Delays resulting from weather or terrain can greatly impact your budget, particularly when a hotel or hostel stay is required. When making plans, allow for a margin of error and never stress or injure yourself in an attempt to make a deadline on the trail.

So how far can you expect to hike in a day? This largely depends on weather, terrain, how much weight you carry, and your physical condition. A hiker in good shape can expect to travel at a speed of two to three miles per hour over moderate terrain. For areas of extreme elevation gain and difficult footing, hiking speeds can drop to a mile an hour or even less. On flatter areas of the trail (such as in Maryland or certain sections of Virginia), hikers may achieve speeds of over four miles per hour. Typically, a long-distance hiker averages anywhere from ten to fifteen or even twenty miles a day. Some hikers can crank out daily mileage in excess of twenty miles, and, on the odd occasion, hikers have been known to tackle thirty to fifty miles in the span of a single day. When planning your hike, remember to factor in a resupply stop every three to five days and a day of rest about once a week.

> There is an online AT thru-hiker calculator at http://tomjanofsky.com/at/. Plug in your start date, estimated zero days, and daily mileage, and it will supply an estimate of how long your thru-hike will take.

AN OVERVIEW OF WHAT YOU'RE GETTING YOURSELF INTO

The southern terminus of the AT is atop Springer Mountain. The seventy-five miles of trail that run across Georgia cut through the Chattahoochee National Forest and include some of the tougher climbs and descents on the AT even though the elevation stays between a modest 2,500 to 4,500 feet. This area was made famous in the movie *Deliverance*, and it's rumored that the infamous albino banjo player lived close to the trail. Northbounders need to be aware that during the months of March and April the trail may be congested, a problem when looking for shelter space or a place to pitch your tent at the end of the day. It's good to get to shelters as early as possible during March and April, as space is at a premium during this time of year. Walasi-Yi Center at Neels Gap is a popular area of civilization right on the trail, and one may find resupply, a hostel, and gear upgrades there.

The AT runs along the border of Tennessee and North Carolina for quite a distance. The North Carolina section of the AT feels remote and fairly wild. Its eighty-eight miles traverse some very well-graded trails (but also some steep climbs) from the Georgia/North Carolina border to the Nantahala River (home of the Nantahala Outdoor Center, a place of rest, restaurants, and rafting for hikers). The trail crosses the Stecoah-Cheoah Mountain area and includes access to unused fire towers and great views, especially those from Cheoah Bald. The section of the AT that runs along the state of Tennessee covers some of the largest extremes in elevation found on the trail (anywhere between 1,300 to over 6,600 feet) and contains the beautiful Roan Highlands. Tennessee offers hikers a true experience of roughing it as it doesn't provide a single privy. For the north-bounder, Fontana Dam and Lake precedes the Smokies. This large dam was created on the Little Tennessee River by the Tennessee Valley Authority and was completed in 1945. Adjacent to the dam is Fontana Village, a small collection of buildings providing services to hikers. The highlight of the North Carolina and Tennessee section of the trail is the Great Smoky Mountains National Park. While hiking the Smokies, you will encounter Clingmans Dome, the highest point on the AT. Due to long-standing bitterness from Appalachian Trail land acquisition disputes, there is a history of poor relations between hikers and the communities in the area between Elk Park, Tennesee, and Hampton, Tennessee. There are reports of past hiker abuses, but these incidences are rare. Generosity and kindness generally abound in the south.

Virginia is the longest section of the trail, covering around 550 miles. Long-distance hikers claim that Virginia is the never-ending state, and the long walk through this state can cause the "Virginia blues" for some. However, Damascus, near the state's southern end, provides a welcome place for hikers to relax. The annual Trail Days festival in Damascus provides a place for long-distance hikers, past and present, to gather and celebrate life on the AT. Virginia contains a broad range of scenery and trail conditions. It is popular belief that Virginia is flat, but don't be fooled, because this state contains some pretty invigorating terrain. Virginia features the Mount Rogers region, the George Washington National Forest, and the Jefferson National Forest. Strange rock formations exist in the central region of the state, including the infamous Dragon's Tooth (be careful not to get lost in the labyrinth of rocks and ladder rungs climbing to or from it). Highlights of Virginia include the perfectly groomed and bear-filled Shenandoah National Park as well as Grayson Highlands, where herds of wild ponies run free. Northern Virginia presents difficult cross ridge walking. South of Harpers Ferry is an area known as the "roller coaster," where there are many PUDs (pointless ups and downs)—the ridges undulate up and down in a series of small but trying elevation gains and losses.

Only four miles of the AT run solely in the state of West Virginia. The highlight of this state is historic Harpers Ferry, home to the Appalachian Trail Conservancy's headquarters. From Harpers Ferry, it is easy to get to Washington, D.C., via Amtrak and commuter rail service. Northbound thru-hikers should anticipate being in Harpers Ferry by July 4 to be on schedule to summit Katahdin before its seasonal closing.

The AT travels forty-one miles through Maryland. The southern tip of the Maryland AT follows the well-graded C&O Canal towpath, then travels along South Mountain's ridgeline. It passes through Dahlgren Campground and Gathland State Park and is an easy walk compared with the rest of the trail. This stretch of the trail is where the Hike Across Maryland (also known as the Maryland Marathon) event is held. It is an informal race where hikers try to walk across the entire state (with elevations changing from 230 feet to over 1,800 feet) in a twenty-four-hour period.

While the southern segment of Pennsylvania is relatively gentle in terms of terrain, the northern part of the state is notoriously rocky (giving the state its nickname, Rocksylvania) and has claimed the lives of many boots and hikers' feet. Pennsylvania is home to many rattlers, which lurk among its rocks, and it lacks ample water sources. The Palmerton EPA Superfund Site (near Lehigh Gap) is an area of residual environmental devastation caused by zinc smelting and is marked by a barren, treeless landscape, which is in the process of slowly recovering. One of the highlights of this state is Duncannon, where the infamous Doyle Hotel—home to notoriously inexpensive Yuengling beer, burgers, and rooms—plays host to many long-distance hikers. Another is Pine Grove Furnace State Park, which marks the halfway point of the AT.

Many hikers find New Jersey to be one of the most enjoyable mid-Atlantic states on the AT. The trail through this state features gentle terrain and boggy wet areas. It sports a mile-long elevated wooden walkway, known as the Jersey boardwalk, across the Pochuck Creek and floodplain area. Though the trail in this state is near much industry and developed land, it has a remote feel and is home to many bears that have been crowded out by nearby development. Both New Jersey and New York sport many road crossings and eating establishments close to the trail, providing hikers with many deli options.

The eighty-eight miles of trail in New York run close to many developed areas and present the doubled-edged sword of frequent resupply stops at the cost of a higher incidence of road crossings, littering at shelters, and other problems connected to a lack of remoteness. Harriman State Park, a park on the western shore of the Hudson River, is home to the Trailside Museum and Wildlife Center and has the lowest point of elevation on the trail (at a mere 124 feet). Southern New York can be brutal and rocky, while the northern half of the state (just north of Bear Mountain Bridge) is gentle and rolling. Near the Connecticut border, a commuter rail intersects the trail, allowing hikers weekend-only access to an easy train ride to Grand Central Station in midtown Manhattan (a station providing weekday service is nearby at another rail station farther down Route 22).

Connecticut is the gateway state to New England. For NOBOs, Connecticut is a reintroduction to more elevation and a sneak preview of what is to come farther up the trail. This state has a lot of trail laid out next to rivers, making it gentle and scenic in many parts (a small part of it is even wheelchair-accessible). The gentle parts of the trail are punctuated with brief challenging climbs and descents. Connecticut is known for its hiker-friendly quaint yet pricey towns, such as Kent, Salisbury, and Falls Village.

Massachusetts is the state that marks the beginning of more truly mountainous terrain for hikers traveling northbound. Mountains such as the lighthouse-crowned Mount Greylock punctuate the trail and offer great views of the surrounding countryside. Like New York, Massachusetts offers many opportunities to enjoy civilization with its easy access to towns and extensive bus service access. The tiny town of Dalton boasts two free hiker hostels run by a couple of its most generous citizens.

Vermont is where the AT and the Long Trail share the same path for about one hundred miles before parting ways at Maine Junction. The Inn at Long Trail is a favorite pit stop for AT hikers and LT hikers alike. The trail in this state is markedly more remote and features trail running across the ridges of the Green Mountains and more elevation gain and loss than in the mid-Atlantic states. It is not uncommon for hikers to see moose tracks here, and the trail is punctuated with boggy areas traversed by puncheons: small wooden bog bridges that cross the marshy areas of the trail. Summits at ski resort mountains, such as Killington and Stratton, provide spectacular views. One of the more interesting man-made features of this state is the Clarendon Gorge suspension bridge, built as a memorial to a hiker who was killed trying to ford the river in that area.

New Hampshire has the difficult terrain that characterizes the northern New England segment of the AT. This state is best known for the White Mountains (known more familiarly as the Whites). These mountains were so named because of early European settlers who spotted the white snow that covered the peaks even in the summer. This is a challenging stretch of trail, much of which is above timberline and sometimes features severe weather (Mount Washington, a peak in the Whites' Presidential Range, is home to the worst weather in the world). It's important to plan ahead and bring extra clothing and gear when traversing the Whites as there can be dangerous weather conditions any time of year. This area features a series of warming huts run by the AMC. Due to the way these huts are spaced, they can have a big impact on your daily mileage. Camping between huts is largely restricted, but many long-distance hikers save money and extend their mileage by stealth camping. The Whites are bookended by two very hiker-friendly towns, Gorham and Glencliff.

Maine is the most difficult of all of the states on the AT. In Maine, hikers can expect to have very low mileage and a lot of fatigue. Fortunately for weary hikers, Maine provides some exceptional beauty and, of course, hospitality such as at Shaw's Boarding House in Monson. The southern section is home to the Mahoosuc Range, which contains the toughest mile on the trail, Mahoosuc Notch. Mahoosuc Notch is a mile-long, boulder-strewn ravine (a description that does not even begin to do the place justice). In the central section, a hiker may cross the Kennebec River via a canoe ferry that has a white blaze painted on its bottom (fording is very dangerous and not recommended). Throughout the entire state, there's an abundant amount of water sources, and fording can be an issue for hikers. The northernmost stretch of the trail, directly before Katahdin, is known as the "one-hundred-mile wilderness" and is relatively flat and easy to hike compared with the rest of the state. Despite the name, this area is not as wild or unpopulated as one may think. It's been a working forest for hundreds of years, full of the bustle of the local lumber industry. At the northernmost trail terminus in Maine is Baxter State Park, home to the infamous Katahdin. Originally called *Kette-Adene* by the Abenaki people, this mountain was believed to be inhabited by the feared god, Pamola. It is the highest mountain in the state of Maine and offers a challenging day hike or a fitting end to a thru-hike.

HIKE YOUR OWN HIKE

As you can see, there's definitely more than one way to hike the Appalachian Trail. Along the AT, you'll hear the saying, "hike your own hike" (also known as HYOH). *Purists* are hikers who walk past every single white blaze on the trail and refuse to blue-blaze, slack-pack (when a hiker's gear is shuttled ahead by a support vehicle), or skip any parts of the trail by yellow-blazing (hitching a ride past a section). However, some hikers feel that blue-blazing and side trips are essential to their hiking experience. Some hikers opt to slack-pack a portion of their hike, carrying only a daypack with the essentials, and some even rent canoes to *aqua-blaze* the Shenandoah River. Hostels and outfitters who provide slack-packing services are listed in the guidebooks.

While the subtle nuances of "hike your own hike" entail many different things to each hiker, the meaning of the motto essentially boils down to developing an accepting attitude toward the way your fellow hikers choose to follow their journeys. There is no right or wrong way to hike the trail so long as you hike your hike with respect for others and the environment around you.

9

Mail Drops and Bounce Boxes

It was Christmas season and I learned from the drunk up the hill,
who did the trick every Christmas, that they would hire damned
near anybody, so I went and the next thing I knew I had this leather
sack on my back and was hiking around at my leisure.

—Charles Bukowski, *Post Office*

The quote popularly associated with the United States Postal Service, "Neither snow, nor rain, nor heat, nor night . . . ," addresses the perils of the long-distance hiker to a tee. Many hikers are logistically dependent on the U.S. Postal Service for their food, medicine, gear, and other necessities. Mail drops and bounce boxes are a popular method of resupply on many long trails and are particularly so on the Appalachian Trail because of its close proximity to towns.

THE PROS AND CONS OF MAIL DROPS

A *mail drop* is a prepackaged box of goods sent to a hiker while he or she is on the trail and consists of food, gear, maps, or other supplies. Mail drops are assembled by a hiker as part of the preparation process and are sent by a support person (usually a friend or family member) as the hiker progresses up the trail. Mail drops are typically sent to post offices in trail towns but may also be sent to outfitters, hostels, and other trailside businesses.

There are benefits and disadvantages to using mail drops. Some hikers complete long hikes without ever using the post office, while others will have mail drops numbering well into the double digits. There's no right or wrong way to resupply, and the choice to use mail drops is one of the many decisions you need to make before your hike.

So what are the pros to having the USPS help with resupply? By using mail drops, you aren't dependant on what a town has to offer. Some town resupply offerings are far from attractive, offering only potato chips and Ring Dings for dinner options. Using mail drops allows you to carefully

tailor your meals to fit your tastes and specific dietary needs (this is especially important for hikers with food allergies or who follow certain dietary
lifestyles such as veganism). It also allows regular access to spare gear,
medications, and other goods that you may not be able to find at all
resupply points along the trail. Unfortunately, some remote resupply
stores take advantage of the lack of competition by jacking up their prices,
and many hikers who use mail drops feel that they save money by buying
their food in bulk and preparing it (drying and/or packaging) at home.

If timed properly, picking up mail drops saves time in town and can
change a *zero* (a day with no hiking mileage) into a *nero* (a day with at least
a few miles hiked) by eliminating the need to run around from store to
store searching for supplies. This is helpful in towns that are spread out
over large areas. One of the biggest perks of using mail drops is that getting mail can be a real morale boost, especially when you're out on the
trail and feeling disconnected from loved ones at home. While a hiker may
not rely heavily on mail drops, he or she may end up requesting General
Delivery mail at some point on the trail for this reason.

Mail drops aren't a perfect resupply method, however. Some thru-
hikers believe they are too much of a hassle. Many hikers plan mail drops
as a way to kill time during the planning stages before a long hike—planning that may not pan out during an actual hike. Mail drops also create excessive postal costs. While some hikers save money by buying in bulk and
preparing backpacking meals at home, others discover that the shipping
fees even out the score when it comes to overall resupply costs. A risk of
having multiple months of prepared food is the possibility of tiring of the
menu, regardless of how elaborate or appealing it seemed when you created it. There's also the horrible prospect of not being able to complete
your hike and being confronted with and taunted by many months' worth
of ramen when you arrive home.

While using mail drops adds the element of predictability to your resupply, it may hamper your schedule. Many hikers don't enjoy being held
to a schedule while doing a long-distance hike. I've encountered many AT
hikers in the process of either speeding up or dawdling in order to arrive
in town during post office business hours. For some, planning daily
mileage around postal hours isn't a big deal, but for others it is the horror
of horrors. Remember, many small town post offices have very limited
hours of operation and, of course, no post office is open on holidays. Finding yourself in town on a Saturday night during a three-day weekend can

force you to take two zero days until the post office reopens on Tuesday. Fairly large hassles result when mail drops are either missed or lost, severely cramping a hiker's schedule, menu, and sense of well-being.

Register box

THE INS AND OUTS OF MAIL DROPS

Successfully preparing and shipping mail drop boxes is a fairly straight-forward process, though it does require knowing a few tricks of the trade (both postal and hiker trades, that is). The United States Post Office (www.usps.com) provides a service called General Delivery mail, which allows travelers to pick up mail addressed to them at any post office destination. All that's needed to use this service is a post office's town location and zip code and the estimated date when you expect to pick up the package. Post office addresses and zip codes are provided at the end of this chapter and may also be found in major guidebooks such as the *Appalachian Trail Thru-Hikers' Companion* or *The Thru-Hiker's Handbook*.

*D*o *not* send packages via UPS or FedEx to a post office because the office will not accept them! This is especially important to consider when manufacturers send new or repaired gear to you on the trail. Using UPS or other mail services is fine when shipping to a non-USPS location such as a hostel or private residence.

Sending mail drops to hostels and other businesses is an alternative to sending packages to a post office. Always call ahead and check the amount of time a package may be held, and inquire about the practices for handling mail. Outfitters and hostels typically have longer hours of business, but bear in mind that some places may charge a fee for holding boxes.

When shipping a package or letter for General Delivery, it's a good idea to send it Priority or First Class Mail (Priority Mail is First Class Mail that weighs more than thirteen ounces). Priority Mail comes with free packaging, may be forwarded free of charge, and can be insured (this is especially important when forwarding expensive items such as seasonal gear). Allow a few weeks for shipping a mail drop or bounce box. Keep in mind that the post office will only hold a package for thirty days—some for less than that if the hiker traffic is especially high and the office's storage space gets crowded. It isn't necessary to send mail First Class or Priority, and if you don't want to take advantage of forwarding and other services, you can ship things more inexpensively at Parcel Post rates. Packages sent via Parcel Post mail can be insured but generally take longer in transit than Priority packages. Sending particularly dense and heavy items in Priority flat-rate boxes can save you money as these packages come with a preset postage rate that will not increase, regardless of how much the contents weigh.

When addressing a package, write the information clearly using a waterproof and smudge-proof marker or pen. Be sure to use the hiker's legal name, the name shown on his or her photo ID. This is vital since a hiker

> **SAMPLE GENERAL DELIVERY
> ADDRESS LABEL**
>
> Jane Doe (hiker's name)
> c/o General Delivery
> City, State, and Zip Code of post office
> Please hold for AT Hiker
> Estimated date of arrival

must show photo ID when picking up General Delivery packages at the post office. A trail name may be put on the package in addition to the legal name. If two hikers share a package, put the names of both people on the package so either can pick it up. It's preferable to use the Priority address labels supplied by the post office, and it's strongly recommended that the sender write a return address on the upper-left-hand side of the package in case the package goes missing.

When assembling your mail drops, it's a good idea to make a list of what's in each box. Carry a copy of this list in your pack or keep it in your e-mail account where you can refer to it. By doing this, you can avoid opening Priority Mail containing unwanted items and, instead, can bounce it ahead. It is free to forward Priority Mail to a new address unless it has been opened. Keep track of what is being sent to you in order to avoid missing packages.

When packing your mail drop boxes, use vacuum sealing, packing peanuts, or anything else that ensures your supplies arrive at the post office intact. You may want to consider using recycled lidded buckets (such as those used for drywall compound) if you intend on using mail drops and bounce boxes frequently. A plastic bucket is sturdy, may be easily opened and resealed, and keeps its contents safe and dry. If you use recycled boxes, make sure all of the writing on the box is covered up or crossed out to avoid confusion. The USPS provides Priority Mail boxes free of charge (see their web site or call 800-ASK-USPS for ordering information).

If you're keeping an online trail journal, you may want to provide your mail drop information on it. This is a great way to solicit surprise goodies and words of encouragement. When posting this information on your journal, be sure to give your readers clear directions on how to send General Delivery mail. Also list the post office towns and zip codes and your estimated times of pick-up. Prior to your hike, you may want to send out a mass e-mail to family and friends with mail drop instructions as well.

BOUNCE BOXES: CHEAP MOBILE STORAGE

A *bounce box* is similar to a mail drop box but, instead of being sent from home to a single location, it follows a hiker up the trail and is bounced

ITEMS TO INCLUDE IN MAIL DROPS AND/OR BOUNCE BOXES

- Freezer bags for repackaging food
- Sharpie markers, packing tape, and other materials for forwarding your box
- Extra food, especially goodies that may be difficult to find in trail towns
- Vitamins and medications
- Town clothes
- Batteries
- Extra first-aid and hygiene supplies
- Spare gear parts and a repair kit (including materials such as seam sealant and waterproofing spray)
- Maps and guidebook sections
- Chargers for MP3 players, cell phones, and other electronic devices
- Laundry soap, shampoo, body soap, lotions—anything that makes you feel comfortable and clean when in town
- Solid fuel tablets
- Febreze (this stuff is great for deodorizing pack straps, hotel rooms, clothing—anything a stinky hiker may come into contact with)
- Seasonal clothing and gear
- Paperback books
- Stationery materials such as envelopes and paper
- Film or spare memory cards for cameras
- Contact information for friends, family, and gear manufacturers
- Spare eyeglasses or contact lenses

ahead to a number of post offices along the way. Bounce boxes are useful when a hiker wants to switch out seasonal gear or ship excess supplies ahead. It's also a good way to ship food and other supplies ahead to areas that may be lacking in variety or convenience.

A bounce box combines the ease of mail drops with the built-in flexibility of creating them and sending them while en route. You may want to construct a bounce box with all of your essentials to follow you up the whole length of the trail. This is a good option if you aren't able to obtain a support person to mail supplies to you from home. A bounce box is a good way to transport supplies needed only in town. These town supplies include items such as shampoo, laundry detergent, and a clean set of town clothes.

You can forward Priority and First Class Mail for free if the mail is unopened. To avoid missing late packages, fill out and sign a forwarding form every time you pick up a mail drop. That way, any mail that arrives at the post office after you're gone will be sent up the trail to meet you at your next mail drop location. If you prefer, you can have all mail forwarded to your home address from a post office so that you can have cards and letters to greet you once you complete your hike.

Be aware that there are limits to what you can send in the mail. For example, there are restrictions placed on shipping explosive or flammable materials such as stove fuel. When in doubt, check with your local post office or contact USPS through their web site or by calling 800-ASK-USPS. Avoid mailing things that could leak or spoil and, if you do mail something that could melt or leak, double-bag it in sturdy freezer bags. Also keep in mind that postage is charged by weight. This should be good incentive to keep superfluous items such as your lucky rock collection out of your mail drop or bounce box.

Though not utilized by every long-distance hiker, mail drops are a worthwhile strategy for resupply. There's a useful article entitled "Mail Drops/Resupply Advice" on www.whiteblaze.net located in the links section under "AT Resupply Info." The Appalachian Trail Conservancy web site (www.appalachiantrail.org) offers valuable information about mail drops and bounce boxes as well. Go to the "Hike the Trail" heading and click on the "Thru-Hiking" link to find the "Resupply and Mail Drops" page. On your trip you will encounter rain, hail, sleet, and dark of night; but if you opt to use mail drops and bounce boxes, there will be a package full of goodies waiting for you at the post office at the end of a rough day.

POST OFFICES (WITH ZIP CODES) LISTED BY STATE

Check your guidebook for distances from the trail and recommended mail drop locations. *Towns marked with a star are popular resupply and rest stops for hikers.

Georgia

Suches	30572
Helen	30545
Hiawassee*	30546

The AT travels along the North Carolina/Tennessee border, offering access to post offices in both states at sporadic intervals. Please note that the North Carolina and Tennessee post offices are listed here by state, rather than by their sequence on the trail.

North Carolina

Franklin*	28734

Bryson City	28713
Fontana Dam*	28733
Hot Springs*	28743 (town is on the AT)
Elk Park	28622

Tennessee

Gatlinburg	37738 (This is the halfway point in the Smokies. If you choose to resupply, note that the post office is fifteen miles away from the AT.)
Erwin*	37650
Unicoi	37692
Roan Mountain	37687
Newland	38657
Hampton	37658
Shady Valley	37688

Virginia

Damascus*	24236 (town is on the AT)
Troutdale	24378
Sugar Grove	24375
Marion	24354
Atkins	24311
Bland	24315
Bastain	24314
Pearisburg*	24134 (post office is a mile or less from the AT)
Catawba	24070 (post office is a mile or less from the AT)
Daleville*	24083 (post office is a mile or less from the AT)
Cloverdale	24077
Troutville	24175
Buchanan	24066
Big Island	24526
Glasgow*	24555
Buena Vista	24416
Lexington	24450
Montebello	24464
Waynesboro*	22980
Elkton	22827
Luray	22835
Front Royal*	22630

Linden   22642 (post office is a mile or less from the AT)
Bluemont   20135

West Virginia
Harpers Ferry*   25425 (town is on the AT)

Maryland
Boonsboro   21713
Smithsburg   21783
Cascade   21719

Pennsylvania
Blue Ridge Summit   17214
Waynesboro   17268
South Mountain   17261
Fayetteville   17222
Mount Holly Springs 17065
Boiling Springs*   17007 (town is on the AT)
Duncannon*   17020 (town is on the AT)
Bethel   19507
Pine Grove   17963
Port Clinton*   19549 (town is on the AT)
Hamburg   19526
Slatington   18080
Walnutport   18088
Palmerton*   18071
Danielsville   18038
Wind Gap   18091 (post office is a mile or less from the AT)
Delaware Water Gap* 18327 (town is on the AT)

New Jersey
Branchville   07826
Glenwood   07418
Vernon   07462

New York
*Unionville   10988 (town is accessible from the New Jersey section of the trail before
                   Glenwood, post office is a mile or less from the AT)

Greenwood Lake	10925
Bellvale	10912
Warwick	10990
Southfields	10975
Arden	10910 (post office is a mile or less from the AT)
Bear Mountain	10911 (post office is on the AT)
Fort Montgomery*	10922 (post office is a mile or less from the AT)
Peekskill	10566
Stormville	12582
Poughquag	12570
Pawling	12564
Wingdale	12594

Connecticut

Gaylordsville	06755
Kent*	06757 (post office is a mile or less from the AT)
Cornwall Bridge	06754 (post office is a mile or less from the AT)
West Cornwall	06796
Sharon	06069
Falls Village	06031 (post office is a mile or less from the AT)
Salisbury*	06068 (post office is a mile or less from the AT)

Massachusetts

South Egremont	01258
Sheffield	01257
Great Barrington*	01230
Monterey	01245
Tyringham	01264 (post office is a mile or less from the AT)
Lee	01238
Becket	01223
Dalton*	01226 (town is on the AT)
Cheshire	10225 (town is on the AT)
Adams	01220
North Adams	01247
Williamstown	01267

Vermont

Bennington	05201

Manchester Center*	05255
Danby	05739
Wallingford	05773
Rutland	05701
Killington*	05751 (post office is a mile or less from the AT)
Woodstock	05091
South Pomfret	05067 (post office is a mile or less from the AT)
West Hartford	05084 (post office is a mile or less from the AT)
Norwich	05055 (post office is a mile or less from the AT)

New Hampshire

Hanover*	03755 (town is on the AT)
Lyme	03768
Wentworth	03282
Warren	03279
Glencliff*	03238 (post office is a mile or less from the AT)
North Woodstock	03262
Lincoln	03251
Bartlett	03812
Mount Washington	03589 (this post office is on the AT but is closed periodically for severe weather)
Gorham*	03581

Maine

Andover	04216
Oquossoc	04964
Rangeley	04970
Stratton*	04982
Caratunk*	04925 (post office is a mile or less from the AT)
Monson*	04464
Millinocket	04462

10

Flora and Fauna

The best things about animals is they don't talk much.
—Thornton Wilder

The Appalachian Mountains have an impressive diversity of resident organisms. The southern Appalachians alone house more than a hundred species of trees, and the Smokies provide a habitat for twenty-seven species of salamander, forty species of fish, fifty different mammals, and two hundred different bird species. There are two hundred species of plants on the AT that are found nowhere else in the world. It is an area of protected corridors containing some of the country's greatest natural treasures.

The AT is not true wilderness by any stretch of the imagination, and it runs past (and even through) many developed areas. Much of the forest that the trail runs through is second-growth, a renewed wilderness that was once farmland or timber lands. Unfortunately, many of the larger animals that once lived along the Appalachian corridor have been eradicated through human presence, though some creatures, such as the black bear and bobcat, remain. Ironically, the loss of wildness can be most felt in the public park lands especially set aside for conservation, where animals are habituated by repeated contact with humans. However, the Appalachian Trail is the best possible compromise of human access to the wilderness and is still very much an untamed place, offering up spectacular wildlife and plant encounters.

The AT hosts wildlife from the tiny shelter-dwelling mouse to the behemoth of Maine, the moose, which can weigh as much as a compact car. Nonnative species such as wild boar, introduced by the British in the 1930s for sport hunting, roam the Smokies area, while established native species such as bobcat, white-tailed deer, black bear, and coyote hold their own on almost the entire length of the trail. Smaller mammals such as otter, beaver, skunks, raccoons, rabbits, squirrels, chipmunks, shrews, mink, muskrats, and mice can be found on the trail as well. There are a number of animals on the rare species list that you may encounter on the trail, including the exotic-sounding Allegheny wood rat and the fence lizard. Black bear and eastern timber rattlesnakes, both frequently spotted on the trail, are also on this list. The mountain lion population, once driven off the land by development, is even rumored to be making a comeback on certain sections of the trail.

HOW TO NOT HAVE YOUR FACE EATEN: GENERAL ANIMAL SAFETY

Habituation occurs when animals lose their fear of humans through repeated contact and, in extreme cases, become aggressive. Aside from the rare run-in with a habituated bear hungry for hiker food or a mouse who has chewed through someone's pack, animal encounters are generally not fraught with peril. It's the animals that we fear the least (porcupines, mice, raccoons, and so on) who do the most damage, making off with deliciously salty, sweat-soaked socks and chewing holes through tents to get at the tasty hiker treats inside.

Keep in mind that wild animals are more afraid of you than you are of them, and they generally leave you alone if you give them wide berth and respect. It's good to know about a species' particular behaviors to help protect yourself during encounters. For example, moose are most dangerous during the fall rutting season, and protective mothers are best left alone when with calves. The same holds true for mother black bears that are on the defensive when accompanied by their young. Practice common sense and stay far away from wild animals. Never feed or interact with them. The black bear problems in the Smokies arose from uninformed park visitors feeding the bears and failing to respect them as large, wild predators.

By far, the most destructive creatures on the AT are small mammals such as mice, raccoons, and porcupines. Mice are found in abundance in most shelters and cause a lot of havoc with hiker equipment and food supplies. Many shelters supply mouse bells, odd-looking devices made from a hanging line with an upturned can hanging from it. In theory, the can keeps mice from shimmying down the line to your food bag, though many agile and cunning mice have learned ways to get around these devices. When storing your pack in the shelter, leave it open so that rodents don't chew holes in it in an attempt to explore its contents. Also, don't sleep with your head close to the shelter wall as this area tends to be a mouse highway and they have no qualms about running over your face as you sleep.

Raccoons and skunks can also be a nuisance. Food should be bear-bagged to keep it out of their path.

Porcupines and deer are particularly attracted to the salty sweat residue on trekking poles, socks, shoes, and other items. On the AT, deer have made off with expensive Leki poles and porcupines have gnawed holes in hiker socks, ruining them. Porcupines mostly reside in the New England states (Vermont is home to the most unruly of them), and some of the shelters in those areas are built with a deacon's seat, an additional short wall across the front entrance, to keep them out. Porcupines aren't necessarily dangerous, but their quills can do damage to trail dogs and overly curious (read: stupid) hikers. Quills need to be removed as soon as possible from the skin as they can become deeply embedded and cause serious infection. When camping in porcupine country, be sure to hang your gear up off the ground out of porcupines' reach.

Most suburban and rural dwellers have dealt with precocious skunks and raccoons and their inventive ways of getting into human food and garbage. Give these animals, especially skunks, a lot of space, and be sure to keep good-smelling food suspended in a bear bag where it can't be reached. Skunks and raccoons are highly habituated animals and have been sharing space with humans for a long time. They are commonly found at campgrounds where there are trash cans and sloppy campers supplying a wealth of tasty food. Avoid setting up your tent near trash cans that may attract midnight

> When staying in a shelter, leave the zippers and other closures on your pack open. Curious mice who are denied easy access to the insides of a pack will chew through the fabric to explore. Leaving an open pack (without any food in it, of course) can spare you from annoying rodent damage.

visitors. Don't ever stash food in your tent, cook in your tent, or do *anything* that could leave the inside of your tent smelling edible to animals. Raccoons and mice are especially inventive when it comes to obtaining food and won't think twice before gnawing holes in an expensive tent.

When in the backcountry, you need to remember that you are in the animals' territory, not the other way around. Keep in mind that wild animals are not the same as domestic pets and that, in the case of larger mammals, there's always a chance of an unpredictable or perilous encounter. It's good practice to always secure your food in a high, inaccessible space and keep it away from your sleeping and gear-storage areas. If you go into the woods with some respect and knowledge, animal sightings are a thing of beauty and pleasure rather than fear and discomfort.

PLEASE, DO NOT FEED THE BEARS

Of all the animals found along the AT, black bears command the most respect. Unlike grizzly bears found out west, black bears lack the aggressiveness that makes the grizzly legendary. There's an old hiker saying that while a black bear will climb up a tree to get you, a grizzly will just knock the tree down. While black bears are much more benign than grizzlies, hikers should exercise caution when in black bear country. Black bears are generally shy creatures and make an effort to avoid human contact. It's possible for a hiker to thru-hike the entire length of the AT without ever having the opportunity to see a bear.

There are a number of locations along the AT with particularly notorious bear populations. Areas most highly populated by black bears are in Georgia, the Nantahalas, Smokies, Shenandoah, and New Jersey. The Smokies have long been an infamously bear-ridden area of the AT, and some shelters still sport chain-link-fence enclosures to keep the bears and people separated. In New Jersey, bear hunting was reintroduced and this may eventually impact the large habituated population in the area.

Watch for signage indicating the presence of nuisance bears. Maintainers, ridge-runners, and other hikers may post notices in the registers or hang signs at the shelters warning hikers of any unusual bear activity. I've heard that such signage is sometimes hung as a precautionary measure and doesn't necessarily point to a specific recent bear incident. Regardless, take heed and exercise caution in areas with the reputation of having bear problems. And keep in mind that while areas with bear problems are managed to keep hikers safe, this management relies on your ability to responsibly share the bears' habitat. Parks and maintainers provide bear cables and bear boxes, devices designed to keep hiker food safely out of reach. Use these devices. Not only do they help to keep your food safe, they help to protect the resident animal populations from the problems associated with habituation.

Habituated bears who have learned to associate hikers with food pose the largest threat. These bears have lost all natural fear of people and may happily mug you (i.e., steal your pack right off your back much the same way a guy with a ski mask steals a purse). A threatened and aggravated bear displays signs of distress such as pawing at the ground, making noises, or charging. If this behavior occurs, back away slowly from the bear, never turning around or running. Never stare at a bear as bears read this behavior as a challenge; and if you encounter an aggressive bear, talk to it in a low, comforting voice. If followed or approached by a bear, change your course of direction. If the bear continues to pursue you, confront it at a distance by shouting, waving your arms and trekking poles, or throwing sticks or rocks in its direction. If you're hiking in a group and encounter an aggressive bear, have the group band together and make noise and motion to confuse the bear into thinking that you're one large creature.

There are two schools of thought on how to behave if actually attacked by a black bear. Some feel that you should lie on the ground and the bear will eventually leave you alone, and this is the approach more often taken with grizzlies. Others strongly feel that if attacked, a hiker should fight a black bear because aggression sometimes acts as an effective deterrent (never initiate bear fights, of course).

Never climb a tree to get out of a bear's way as black bears are excellent climbers. There's a myth that black bears aren't able to run down hills quickly because of their short front legs. This is not true at all—they can book it down an incline just as fast as a fleeing hiker, if not faster. Always leave your pack on when you encounter a bear. You are far less likely to be mugged if the pack is on your back. On a final cheerful note, in the event of a mauling, the pack provides your body with additional protection.

Occasionally, hikers wear bear bells to help alert bears of their presence, or they carry bear mace as a form of self-defense. It is your personal choice to use mace, but it's preferable to avoid negative bear encounters using common sense rather than resorting to defense tactics. Talking, whistling, or singing while hiking in bear country is adequate for warning them of your presence and avoiding surprise encounters. Be sure to make a lot of noise in foggy and windy conditions or if there's a loud water source nearby, as these sorts of environments make it difficult for a bear to detect your presence. Be on the lookout for natural signs that indicate the presence of bear. Look for prints on the ground, scat, or scratch marks on trees to determine the presence of bears in the area. Negative bear encounters are extremely rare on the Appalachian Trail and are easily avoided by using common sense and respect.

BEAR-BAGGING

The only reason that bears interact with humans is to gain access to their food. The best way to keep bears from becoming habituated and potentially dangerous is to handle your food correctly in the backcountry. The technique of bear-bagging, putting your food in a bag that is hung from a tree limb, keeps food safe from hungry bears and other animals. As well as keeping food physically out of reach, some feel that bear-bagging keeps the scent of the food off of the ground and away from animals' radar.

Though it sounds easy enough to hang your food from a tree limb, bear-bagging has been elevated to the status of an art form, and there are various techniques. The standard rule of thumb is that a bear bag should be hung at least ten feet off the ground and ten feet away from the base of the tree (and away from other limbs that could support a bear) and at a distance of two hundred feet or more away from camp. This ideal is rarely possible to achieve, of course, since trees on the AT never look the way they do in bear-bagging illustrations in hiking books.

You'll need two things to bear-bag your food: cord and a waterproof food bag. It's important that the bag is waterproof so that your food doesn't get ruined hanging outside in heavy dew or rain. Carry about forty feet of lightweight cord (³⁄₁₆-inch is an ideal size), which can be purchased at an outfitter or hardware store.

The *traditional method* of bear-bagging involves tying one end of the cord to your bag and heaving the remainder of the line over an ideally situated limb. If the cord is too light to gain enough momentum when you throw it, tie a small rock or stick to the end of it or make a rock-filled pouch out of a bandana tied to the end of the cord. Pull the bag into the air and tie off the end of the line to a rock, tree trunk, or branch. Bears are clever and many are able to defeat the traditional bagging system. However, not too many hikers lose their food to bears on the AT when correctly using traditional bagging, and this was my method of choice in bear country.

The *counterbalance method* involves hanging two bags over a limb, with one bag on each side. To do this, tie one end of your cord to the first bag. Heave the cord over a tree limb and draw the bag up as high as it can go. Reaching up, tie the second bag to the other end of the cord. Using a trekking pole, push the second bag up, using the first one as a counterweight. When both bags are hanging parallel to one another at least ten feet off the ground, it makes a difficult target for bears. Use your trekking pole to reach the bags when breaking camp in the morning.

Another option is to tie a line at least ten feet off the ground between two trees and hang your food bags off of it. This method is pretty easy to defeat, especially for squirrels and other acrobatic small mammals. Less often used methods are the Marrison and PCT methods, techniques utilized in grizzly country and equaling rocket science in their complexity. The *PCT method*, named so for its use on the Pacific Crest Trail, utilizes cord, a carabiner, and a stick tied to the line to act as a stopper when line is drawn through the carabineer to mimic a counterbalance effect. The *Marrison method* makes use of two carabineers that act as a pulley system to draw food up and out of harm's way. There are ready-made bear-bagging systems available. While this might be a lot more cru-

So what should you store in a bear bag? Anything that has an odor, such as dirty pots, trash, soap, toothpaste, and food needs to be stored safely. Keep in mind that wild animals have an unusual palate and may find things such as dirty toilet paper appealing.

cial in grizzly country, the additional investment isn't worth it on the AT where simple bagging methods are typically effective.

There are alternatives to bear-bagging. Some campsites with known bear activity provide hikers with bear boxes, small metal lockers for food storage, or a tall metal pole for hanging packs and food bags. Bear canisters, bear-proof food containers that are carried in the pack, are more predominantly used on the western trails in grizzly country. Some AT hikers use an Ursack (www.ursack.com), a product made of high-tech Vectran fabric that is reportedly bulletproof and impervious to bears and other critters. Though it may seem like overkill, the Ursack is a great device for keeping mice and other small mammals out of your food.

Cooking on the trail is somewhat different from cooking in your kitchen. All creatures from mice to bears are interested in what you have to eat, so it's important to protect your food. When animals and hiker food are kept apart, everyone is able to co-exist peacefully. It's only when animals such as bears come to associate humans with food that problems start to occur. While this is a larger concern in bear country, it is something to keep in mind even if there are only raccoons, porcupines, and other small mammals in the area (which is pretty much everywhere you'll be camping). These small animals can do as much, if not more, harm as bears.

A WORD ON MOOSE

Moose can be especially tricky to deal with during the rutting season or when with calf. Again, negative encounters can be avoided by being aware of when you are hiking in their territory, which spans northern Massachusetts to Maine, and by keeping your distance. As with bear, an aggressive moose can be deterred by a group of hikers grouping together and making a lot of noise and motion. To the myopic moose, a group of hikers appears to be one large and threatening creature. If a moose charges you, run behind trees. Strangely enough, a moose falls for this "out of sight, out of mind" tactic and may be less inclined to pursue you. If a moose is really persistent, you may want to curl up in a ball, which will likely cause the moose to become disinterested in you.

ANIMAL-BORNE DISEASES

Encounters with animals may pose a threat to hikers by introducing communicable diseases that can pass between species. Among these are rabies and hantavirus. Though rare, these diseases may be present on the AT and are worth knowing about.

Rabies

Rabies, a virus affecting humans and certain animals, can be fatal, causing severe encephalitis and myelitis if left untreated. The virus is most commonly transmitted through an animal bite or contact of saliva with an open wound. A vaccination for rabies may be given after a person has been exposed to it. This vaccination is effective as long as it is administered before the onset of symptoms. If rabies is left untreated, symptoms appear anywhere from a few weeks to years after exposure to the virus. It's important to avoid close contact with any animals, particularly raccoons, bats, skunks, or domestic animals such as dogs that display rabies symptoms.

Rabies may manifest itself in humans in a number of ways. It can lead to paralysis and apparent calmness or can cause wild and erratic behavior. Symptoms include any number of neurological, cognitive, and psychological disturbances; all leading to death. If you are bitten by a wild animal, seek medical attention immediately. If you encounter an animal displaying signs of rabies, notify a ranger, ridge-runner, or other authority as soon as possible.

Hantavirus

Hantavirus, short for hantavirus pulmonary syndrome (HPS), is a virus transmitted through mouse saliva and waste. The virus may travel through the air in dust and be inhaled by humans. Hantavirus was first recognized in the U.S. in 1993, and, since then, a few hundred people have been diagnosed with it (in 1994, it claimed its first AT hiker).

This disease is violent and potentially deadly but very rare. Its symptoms include aches, fever, fatigue, headaches, vertigo, nausea, diarrhea, and vomiting. Accompanying these symptoms are breathing problems, coughing, and restricted feeling in the lungs. Not all people infected with hantavirus experience these symptoms, though. If a person displays respiratory or other symptoms, he or she should seek medical treatment. Like

other viral infections, there is no cure for hantavirus. Since mice are hantavirus carriers, it's important to discourage them from infesting shelters
(a seemingly impossible task). Keep all of your food hung on mouse bells,
and never purposefully feed shelter mice.

PLANT LIFE

Trees are what gives the AT its signature green tunnel feel. Many of the
forests that the AT runs through are second-growth, meaning the trees living there are the product of re-growth occurring after the original forest
was cleared for lumber or farmland. There are still a few old-growth areas
along the eastern woods, but they are few and far between. The trail sports
a variety of types of forest such as mixed deciduous, southern Appalachian, transitional, and boreal. Within these areas, very unique group-
ings of trees grow.

The boreal forests of New Hampshire and Maine, which sport growths
of krummholz, a stilted form of spruce and fir found near tree line, are
quite different from the southern hardwood forests that are host to large
oaks and hickories as well as the beautiful rhododendrons that blossom in
spring. These various forests display a wealth of species, with the southern Appalachian forest boasting more tree species than any other forest in
North America.

Along with the trees, the AT is home to a large variety of other plant
life. Depending on the season, the AT is a riot of colors and scents due
to the abundance of wildflower species. Jack-in-the-pulpit, pink lady's
slipper, and columbine are but a few of the many species of flower found
on the trail. There is also the unique glowing foxfire found in the southern states. The trail hosts rare and endangered plant species such as the
Roan Mountain bluet (which grows in only nine sites in the world, all of
which are near the AT) and the Robbins cinquefoil. The AT provides a
protected corridor for these species to survive unharmed by encroach-
ing development.

There are plants along the AT that are edible (or have edible fruits),
though hikers are strongly discouraged from making use of them. Along
the trail, there are blueberries, blackberries, ramps (a type of wild onion
that grows in the south), edible mushrooms, wild watercress, ginseng, and
other tasty plants. So why shouldn't you gorge yourself on your forest
food finds? Animals rely heavily on edible plants as a source of nutrition.
If every hiker were to graze on plants, large swaths of forest would be
stripped of some essential animal food sources. There's also an inherent

danger associated with eating wild plants or fungi, particularly the many species of mushrooms that the AT supports. Some plants can be highly toxic, and, if misidentified and consumed, can pose serious health risks. There are also environmental pollutants that can appear in plants in trace amounts. It is not recommended, for example, to eat the blueberries growing alongside the trail near the Lehigh Gap in Pennsylvania, an area that is still recovering from industrial pollution.

POISON IVY, POISON OAK, AND POISON SUMAC

There are a few poisonous plants found on the AT. These plants secrete urushiol, a sap that causes allergic skin reactions (one of the most common allergies in the country). For most people, simple skin contact with any of these plants is sufficient to cause rashes and other reactions. Urushiol can be transported from skin to skin, clothing to skin, and through smoke when plants are burned. After exposure, it normally takes a day or so for symptoms, such as redness and itching, to appear. More severe reactions may include swelling and blistering.

Companies such as Burt's Bees manufacture special soaps designed to combat poison ivy. If you're especially allergic to poison ivy, poison oak, and poison sumac exposure, using barrier creams such as IvyBlock will reduce or prevent allergic reactions. Wipes such as IvyCleanse and cleaners such as Zanfel remove urushiol, preventing rashes after exposure.

If you come into contact with any of these plants, wash exposed areas of skin (preferably with hot water and soap) and remove and wash clothing that has been exposed. Use alcohol wipes to thoroughly clean exposed skin. Don't let affected skin come into contact with eyes or other parts of your body (or someone else's). You can treat the itch and irritation with over-the-counter products such as calamine lotion and antihistamines. If you have a rash that won't clear up or is very painful, contact a doctor. The best approach to avoiding allergic rashes from these plants is to be able to identify and avoid them. Useful information on poisonous plants (including photographs) can be found at poisonivy.aesir.com, www.poison-sumac.org, and www.poison-ivy.org.

THE AT IS FOR THE BIRDS

The Appalachian Trail is home to a number of both rare and commonly found birds. The higher elevation creates a climate zone similar to that of Canada and the more northern edges of the United States. Bird species along the trail range from tiny songbirds to larger game and predatory birds. Rare species such as the Cooper's hawk and the northern raven may be seen, as well as many others.

The wooded corridor shielding the AT is full of the sounds of bird call, woodpeckers tapping on trees,

> One of the most famous birds on the AT is the whippoorwill that sounds every morning at the Vandeventer Shelter and is rumored to be the spirit of a woman who was murdered there many years ago.

and the drumming of grouse wings. In the spring, hikers may encounter a mother grouse limping along, attempting to lure them away from her young. Hikers at higher altitudes encounter vultures, hawks, and other predatory birds soaring on thermals around them.

DOGS AND OTHER DOMESTIC ANIMALS ON THE TRAIL

Thru-hiking with man's best friend may seem like an ideal experience. Dogs are a great source of companionship and safety for hikers. Keep in mind that taking a pet on a long-distance hike is a huge responsibility, one that needs to be considered carefully. A dog may affect your hiking speed, restrict where you can stay, complicate the logistics of your trip, and generally create more work for you. If this sort of effort isn't a deterrent and you're willing to shoulder the responsibility of hiking with your canine companion, it can be a gratifying experience.

So what sort of dog makes a good hiking partner? Ideally, a trail dog should have good manners and not be aggressive or combative with humans or other dogs. It should be able to heel, sit, and follow other simple commands even with distractions. Along with being well-trained, the dog should be relaxed, personable, and able to deal with new people and situations on a day-to-day basis. If your dog is prone to making a lot of noise—howling, barking, or growling—the trail is not the place to bring it. Aside from frightening or annoying other hikers, loud dogs scare off wildlife, eliminating the chance animal encounters that greatly add to a hike. A trail dog taken on a long hike should be mature, in good shape, and have previous backpacking experience. An overly young or old dog may not be able to handle the physical or mental stresses of the trail.

> Take your dog to a veterinarian before going on a long-distance hike. Your vet is a great resource for preventative health information and will be able to administer the necessary shots and prescribe heartworm pills or other medications as needed. Trail dogs should have up-to-date rabies vaccines and wear their rabies tags on the trail.

Your dog should be willing to pull its own weight by carrying a small dog pack designed for its height and weight. Many hiking dogs will help their owners carry food and other supplies. Companies such as Mountainsmith (www.mountainsmith.com) and Granite Gear (www.granite gear.com) manufacture special packs for canine hikers.

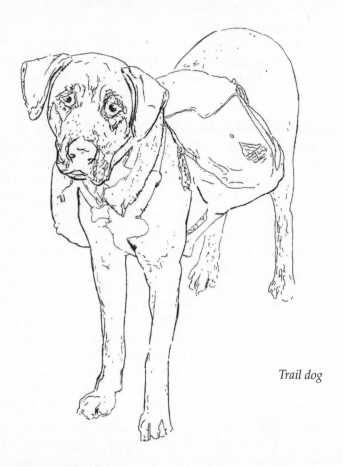

Trail dog

When you hike with a dog, you'll encounter many hikers who are dog lovers, but there are also those who would prefer not to hike with or share a shelter space with a dog. Be respectful of others and keep your dog away from the insides of shelters in all but the worst weather, and allow them in, even then, only with the consent of the hikers inhabiting it. Your portable shelter should have enough space to protect both you and your pet during bad weather.

If hiking in a heavy-traffic area with a dog with less than perfect heeling skills, use a leash as a matter of courtesy and safety. I was hiking near Sages Ravine in Connecticut when a massive Doberman belonging to day hikers bounded toward me out of nowhere. While the dog ended up being friendly, its owner's negligence managed to shave a few years off of my life and temporarily ruin my hike. Respect leash laws in towns and on national park service lands. Clean up after your dog, either by burying its waste or packing it out with your garbage. Don't allow your dog to beg for food, damage gear, or harass other hikers. It's important for your dog's well-being as well as that of the environment to keep it away from wildlife.

There are a few areas of the AT where dogs are prohibited (unless they are service animals such as seeing-eye dogs). These are the Smokies, the Trailside Museum and Wildlife Center in New York, and Baxter State Park. Make arrangements well in advance to board your dog if you hike the Smokies or Baxter. While hiking the Smokies, many hikers

> Make sure your dog always wears a collar with identification tags on it. These tags should include your name, mailing address, telephone number, and e-mail address.

have their pet boarded then shuttled to meet them at the end of the park's restricted area. Boarding information is available in the major guidebooks. Be judicious about with whom you leave your dog, asking other hikers and locals for recommendations on quality facilities.

Having a dog with you while you hike poses other restrictions. Getting a hitch into town or utilizing public transportation can be difficult or even impossible with a dog. Staying at certain bed and breakfasts, hotels, campgrounds, and hostels is prohibited with a dog. It's a good idea to call ahead before trying to stay at these sorts of places. Simple town chores such as eating in a restaurant, shopping, or going to the laundromat may be complicated when traveling with a dog. Also, some obstacles on the trail itself may not be dog-friendly, including stiles (the wooden ladders leading over fences) and steep rock climbs, particularly those involving steps or ladders.

Dogs require special care on the trail. Like a small four-legged hiker, they are asked to perform repeated strenuous tasks day after day. Keep your dog well-hydrated, stopping often for water when the temperatures are high or when traveling on rough terrain. Some dogs have a tendency to keep going well after reaching a stage of exhaustion, so keep an eye on your pet and strictly impose frequent breaks. You may want to clip a dog with a heavy coat during hot summer months, and always allow your dog to take full advantage of ponds, lakes, and streams to cool off (just be sure to keep the dog away from water sources that hikers use for drinking and cooking).

When traveling with a dog, you need to consider the animal's needs in your resupply logistics. The amount of food a dog eats during the course of a day varies, and you need to get a sense of what to carry before you hit the trail. You should bring along the dog's medications, such as heartworm pills, as well as a small first-aid kit focused on the dog's particular needs. Most towns have a general resupply option, but dog food may be difficult to come by, especially if your pet has special dietary needs. You may want to consider frequent mail drops with dog food and other supplies.

> Veterinarian services, primarily available in larger towns, are listed in the guidebooks.

Dog food tends to be heavy and dense, so you don't want to carry too much of it at a time. On the upside, it does store and pack well and won't spoil easily.

> If you encounter a stray dog on the trail, avoid interacting with it and tell an authority such as a ranger about its presence. Loose hunting dogs are an issue in the south during hunting season, and though these dogs are usually friendly, it's best to leave them alone.

Aside from dogs, other pets have made appearances on the AT. The trail has hosted miniature pigs, goats, ferrets, and a host of other creatures. In the Smokies, you may encounter horses on the AT because that section of the trail is open to pack stock. Whether your pet is exotic or not, hiking with it can be a rewarding experience. More information on hiking with dogs may be found on the ATC web site at www.appalachiantrail.org (click on "Hike the Trail"/"Plan a Hike"/"Hiking with Dogs").

SLIMY STUFF: REPTILES, AMPHIBIANS, AND FISHES

The most well-known of the reptiles, amphibians, and fishes of the AT is the diverse collection of salamanders, including the awe-inspiring hellbender. There are other creatures of interest living along the AT such as the fence lizard, triangle floater mussel, and the Appalachian brook crayfish. The bodies of water flowing through or under the trail host fish species such as trout, bass, and catfish, and other damp or hidden areas are home to turtles, frogs, and toads. Most hikers encounter a number of snakes from the benign garter snake to more treacherous ones from the pit viper family.

A snakebite is a fairly rare oc- currence, and death from a snakebite is even rarer. Pit vipers are a venomous group of snakes so named because they contain heat sensors located in small pits in the head. There are a number of pit vipers found on the AT, such as

> **C**oral snakes, found primarily in the southern Appalachian mountains, are not pit vipers but are also venomous. They resemble non-poisonous snakes such as the scarlet kingsnake but have a particular color pattern where the red and yellow bands touch one another.

water moccasins (also known as cottonmouth or cottonmouth water moccasins), copperheads, and rattlesnakes. There are many different types of rattlers (timber rattlers are commonly found on the AT), but they are all characterized by rattles on their tail and the buzzing or rattling sound they create when threatened.

A pit viper may be identified by its large fangs, deep pit indentation in the face, triangular head, and vertical elliptical pupils. Of course, in order to identify a pit viper, one must get dangerously close to the snake. It's a good rule of thumb to avoid handling any snake, even if you feel confident that it's not a harmful type. This goes for dead snakes as well as live ones, as freshly dead snakes still have a bite reflex.

A person suffering from a poisonous snakebite begins to show symptoms within five minutes of receiving the bite. The first symptom of a poisonous bite is swelling and redness around the bite wound, later turning to a purplish discoloration. A coral snakebite will not cause immediate symptoms. Swelling continues for over a day and may eventually affect the entire limb. Numbness and blistering affect the wound a few hours after its occurrence. The body's reactions to a poisonous snakebite are complex and include nausea, rapid heartbeat, weakness and dizziness, low pulse, excessive perspiration, fever, convulsions, darkened vision, and headache.

The old-fashioned field treatment for a venomous snakebite was to incise the area of the bite and suck the venom out with the mouth. This is no longer recommended. There are snakebite kits available on the market that include a suction pump to draw the venom from the wound. Very few people carry these kits because they're bulky and not overly effective in treating bites. When a person is bit by a pit viper, the best approach is to reduce the spread of venom throughout the body and keep the vital signs going. Send someone for medical help immediately. If you witness a snake bite a victim, move the victim away from the snake to avoid multiple bites. Make the victim lie down to help reduce the spread of venom.

Remove tightly fitted garments, rings, or other things that could be affected by swelling. The bite wound shouldn't be elevated above the heart; instead, keep it at the level of the heart. Clean the wound to help avoid infection and do not use a tourniquet or ice.

Prevention is one of the best measures against snakebites. Be careful where you place your hands and feet, and be on the lookout for snakes in ideal habitats such as warm, rocky ledges. Poisonous snakes are prominent in the southern states, Pennsylvania, and the southern portion of Massachusetts. Rattlesnakes often create a rattling sound as a warning to intruders, but this is not always the case, so never rely on sound alone when walking through snake country. Avoid night hiking in snake-ridden areas. If you run into a venomous snake, give it space and leave it alone. Never kill a snake as they are useful in keeping down the number of mice and other pests.

THE TINY WINGED MONSTERS FROM HELL: INSECTS (AND SPIDERS)

Insects are the bane of many hikers' existences. Any hiker who's struggled through New Jersey in the height of mosquito season or who's slogged through Maine in black fly season will attest to that. From the merely annoying no-see-um to the gypsy moths that are destroying the foliage in Maryland and Pennsylvania, insects are a force to be reckoned with. Hikers take a variety of approaches when combating bugs. Those who don't shy away from heavy chemicals douse themselves in DEET, while the more sensitive use natural oils, eat vitamin B, or wear a bug net. Simple preventative moves such as wearing gaiters and lighter-colored clothing are something every hiker can do. Regardless of your strategy, bugs are out there and you'll have to hike with them.

Wearing light clothing and long-sleeved shirts and pants, tucking in your shirt, and wearing tall gaiters are strategies for lessening exposed skin to hungry insects. I have heard of hikers wearing flea collars treated with permethrin to ward off ticks, but perspiration can quickly negate the effect of this chemical. There's also a line of clothing called Buzz Off, which is treated with permethrin and helps to keep insects at bay (www.buzz offoutdoorwear.com).

Many insect repellents are carcinogenic, act as neurotoxins, or have other serious side effects. A long-distance hiker is subjected to prolonged exposure to these chemicals and should be aware of the potential long- and short-term health risks. Always read the safety precautions and directions for use, and exercise common sense. Don't use repellent if you have open wounds, sunburn, or other preexisting skin irritations, and avoid contact with eyes and other mucous membranes. If you notice an adverse reaction to a repellent such as rash, dizziness, heart palpitations, or nausea, immediately wash it off. Use repellent sparingly and preferably on clothing rather than bare skin (never wear repellent underneath clothing). Use spray repellents in a well-ventilated area away from water sources, food, and other hikers. Repellents create a layer of chemical vapor that confuses insects and keeps them from finding you. Repellents don't work the same as insecticides, which kill the insects rather than merely keeping them at bay.

POPULAR INSECT REPELLENT CHEMICALS

Note that these chemicals are the basis for most commercial repellents and are marketed in a variety of forms and mixtures.

DEET (chemical name, N,N-diethyl-meta-toluamide)—By far, DEET is the most effective repellent for ticks and mosquitoes. DEET products are available in concentrations of 5 percent to 100 percent, in spray and lotion form. The stronger the concentration, the longer it works. This chemical is harmful to synthetic materials and may cause rashes and other allergic reactions when applied in higher concentrations.

Dimethyl phthalate (DMP)—DMP has been used on fabrics to make them insect-deterrent and can also be directly applied on the skin. It is an irritant for mucous membranes and has potential health risks.

Picaridin—This is an especially effective chemical for warding off mosquitoes (possibly more so than DEET) and also deters ticks.

MGK-264 (N-octyl bicycloheptene dicarboximide)—When used in conjunction with DEET and R326, MGK-264 helps to create a broad-spectrum repellent. This repellent is less easily absorbed into the skin than DEET, yet is a suspected carcinogen.

Permethrin—This chemical lasts for weeks when applied to clothing and other materials such as tents and is used in this manner rather than directly on skin. Materials treated with permethrin may be effective for up to six weeks (keep unused treated items in plastic bags to prolong effectiveness).

R-326 (Di-n-propyl isocinchomeronate)—This chemical is most effective at repelling flies, gnats, and no-see-ums. You only need to use small quantities of it, and it isn't readily absorbed into the skin, posing less of a health risk.

Along with these basic chemical repellents, there are other methods of repelling insects, such as herbal repellents based on essential oils. Check to see if an essential oil product is registered with the EPA before using it as

COMMON HERBAL REPELLENTS

Catnip—A homemade repellent can be made utilizing catnip. Place catnip along with other herbs from the mint family (such as pennyroyal and spearmint) in apple cider vinegar. Soak for two weeks, mixing the concoction every day, strain, and rub on skin for a safe and inexpensive repellent.

Cedar oil—This is a safe non-pesticide repellent that can be used on pets and children. It may be used directly on clothing with no damage and is especially effective for mosquitoes.

Citronella oil—This is a lemon-scented oil extract of the Eurasian grass *Cymbopogon nardus*. It isn't a pesticide and smells relatively pleasant, but isn't very effective. Citronella oil may cause an allergic reaction in some individuals.

Lavender oil—This essential oil typically works for thirty minutes or so. It cannot be used on toddlers.

Oil of lemon eucalyptus (P-menthane 3,8-diol)—Eucalyptus oil has a number of medicinal uses and is the most effective herbal repellent available, providing up to two hours of protection. For health reasons, only apply it a couple of times a day.

Soybean oil—Soybean oil provides one to three and a half hours of mosquito protection and is generally thought to be almost as effective as oil of lemon eucalyptus.

ALTERNATIVE REPELLENTS

Along with the standard chemical and herbal repellents, there are alternatives (usually derived from household products). The following is a list of repellent options, many of which are inexpensive and readily found in grocery or drug stores:

Avon Skin-So-Soft—Avon Skin-So-Soft bath oil may be mixed with water or alcohol as a safe bug repellent. Skin-So-Soft Bug Guard Plus is now marketed by Avon specifically as an insect deterrent. It is not very effective compared with other products, but has no known side effects and helps to keep mosquitoes at bay. It also helps stinky hikers smell better.

Garlic—Some hikers believe that ingesting large amounts of garlic helps to ward off insects. However, the amount of garlic one would have to eat in order for this to be effective is prohibitive.

Mosquito coils—Mosquito coils are an insect-repelling incense. They are useful for deterring mosquitoes, gnats, biting flies, and no-see-ums. The smoke produced by these coils is a pollutant and poses health hazards.

Rubbing alcohol—Though it shouldn't be used regularly, rubbing alcohol can be applied to the skin to act as a deterrent against mosquitoes.

Vanilla—Pure vanilla (found at health food stores) mixed in a ratio of one part water to one part vanilla smells nice and helps to repel. Don't use the cheap extract that contains alcohol.

Vicks VapoRub—Though it stinks, it is safe, and is reported to do some good with repelling insects.

Vitamin B—There is no solid evidence that ingesting vitamin B successfully repels insects, yet some hikers swear by it.

some unregistered products contain dangerous concentrations of essential oils. Absolutely avoid products that contain more than 10 percent essential oils and be wary of those that contain more than 3 percent. I have a strong chemical sensitivity to DEET but, fortunately, I've discovered an herbal product, All Terrain's Herbal Armor, which offers protection against no-see-ums, mosquitoes, ticks, and other pesky insects.

Bee Stings

Bee and wasp stings are merely an uncomfortable nuisance, except for the occasional person who has an allergy to them. In these instances, stings can prove very dangerous or even fatal. Hikers who know they have an allergy to bee stings should carry a bee sting kit (a prescription epinephrine kit). If you stumble upon a bee or hornet nest, it's best to run for brush or water to thwart the hive if they attack. Africanized bees may be found along the trail. These bees are very aggressive but are no more poisonous than other types of bees.

If you are stung, carefully scrape the stinger out of the skin (pulling it out may release more venom) and sterilize the bite area with an alcohol wipe to prevent infection. Swelling and pain may be managed with the application of ice to the bite area and by taking NSAIDs (nonsteroidal anti-inflammatory medication). An antihistamine may also help to reduce the risk of swelling associated with stings. Seek medical attention if you are known to have an allergy or if you experience excessive swelling, dizziness, hives, tightness in chest and throat, nausea and vomiting, or difficulty breathing. If you experience many stings, seek medical help even if you aren't allergic because cardiovascular and kidney complications may arise.

Spider Bites

The Appalachian Trail is home to the black widow and brown recluse spiders. These spiders are more prevalent in the southern part of the trail. If you are bitten by a spider, try to safely capture the insect to show to a doctor. This helps in determining the treatment and the severity of the bite. Spider bites should be washed or disinfected with an alcohol wipe, covered in antibiotic cream, and iced to reduce swelling. Pain can be managed with over-the-counter NSAIDs. Seek medical help as soon as possible. There is no antivenin available for brown recluse bites but treatments may help to ease symptoms. The sooner a spider bite victim seeks treatment, the greater a chance of a fast recovery.

The brown recluse, also known as the violin spider (due to the violin-shaped marking on its back), is often found in warm, dry, enclosed areas such as privies and shelters. The venom from this spider's bite is very toxic and typically causes redness, itching, a bull's-eye pattern around a blister, or black ulcer or blister at the site of the bite. It is not uncommon for the bite to be painless and easily ignored. The spider's poison may cause headache, fever, nausea and vomiting, general fatigue and aches, kidney damage, coma, or even death. Necrosis (dead tissue) is commonly associated with brown recluse bites. This is when an opened ulcer resulting from the bite becomes infected and the living tissue surrounding it begins to break down.

Less common on the AT is the black widow spider. Like the brown recluse, this spider likes to live in dark, dry, enclosed areas. In the south, the black widow is characterized by an hourglass-shaped marking on the underside of the abdomen. In the north, this spider has a row of red dots running down its upper abdomen and bars on the underside. The coloration of the northern black widow may vary to a good extent. Bites from these spiders don't always cause reactions because the bites don't always contain poison. Death resulting from a black widow bite is very rare. This spider's poison causes a bull's-eye rash. Reactions include muscle cramping, weakness, headache, sweating, nausea and vomiting, increased blood pressure, and respiratory problems. If any of these symptoms occur, the bite victim should seek medical attention as soon as possible. Treatments may include narcotics or the use of antivenin.

Non-poisonous spiders may also give painful bites. These bites may resemble those of the brown recluse without the same physical symptoms associated with it. Though these bites are not poisonous, they may cause necrosis in tissue. It's important to clean bite wounds and to seek medical help if the wound fails to heal normally.

Lyme Disease

It's important to regularly check yourself for ticks, the carrier of Lyme disease and other bacterial infections. Typically, a tick rides on its host for a period of time, looking for a dark or hairy place to feed before it bites. Regular tick checks help to increase the chance of finding a tick before it's begun the feeding and subsequent infecting process. Ideally, you should check for ticks every few hours in heavily infested areas. When looking for ticks, pay special attention to the hairline, groin, armpits, and other good hiding spots on the body. Take measures to repel ticks by wearing light clothing and gaiters and by using a chemical bug repellent.

Lyme disease is one of the major health concerns for AT long-distance hikers; its occurrence is not as rare as one may think. This disease is caused by a bacterial infection from the spirochete *Borrelia burgdorferi* (also known as *Bb*). Spirochetes live in warm-blooded animals and are transferred from host to host via the *Ixodes* ticks (such as deer ticks, also known as black-legged ticks). Despite the popular misconception that it was discovered in Lyme, Connecticut, in the 1970s, this disease was documented well over a hundred years before (however, the first positively diagnosed case in the United States was discovered in the mid-seventies).

The disease is spread through ticks in the nymph stage, which occurs between May and August. Peak tick season is April through September, though ticks may be found at any time of the year. The areas of the United States with the highest incidences of Lyme disease are New York, Connecticut, New Jersey, and Pennsylvania.

If untreated, Lyme disease can lead to serious health problems. This disease is known as "the great imitator" because of its varying and inconsistent symptoms. Symptoms of an early-stage infection may include headaches, joint stiffness, general aches and pains, and tiredness, and is often mistaken for the flu. Some (but not all) infected people get a bull's-eye rash or a skin irritation that resembles a bruise after exposure. The long-term effects of Lyme disease are severe and affect many areas of the body, including a person's psychological state. The symptoms include headaches, fatigue, muscle pain, neurological and cognitive disorders, depression, vision issues, skin rashes and tumors, heart troubles, joint pain, liver abnormalities, loss of function in the digestive tract and lungs, and pregnancy problems.

The good news about Lyme disease is that, with proper action, it can be prevented or successfully treated. Infection usually takes thirty-six hours to occur when a tick feeds, so frequent tick checks can reduce the risk of getting the disease. Testing for Lyme disease is expensive and not always accurate. Blood tests check the level of Bb antibodies, the immune system's reactivity to Bb, or the level of Bb proteins in the blood. Diagnostic tests have become better in recent years, notably with the introduction of the Polymerase Chain Reaction (PCR) test that analyzes spinal or joint fluid for the presence of Bb DNA. Lyme disease is usually treated with antibiotics such as cefuroxime, doxycycline, or amoxicillin. Be aware that a person who's been infected with Lyme disease is able to catch the disease again, since the human body doesn't develop immunity to it.

When the disease is caught in its early stages, an infected person stands a good chance of having a complete and rapid recovery. This is why it's important to be on the alert for tick bites and the occurrence of early-stage Lyme symptoms. An FDA-approved Lyme disease vaccine, LYMErix, used to be available to those at risk (such as hikers), but the vaccine was taken off the market in 2002 due to a lack of demand. Some hikers may opt to take courses of antibiotics on a preventative basis to combat the onset of Lyme disease, but this is a strategy that you need to discuss with your health care provider as it can have undesirable consequences.

If you find a tick feeding on you, don't touch it with your bare hands. Instead, gently remove it using a pair of tweezers (such as those found on some multi-tools), grasping it at the base of its head and gently pulling it up and away from the skin. After finding a tick, be alert to the onset of Lyme symptoms and consult a doctor as soon as possible if a rash or flu-like symptoms occur. It's ideal to start treatment immediately since antibiotics are relatively harmless and inexpensive (and the tests sometimes give false negative results and may further delay necessary treatment).

If you hike with a dog, check the dog regularly for ticks as they can transport the ticks to humans. Lyme disease may not produce symptoms in all dogs, but when symptoms are displayed, they are similar to those seen in an infected human. You may want to have your pet wear a tick-repelling collar or use a pet-friendly chemical tick repellent such as Frontline Plus. A Lyme disease vaccine is available for dogs, so before beginning your hike you should discuss this option with your veterinarian.

Be aware that during the summer of 2006, the FDA issued a warning about the injectible Lyme treatment known as bismacine and chromacine. This treatment contains heavy metals that can cause cardiovascular and kidney failure.

If you suspect that you may have Lyme disease, tell your doctor that you've been bitten by a tick. Due to its ambiguous symptoms, Lyme disease is often misunderstood or overlooked as a potential health condition, and it's your responsibility to assertively communicate your concerns about Lyme disease to your health care provider. The Lyme Disease Foundation, Inc., a leading foundation for research and education on Lyme disease, has a web site that provides many resources, including tick identification and a database of medical practitioners (available for a fee) who are knowledgeable about Lyme disease (www.lyme.org).

Rocky Mountain Spotted Fever

Spread by the American dog tick in the eastern part of the United States, Rocky Mountain spotted fever is a rare but serious bacterial infection that may cause death. The disease is caused by a species of bacteria, *Rickettsia rickettsii*, and incidents of it have been reported throughout the United States, typically in Virginia, Georgia, and the Carolinas. In the Rocky Mountain states, the disease is generally spread by the lone star tick, and the illness got its name from the Rocky Mountain region where it was first identified. The American dog tick is most prevalent during spring and summer but may be present any time of the year, depending on the conditions.

Rocky Mountain spotted fever is contracted from a tick when it breaks the skin during the feeding process. A person may also contract the disease through contact with the tick's feces or blood, so it's important to avoid handling the tick with bare hands (never crush a tick with your fingers). If someone removes a tick from another's body, that person should take care not to make skin contact with the tick, especially if she or he has cuts and scrapes on the hands. After removing the tick, sterilize the tweezers and the bitten area with an alcohol wipe. The general precautions to take to avoid exposure to the American dog ticks are much the same as with black-legged ticks and include the use of insect repellent and frequent tick checks (since it takes several hours for a tick to transmit the illness).

Like Lyme disease, Rocky Mountain spotted fever can be treated successfully if detected early enough, so be alert to symptoms. Fatal results can occur (more typically with older adults and young children) if the infection is left untreated and allowed to spread throughout the body. The signs of this disease occur within two weeks of exposure and may include sudden high fever, headache, muscle pain, red eyes, restlessness, sore throat, and nausea. The characteristic widespread spotty rash may occur anywhere from two to ten days after exposure but is not always present on infected people. This rash typically begins to appear on the legs and arms, and then spreads to the trunk of the body, rarely affecting the face. It is essential to seek treatment as soon as you begin to show symptoms because, if left untreated, this illness has the ability to cause heart, liver, kidney, lung, and other organ damage. It may also cause severe joint problems or meningitis (an infection of the fluid surrounding your brain and spinal cord). Some people only show very minor symptoms, but this is rare.

Diagnosis is done through blood tests, but antibiotic treatment can begin before test results are obtained. Antibiotics such as tetracycline or chloramphenicol are used to treat Rocky Mountain spotted fever with great success rates if the illness is caught early. Some people require hospitalization for this disease, while others merely require bed rest and a course of antibiotics. It is not known whether or not a person develops immunity to the illness, so caution should be exercised even if one has had the illness before.

Ehrlichiosis
Ehrlichiosis is transmitted by the deer tick (and the lone star tick, which doesn't live on the AT). Appearing one to three weeks after exposure, the symptoms that appear are usually not overly severe, though this disease is occasionally fatal. The symptoms of this disease include fever, aches, cognitive disruptions, nausea and vomiting. Rarely, a rash accompanies ehrlichiosis but is typically absent. As with some of the other major tick-borne illnesses, treatment for ehrlichiosis is antibiotics (typically tetracycline). It generally takes thirty-six hours of exposure for this disease to take root in the body, so removing feeding ticks before that period of time greatly decreases the possibility of getting ill.

West Nile Virus
West Nile virus was first recognized in the West Nile area of Uganda. The virus made its first appearance in New York City in 1999, and outbreaks have occurred since then. This virus is transmitted through the bite of an infected mosquito (in Asia and Africa, ticks also transmit the virus) and affects humans as well as a number of other animals. Infection with West Nile virus does not cause symptoms in all people. Those who display symptoms develop them a few days to a couple weeks after exposure and may have relatively mild flu symptoms or major problems such as encephalitis, meningoencephalitis, and meningitis. Temporary blindness and weakness may also occur.

A diagnosis can be made with a blood test. This illness and fatality resulting from it are rare. Since this disease is a virus, there is no specific treatment for it. Once a person has West Nile, he or she may develop a long-lasting immunity to it. Use insect repellent specially geared toward mosquitoes if there is a report of an outbreak or especially intense mosquito activity.

Eastern Equine Encephalitis
Eastern equine encephalitis (EEE) is one of the more severe yet relatively rare mosquito-borne viruses in the U.S. The disease is most prevalent in the

eastern seaboard states. Most people exposed to this virus will not develop major symptoms, but if they do, they typically manifest three to ten days after exposure and involve headache, sore throat, fever, seizures, and coma, and may lead to death. EEE can be diagnosed with serum and spinal fluid testing and tissue samples. No specific treatment exists for EEE. Though there is an equine vaccine for EEE, no human one exists. Once infected with EEE, a person will have immunity to it. To help avoid EEE, wear repellent in mosquito-infested areas.

11

Weather Conditions

> *No pain, no rain, no Maine.*
>
> —popular AT saying

The heat, the cold, the beautiful days, and the miserable ones are all a part of the hiking experience. A long-distance hike doesn't afford you the luxury of planning your trip around a warm front, and the longer you're on the trail the more weather conditions you'll encounter. There are ways, however, to deal with the weather to maximize your comfort and safety on the trail. Be smart about your itinerary. A large key to avoiding weather problems is being in the right place at the right time.

> AT hiker Rainmaker developed a fun online tool that allows you to link to the current weather conditions and average weather activity for various points along the trail (www.trailquest.net/weather.html).

Most hikers, for example, aren't going to relish the thought of being on top of Mount Washington (home to "the worst weather in the world") in January. Having the appropriate gear and mindset for the conditions is also essential to successfully dealing with the weather.

THERE'S NO WEATHER CHANNEL OUT THERE

It's nice to have access to the weather forecast, and it is pretty easy to obtain one on the trail from weekend and day hikers (as in, if there are a lot of weekend hikers out, the forecast is typically good), or in town during resupply. Forecast information may help you to decide whether or not you want to stay at a shelter or in town or push on a few extra miles. Having a small radio that picks up NOAA broadcasts or weather reports from local radio stations is convenient, especially in severe weather emergencies.

It's tricky but possible to determine what the weather conditions will be by looking at signs around you on the trail. Large cumuli indicate rain, as will a halo or corona visible around the sun or moon. Due to pressure changes, there's usually a lot of bird activity right before a storm.

There are also obvious signs of approaching weather, such as the sound of distant rumbling thunder or a darkening of the sky. Always keep a small part of your mind tuned-in to the weather to avoid getting caught in exposed areas in dangerous conditions.

BEATING THE HEAT

On hot days, you should take precautions to stay cool and hydrated as it's easier to prevent heat-

It's important to have the right gear for the sort of weather conditions you'll encounter. Hikers who are planning on being out for multiple seasons generally opt to switch out their clothing and sleeping bags as the seasons change. For example, northbound thru-hikers beginning in late March will opt to switch to summer gear after passing over Mount Rogers in Virginia. They will switch back to winter gear in Glencliff or Hanover, New Hampshire, in order to be prepared for the White Mountains.

induced disorders than to treat them. Drink a lot of fluids, but keep in mind that drinks such as beer, tea, coffee, and sugary sodas cause dehydration. Opt to drink water or powdered sports drink mixes. Sweating is the body's way of cooling off, and because you don't have the option of being in an air-conditioned environment, fluid intake is your number one way of warding off heatstroke and heat exhaustion.

TIPS FOR STAYING COOL

- Hike during the morning and evening, using the middle part of the day to rest, eat, and catch up on your trail journal or letter writing. If the temperatures are really high, don't plan a big-mile day.
- Certain accessories can be a big help with heat. Wear a bandana to catch the sweat dripping off your forehead and sport sunglasses or a hat to keep your eyes shaded from the sun.
- Wear loose-fitting, lightweight clothing that wicks perspiration and allows air flow to your skin.
- Try to rinse the sweat off your skin as often as possible since the salts are an irritant.
- Periodically dip a bandana or hat in a cool stream and place it on your head.

Heat Exhaustion and Heatstroke

Weather can be extreme on the trail, and you may encounter temperatures ranging anywhere from the single digits to over one hundred degrees. With extreme temperatures and vigorous activity, such as hours of hiking, come health hazards. Extreme heat can cause dehydration, heat cramps, heat exhaustion, and heatstroke—all of which are a result of a breakdown in the body's ability to regulate temperature. Keep in mind that your body grows accustomed to the varying extreme temperatures it encounters but is more susceptible to heat during the first few hot days of the season.

Heat exhaustion is a combination of dehydration and exposure to hot temperatures. Symptoms of heat exhaustion include dizziness, nausea and vomiting, faintness, and fever-like conditions. This condition is less severe than heatstroke but is still a very serious affliction and may eventually lead to heatstroke if left untreated. A hiker displaying symptoms of heat exhaustion should seek a resting spot in the shade immediately. A mild case of heat exhaustion can be treated with rest and fluids, but severe cases displaying vomiting require hospitalization and intravenous fluids.

Heatstroke is a more severe reaction to heat exposure and may cause permanent physical damage or even death. It is characterized by a rapid pulse; absence of sweat; rapid, shallow breathing; warm, flushed skin; headache; dizziness; cognitive difficulties and hallucinations; fatigue; seizure; and loss of consciousness. Some of the minor symptoms of heatstroke are the same as those of heat exhaustion. Heatstroke is life-threatening and requires immediate medical attention. A heatstroke victim should be placed in a cool, shady area, given lots of fluids, and covered with wet cloths or bandanas. His or her feet should be slightly elevated, and ice or cool damp cloths should be applied to the groin and armpit areas of the body. This condition can develop rapidly, so it's important to be aware of the symptoms and take action immediately if heatstroke is suspected. Often, a victim of heatstroke requires intravenous fluids and hospitalization. After experiencing heatstroke, some people may have a difficult time regulating body temperature for weeks after the incident.

> An uncommon illness associated with hot weather is heat cramps. Heat cramps are painful contractions of the leg muscles brought on by heat and dehydration. It's a disorder usually experienced by people in poor physical condition. Though painful, heat cramps are not overly serious and may be treated by hydrating and resting in a cool area.

Dehydration

Dehydration is damaging to the body in many ways and can occur any time of the year (though it's most common in the warmer summer months). Dehydration is typically caused by excessive sweating, vomiting, or diarrhea. In warmer weather, dehydration can lead to heatstroke, heat exhaustion, and other problems. Being dehydrated may also cause joint injuries. A hydrated body is more able to regulate its temperature and ward off injuries. Dehydration is not just a loss of fluids but also the loss of body salts such as sodium, potassium, calcium bicarbonate, and phosphate.

Use common sense and increase your intake of fluids when it's hot or if you hike a big-mile day. The body obtains water from food as well as drinks; so since backpacking food is dehydrated, you'll need to drink extra water to compensate. Look for pale yellow urine as a sign of good urinary tract health (dark-colored urine can indicate anything from dehydration to kidney damage). Indicators of dehydration include headaches, loss of elasticity in the skin, infrequent urination, dry skin, fatigue, and lightheadedness. More serious dehydration may lead to dizziness, rapid heartbeat and breathing, and cognitive problems.

For mild cases of dehydration, rest in a cool area and drink plenty of fluids. Sports drinks that include electrolytes are helpful for restoring salt and water levels in the body. For more severe cases of dehydration, hospitalization and hydration through an IV may be required. Mild dehydration is a somewhat common occurrence with hikers, but it should be treated seriously and, preferably, prevented.

Sun Protection in the "Long Green Tunnel"

The AT is called the long green tunnel for a good reason. A majority of the trail is covered with trees that provide a substantial amount of sun protection for hikers. You'll be exposed to excessive sun when you travel across balds and pastures and above tree line, and if you hike in winter and early spring when there's no foliage. A lot of hikers hike the entire trail without using any sunblock, but this isn't recommended unless you want your face to look like a leather handbag. If you are fair-skinned or take medications that make you sensitive to sun exposure (such as certain antibiotics), you need to take extra precautions for the short- and long-term welfare of your skin. Along with causing wrinkles, excessive sun exposure can spark a myriad of skin problems, such as benign and malignant skin tumors.

Sunscreen products are rated according to SPF (sun protection factor). SPF ratings typically range from fifteen to forty-five but can be more extreme in their range. A low rating gives minimal protection, while a high rating gives much more. The SPF number is a factor by which the normal amount of safe exposure time in the sun is multiplied (for example, if you can safely spend ten minutes in the sun without sunblock, using a block with an SPF of five allows you to safely spend fifty minutes in the sun). Choose a lip balm and other products that contain an SPF of at least fifteen.

B e careful not to get sunblock on your equipment. As well as leaving a greasy residue, the chemicals in sunblock can be harmful to certain fabrics.

You may want to wear a ball cap or sunglasses for extra protection for the head and eyes. Sunblock may be purchased in small travel sizes and can double as a moisturizer for hikers with dry skin (it also smells nice and may help to mask the hiker smell).

COLD HANDS, WARM HEART: STAYING WARM

Due to its higher elevations, the cold on the AT can be uncomfortable and even dangerous. You'll need to carry much more gear in colder weather, such as a higher-rated sleeping bag, additional clothing, and extra fuel. The cold can make you clumsy and slow-moving, and can create treacherous trail conditions. Freezing temperatures create inconveniences such as malfunctioning stoves and frozen water bottles. I'm a big fan of camping during the winter and have spent many a night in single-digit weather sleeping in the snow. I've learned a number of tactics for staying warm and comfortable in frigid temperatures, making those single-digit nights seem less daunting. The trail is a different world when the temperatures are low, but the payoff for backpacking during cold weather is that you get to see a side of the AT that many fair-weather hikers never get to experience.

A majority of people who hike the AT do so in three-season conditions (spring, summer, and fall), which don't require snowshoes, crampons, skis, or other specialized winter backpacking equipment. However, chilly conditions can be found at almost any time of year, and hikers may find themselves dealing with snowstorms and freezing temperatures during non-winter months. This section covers basic strategies for dealing with cold conditions, but it does not cover specialized winter hiking techniques. Backpacking in harsh winter conditions (such as those found at high elevations in New England during winter months) is an extensive topic. If you wish to tackle backpacking in extreme winter weather, information is available in books such as Michael Lanza's book, *Winter Hiking and Camping: Managing Cold for Comfort and Safety.*

Water can be a problem in colder temperatures. Hikers take for granted that, above freezing temperatures, flowing water fills creeks and water bottles. Once the temperature drops, you need to pay a little more attention to your water situation. If the temperatures are severely cold, you may need to sleep with your water container in your sleeping bag to keep it from freezing solid (wrap it in a waterproof bag to prevent leaks).

Or you may opt to empty your water containers and camp near a reliable flowing source of water. If all else fails, water can be obtained from melting snow and ice. This uses a lot of time and fuel, however, and a piece of snow yields about a quarter of its volume in water.

It's important to stay hydrated in cold temperatures. Though you may not feel as thirsty while hiking in cooler temperatures, it's important to drink at least as much (if not more) as you do during the hottest

Ice can render your water containers useless. Worse, freezing water expands and can damage the container. If you keep water in a bottle overnight, store the bottle upside down. Since water begins to freeze at the top, this allows you to invert the bottle and drink from the unfrozen contents. For hydration bladders, clear the tube out by blowing into it, filling it with air so water will not be trapped and freeze in the tube. Some manufacturers of hydration systems offer an insulator for drinking tubes that helps to prevent water from freezing and clogging the tube.

days of summer. A dehydrated body chills significantly faster than a hydrated one. As a side note, be sure to drink a lot during the day rather than at night. It's a good idea to sleep with an empty bladder because you don't want to be forced out of your tent into the late-night cold to visit the privy. Sleeping with an empty bladder also serves to keep the body warmer since a full bladder absorbs heat and cools the body.

Staying Comfortable

Hiking in cold weather eliminates the sweatiness and stickiness of summer and allows you more food options, since perishable food can be carried in your pack. Despite these perks, cold-weather hiking is not always the most comfortable experience. Many hikers experience shivers, numbness, and other discomforts that keep them awake at night or slow their hiking speed. Hiking in dry cold weather can be pleasant, but when the air turns damp it can be a dangerously chilling combination. Wind chill also plays a large factor in chilling the body, especially in exposed areas such as balds and the tops of ridges.

Use your metabolism to raise your body temperature while you sleep. Eating before going to sleep (especially foods high in carbohydrates) will help you sleep noticeably warmer than if you go to bed with an empty stomach.

The secret to staying comfortable on the trail is to keep moving and let your metabolism heat you up. When you stop for the day, be prepared to dive into your sleeping bag or jacket for warmth. Metabolism plays a key role in the amount of heat your body produces, and a hiker's fast metabolism allows greater comfort in cooler weather than the aver-

Sweat is the main culprit for making clothes damp. When doing big climbs, ventilate your body by removing your hat and gloves and un-zipping your jacket. It's important to cool your body *before* you start sweating.

age person's. This metabolic help is less effective at the start of your hike but increases after hiking for a number of weeks.

Keep your clothing dry, and bring along a spare pair of clothes to wear at the end of the day. Place boots, socks, and other items of clothing in your tent or sleeping bag to keep them from freezing overnight. When waking up on a cold morning, preheat your clothing by slipping them into your sleeping bag with you. You may want to even sleep with extra clothing to fill up air pockets in your bag. Make sure that you have room in your sleeping bag to wear all of your cold-weather clothing (such as a down coat), and be sure not to wear anything too tight as this compromises your circulation, making you colder.

When camping out, sleep in lower elevations and away from bodies of water and windy areas, which can add chilliness to your night. Though it seems counterintuitive, keep your shelter well-vented by leaving the fly

Keep your batteries and butane lighter warm in your pocket so that they'll work when you need them.

partially open because condensation is much more likely to build up in it during cold weather. Getting snow inside your tent causes excess condensation as well.

A stove is essential in cold conditions. A hot drink at the end of a cold day is a luxury, and in the worst case scenario can literally be a life-saver. When hiking in cold weather, bring some extra fuel for making hot drinks, melting snow, and cooking meals for additional calories. Some hikers choose to warm water and place it in a leak-proof bottle to act as a hot water bottle in their sleeping bag (just make sure that your

Winter offers very few daylight hours. Bring along extra batteries for your headlamp, and plan on shortening your daily mileage unless you don't mind hiking during the night. You may want to pack a book, music, or crossword puzzles to keep yourself entertained during the long hours between getting into your sleeping bag and falling asleep.

bag doesn't get wet). Fuels have different tolerances to temperature and have a threshold of coldness in which they won't work. If you do a lot of cold-weather hiking, you may want to carefully reconsider your stove and fuel choices. Butane lighters are fickle in freezing temps, so bring a pack of matches as a backup.

Hypothermia

Hypothermia is a collection of symptoms that occur when the body's core temperature drops below ninety-five degrees Fahrenheit, a temperature at which it is no longer warm enough to function normally. Hypothermia can occur in any season (even in the middle of summer when unexpected weather catches ill-prepared hikers by surprise). Hypothermia is brought about through exposure to cold temperatures, and its effects are accelerated by damp or windy conditions.

There are three basic types of hypothermia: acute, sub-acute, and chronic. Acute hypothermia is when the body's core temperature drops rapidly, and it is a potential killer (this is usually associated with immersion in cold water). Sub-acute hypothermia, the most common type of hypothermia found on the trail, comes from exposure to the cold for hours and is marked by a more gradual drop in the body's core temperature. Chronic hypothermia is a fairly rare physical state linked with preexisting health conditions (rather than environmental conditions), and is not a concern for the average hiker. In its most severe form, hypothermia may lead to death. It is a real concern on the AT, especially in areas where the weather is unpredictable and may catch hikers unprepared (such as the White Mountains, where snow can fall any month of the year).

Signs of hypothermia include shivering, slurred speech, drowsiness or sluggishness, poor cognitive and motor skills, slowed breathing, and pale or bluish colored skin. If left untreated, these symptoms may culminate in cardiac arrest, respiratory failure, and death. Hypothermia can cause an excess amount of urine to be produced in the kidneys, low blood pressure, cardiac arrhythmia, and blood clotting.

Sub-acute hypothermia happens gradually. It begins with shiv-

There are many strategies for avoiding hypothermia, and these all deal with knowing how your body conducts heat and controlling these mechanisms. Some useful strategies are as follows:

- Wear a hat in chilly weather since a lot of body heat is lost through the head. Because of its large arteries close to the surface of the skin, the neck is also an important part of the body to keep covered. A balaclava or neck gaiter does wonders for boosting your body temperature.
- Water cools the body, so stay as dry as possible. Wet clothing loses approximately 90 percent of its insulating properties. Wear tech materials that wick away moisture (never cotton or other water-absorbing materials).
- Avoid fording streams and rivers late in the day when the temperature is dropping.
- Wear windproof and waterproof clothing when the weather is poor, and don't wait until you feel cold to start layering up. Once you've lost body heat, it's hard to gain it back.

ering, the body's way of warming itself through mass muscle contractions. With hypothermia's onset come cognitive and coordination problems. It is not unusual for these cognitive conditions to cause a case of hypothermia denial, in which hypothermia victims fail to realize that they're in danger. Since hypothermia compromises your mental and physical skills as it progresses, it's important to pay attention to this threat, especially if you are traveling alone. If traveling in a group in inclement weather, pay attention to one another and watch for signs of hypothermia.

Hypothermia requires immediate medical attention, and, ideally, a person displaying symptoms of hypothermia should be moved indoors. This is usually not an immediate option on the AT, so the afflicted should be bundled up in dry clothing and a sleeping bag, moved to a shelter, fed warm liquids, and placed near a fire. The trick is to get a hypothermic person as dry and warm as possible given the conditions. Keep the victim horizontal. You may want to use body heat by sharing a sleeping bag with him or her. Watch the person's breathing—he or she may require CPR if breathing becomes too slow or shallow. Don't apply direct heat to a hypothermic person's legs and arms (this forces cold blood to the heart, lung, and brain, causing the core temperature to drop further and may cause a fatal reaction). Instead, warm water on your backpacking stove and place it in bottles on the groin, neck, and chest areas. The worse the case of hypothermia, the more caution you need to exercise in rewarming the body. Never massage a hypothermic person or give him or her alcoholic drinks (alcohol lowers the body's ability to retain heat).

Frostbite

Frostbite is the charming and antiquated name for frozen body tissue. This affliction comes from exposure to the cold and usually affects the skin on the extremities (such as hands, feet, nose, and ears), though it may attack deeper tissue. An area of skin afflicted with frostbite won't have much sensation, looks white, and has a hard feel to it. Frostbite can cause permanent damage, even loss of limb.

Frostbite begins with a characteristic pins-and-needles feeling, followed by an aching pain, and culminates with a total loss of sensation. Hypothermia and frostbite may occur in tandem, and you can prevent both in the same way, by wearing appropriate clothing and avoiding dampness and wind chill. It's important to note that frostbite can be related to poor circulation and tight clothing. Things such as ill-fitting boots can contribute to this condition.

If you suspect frostbite, seek shelter and make sure the affected area is covered with warm, dry clothing. It's important to avoid refreezing frost-bitten tissue as this can cause severe damage. If you're far from shelter and there's a risk of refreezing, it may be best to stabilize the tissue and wait until you reach shelter to fully warm it. Drink warm fluids, and, if you're able to get indoors, soak the frostbitten areas of the body in warm (never hot) water. Be careful not to expose frostbite to strong heat sources such as a fire or radiator, and never rub the affected tissue. Severe frostbite causes blisters and swelling and possibly even gangrene. A health care provider can provide you with sterile dressings and other treatments for severe cases. If frostbite doesn't heal correctly, the afflicted hiker may experience a permanent loss of feeling, fever, discomfort, or drainage. Someone with any of these symptoms must seek medical treatment as soon as possible.

DEALING WITH THE DAMP

The AT is a wet trail. During the summer months, getting caught out in rain showers can be refreshing as the moisture helps the body to cool itself. In colder weather, being damp is a safety risk since it's the leading cause of hypothermia. Even in a scenario where your life isn't at risk, being wet can be miserably uncomfortable.

Dry clothes can literally be a lifesaver. Keep a few articles of dry cloth-ing stashed in your pack in case you get drenched. A waterproof silnylon bag or even a heavy-duty freezer bag can keep your things safe from the elements even if the rain finds its way through your pack cover or liner.

Rain tends to destroy gear and supplies. It causes delamination, spoiled food, mildew, and other problems. Dry all of your gear out on a regular basis, and store moisture-sensitive things such as electronics and journals in a freezer bag. Carry a pack towel or bandana in a waterproof bag to facilitate getting dry quickly.

Thunderstorm Safety

A surprisingly large number of people are capable of surviving lightning strikes, and lightning kills only one hundred to three hundred people glob-ally on an annual basis. Seek cover as soon as you hear or see lightning. Re-member, electrical storms are typically generated from fast-moving fronts and can arise quickly. Pay attention to the weather, especially when hiking on exposed ridgeline or balds, and seek low ground when a storm comes up. Avoid hiking on high ridges, in treeless areas, or near large bodies of water during electrical storms. Try to seek shelter in a small stand of trees at a low elevation, and stay out of caves or rock overhangs since these damp areas are prone to ground lightning.

Cumuli over Chestnut Ridge shelter, Virginia

If you're caught out during an electrical storm, there are a few strategies to minimize the risk of being struck. Stay away from metal objects such as wire fences and buildings. Some hikers believe that it's best to even keep your pack (with its small metal stays) away from you, though wearing a pack may help to distribute electrical shocks away from the heart in the event of a strike. If lightning is close, crouch down on the ground with your hands on your knees. Kneel on your sleeping pad and place items with metal (such as trekking poles) well away from yourself. If hiking in a group, spread out to lessen the possible impact of a lightning strike.

To judge how far away a storm is, count the number of seconds between seeing a lightning flash and hearing thunder. Divide the number of seconds by five as it takes about five seconds for sound to travel a mile. For example, if it takes ten seconds for thunder to be heard after the flash is seen, the lightning strike is two miles away.

If you witness a hiker being struck by lightning, use CPR to revive the hiker's vital signs. Lightning will not leave a hiker with a residual electrical charge, so it's safe to handle a lightning victim immediately after he or she is struck.

Most summertime electrical storms occur late in the afternoon or early evening. Avoid hiking on ridgeline, above tree line, or in open balds and fields during this time of day if storms are in the forecast.

When the hiker is stabilized or if there's someone else to stay with the hiker, go find emergency help. Lightning causes burns, damage to the nervous system, blindness, and deafness. Treat electrical burns from lightning as you would treat any other burn, cleaning it and applying a sterile bandage. Always seek medical help for a victim of a lightning strike, even if the hiker seems fine.

Occasionally, weather on the AT throws you a surprise. Record-breaking heat waves, floods, and snowstorms are all part of its seasonal routine. From the steamy lowlands of the mid-Atlantic to the blustery alpine zones of northern New England, the AT can deliver a wide range of meteorological surprises. Through knowledge and planning, hikers can travel in safety and comfort through most any condition. And keep in mind that perfect warm, cloudless days are best enjoyed after a week of rain.

12

Trail Culture and Traditions

You can tell thru-hikers when you see them on the trail. Though they come in many flavors, they all have a knowledge that cannot be achieved through scholarship but shows in their eyes and their stance and their weary smile. It is a knowledge that cannot find a person through windshields or sunglasses, or the barriers of fresh clothing and fragrance that surround us every day.

—Tanner Critz, *Through-Hiking Vikings*

The AT is a sociologist's dream. It's a place that draws people from all walks of life and puts them in strange and challenging situations, facilitating the creation of some pretty amazing culture and traditions. I've heard the subculture of long-distance hikers accused of being akin to a cult—a cult that wears a lot of polyester, is obsessed with gear, and loves all-you-can-eat buffets. Hiking the AT is perhaps one of the most unique North American traveling experiences. The Appalachian mountain range (pronounced App-a-LATCH-ian in the south and App-a-LAY-chian in the north) has long been a source of culture rooted in the mountains that spawns music, stories, and a society unique to this country. And the numerous long-distance hikers traveling through this area add another layer to the interesting sociological strata.

The AT is a place of legends running the gamut from scary to silly. From the haunted Vandeventer Shelter that was the site of a gruesome murder to the rumored thru-hike of Oprah Winfrey in 1999 (which never happened), the AT is the stuff of which legends are made. For an interesting read on the legends of the trail, check out *Walkin' with the Ghost Whisperers: Lore and Legend on the Appalachian Trail* by J. R. "Model-T" Tate. Tate is a veteran AT hiker and has a lot of information about the spooky elements of the AT's history.

AT LEGENDS

While the topography and weather make the AT what it is physically, the people are what define it in the imagination. The hiker demographic is composed of hippies, hobos, drifters, seekers, wanderers, and pilgrims, and many will agree that it's the people who complete the trail experience. It's difficult, if not impossible, to avoid other people on the Appalachian Trail as millions of people use the trail throughout the calendar year. The numbers of long-distance hikers tend to fluctuate based on a variety of factors such as the economy (a weak economy may bring those unemployed or underemployed out to the trail in droves) or media (the release of Bill Bryson's book, *A Walk in the Woods* is reported to have increased the number of attempted thru-hikes). For many, regardless of what brings them to the trail, the highlight of the long-distance hiking experience is the friendships forged over the many miles.

The story of AT long-distance hikers begins with Earl V. Shaffer, the trail's first thru-hiker and author of the seminal trail account *Walking with Spring*. While Myron Avery, one of the original fathers of the AT, was the first person to hike the entire length of the AT in sections, Shaffer was the first to do it all in one uninterrupted trip. Shaffer undertook his legendary northbound hike in 1948, and then hiked a southbound trip in 1965. His third thru-hike was completed in 1998, at the age of 79, when he became the trail's oldest thru-hiker at that time. Shaffer is an icon of the AT, and, to many, is representative of many of the ideals of long-distance hikers.

The list of AT legends includes Warren Doyle, the hiker who led organized, supported trips along the length of the trail and was influential in making thru-hiking popular. Doyle felt that thru-hiking is a countercultural act and is one of the last means for people to learn to be free in our society. He led nineteen people on a thru-hike in 1975 and has led many other supported group thru-hikes since then. Nimblewill Nomad (www.nimblewillnomad.com) hiked the Florida Trail, AT, and International AT in 1998, and went on to become an author and well-known hiking personality. There's also Bill Irwin, the blind hiker who hiked the length of the trail in 1991 with the aid of his guide dog, Orient. Representing the lady hikers, Emma "Grandma" Gatewood, the mother of eleven children, took it upon herself to thru-hike at the age of sixty-seven after reading a *National Geographic* article about the trail. She continued to be active in long-distance hiking, hiking the trail two more times, and was showered with media attention.

There are hikers who have performed admirable feats of strength and those who have displayed amusing and wonderful characters. Jim "Geek" Adams hiked the AT with his cat, Ziggy, riding on top of his pack the whole way (it is rumored that he and Ziggy even did a fifty-plus-mile day

Some areas along the AT have been featured in films. Burkittsville, Maryland, is where *The Blair Witch Project* was filmed and the movie *Deliverance* was filmed near the AT on the Chattooga River.

together). Cycle Hiker rode his bike to the trail in Georgia and proceeded to thru-hike with the eighteen-pound bike frame strapped to his pack.

THE ULTIMATE TOURIST DESTINATION

The AT is littered with all sorts of fascinating geological formations and quaint towns. From the kitschy clutter of Gatlinburg to the relaxing mineral baths of Hot Springs, the trail offers a wealth of cultural interest. Many

The Doyle Hotel in Duncannon, Pennsylvania

towns can be found along the trail, and it even runs directly through some of them, such as Harpers Ferry, home of the ATC headquarters office where long-distance hikers traditionally have their photos taken for posterity. Probably the most famous town on the trail is Damascus, Virginia, known as the friendliest town on the trail. Damascus offers The Place (a well-known hiker hostel), a host of businesses offering the standard hiker amenities, and, of course, Trail Days. In Duncannon, Pennsylvania, the hiker-friendly Doyle Hotel provides hikers with a place to rest from the rocky trail. Some towns, like Suches, Georgia, are less glamorous. Suches was named so because it was plain and simple, "such as it is."

Along with the towns, shelters and hostels along the trail create memorable waypoints for hikers. Walasi-Yi Inn at Neels Gap in Georgia is the first oasis for northbound thru-hikers where they can resupply and take a shower before heading back into the woods. One of the better-known hostels is Kincora in Hampton, Tennessee. This hostel is owned and operated by Bob Peoples. Bob Peoples is incredibly involved with the trail, and he and his wife know how to pamper long-distance hikers. White House Landing, a hunters' camp in the hundred-mile wilderness of Maine, can be accessed by boat (hikers have to toot an air horn placed by the trail to summon a boat ride across the lake to the hostel). White House Landing has some of the best burgers on the trail. Rusty's Hard Times Hollow, near Waynesboro, Virginia, may possibly be one of the most unique hostel experiences on the AT. It is a rugged little place off the trail equipped with a sweat lodge, resident chickens, and its warmhearted owner, Rusty. It lacks most modern comforts but is a favorite for long-distance hikers.

ODD HABITS: TRADITIONS ON THE AT

Though its history is relatively short, the AT is a place rich with unique traditions. As with any culture, the experience of thru-hiking is accompanied by its own language and practices. Hiker traditions arose in the mid-1970s as thru-hiking became a prevalent activity and more people began taking long hikes.

The tradition of using trail names is one of the most interesting practices for long-distance hikers. A trail name, a nickname used while hiking, is usually based on a hiker's unique characteristic or alludes to a

One of the traditions that northbound thru-hikers participate in is picking up a pebble on Springer Mountain and carrying it all the way to Katahdin, adding it to the final cairn at the trail's northern terminus.

specific episode that occurred in a person's hike (and, trust me, these are not always flattering—just ask the hiker who almost became Mr. Poopy Pants after an unfortunate incident in which he did not look before he sat down). Your trail name becomes your identity on the trail, and hikers use them when signing registers and making introductions. Though this tradition comes off as being corny to some, it's a wonderful way to recreate, realize, or get in touch with a previously untapped facet of your personality while on the trail. Many thru-hikers participate in the tradition of mailing their summit photo to friends and family in the form of a holiday postcard. During my time on the trail, I was known as "BirdLegs" (courtesy of a long-time hiking friend) and went for months on end without being called by the name on my birth certificate.

After a month or so, hikers have their trail legs and can easily pull high mileage. As an experiment with this new level of fitness, hikers have been known to do epic days of mileage, traveling anywhere from thirty to over fifty miles in a single day. One of the better-known institutionalized marathon hiking events on the AT is Hike Across Maryland, also known as the Maryland Marathon. This hike is an organized annual event, but some thru-hikers undertake the challenge on their own when passing through the area. The marathon traverses the forty-one mile distance starting near the Potomac River and crossing South Mountain and the Mason-Dixon Line. It requires a hiker to travel every foot of its length in the span of a day. Another infamous hiking challenge is the Four State Challenge, where hikers attempt to walk from the northernmost point in Virginia to the southernmost in Pennsylvania in a single day, crossing through West Virginia and Maryland en route and effectively hiking in four different states. In New England, the Connecticut Challenge entails a one-day, fifty-two-mile walk across Connecticut from the New York border to the Massachusetts border.

Practical jokes run rampant on the trail, a place where silly humor is much appreciated. One of the more popular pranks is to sneak a rock into a fellow hiker's pack and allow him or her to hike with the extra weight for a while. One 2006 northbounder found a number of rocks placed in his pack by multiple hikers (the pranksters hadn't conferred with one another and had no idea that they all had the same joke in mind).

Halfway through a thru-hike, hikers are confronted with the daunting Half-Gallon Challenge. Make no mistake, this is a feat worthy of a thru-hiker's respectful fear, as it involves eating a half-gallon of ice cream at Pine Grove Furnace State Park store (I recommend Hershey's Moose Tracks, which weighs in at a hefty 3,500 calories). When a hiker is successful, he or she receives a tiny wooden spoon, marking passage into the Half-Gallon Club.

KEEP THE KIDS AT HOME: RISQUÉ CUSTOMS ON THE TRAIL

There are some racier traditions on the AT that call for showing some flesh. The annual summer solstice, the longest day of the year, is celebrated with naked hiking. This is a day when scout troops should be kept at home where their innocent eyes will be safe from the horrors of pale goose-pimply hiker flesh. Typically, hikers walk for a mile or two in the buff before shyly retreating back to their normal stinky garb. Most hikers don't get the chance to drop trou again until Mount Washington, where mooning the cog railway is as much a part of experiencing the Whites as staying at the AMC shelters. The engineers of the train sometimes play along and try to pelt the hikers' bare bottoms with lumps of coal. Unfortunately, mooning hikers have recently found themselves slapped with fines for participating in this tradition.

Nobody loves a festival more than a long-distance hiker. There are a number of noteworthy get-togethers for AT hikers. Most notable is Trail Days, the granddaddy of hiker festivals, held every year in Damascus, Virginia. This festival is typically held the weekend after Mother's Day and includes vendor booths, hiker feeds, music, a hiker talent show, and the famous town parade with water cannons and representatives of the annual "classes" of thru-hikers. Many hikers get off the trail and hitchhike to get to this event, where

> *Rucks* are gatherings held regionally and are small, informal hiker get-togethers that include day hikes, food, and presentations. Contact your local hiking club for more information on where and when rucks are scheduled in your area.

they typically get sucked into doing a number of zeros to enjoy the festival. The town of Damascus' web site (www.damascus.org) provides schedules and other information about Trail Days.

Hot Springs, North Carolina, hosts a trail festival on a smaller scale, known as Trailfest (www.trailfest.net). This annual festival features food and music and is held in the springtime. The Appalachian Long Distance Hiking Association hosts a fall festival dedicated to long-distance hikers called The Gathering. This festival includes the usual food and music but is significant for its informational lectures and presentations. It's a weekend-long educational experience for hikers and is particularly useful for new hikers seeking information about long-distance hiking, particularly thru-hiking (go to www.aldha.org for more information).

While these events are a great resource for new or current hikers, they also provide experienced hikers with opportunities to have reunions and relive a little bit of the hiker life. The Appalachian Trail Conservancy web page (www.appalachiantrail.org) provides a listing of hiker festivals and other gatherings that specialize in providing workshops for long-distance hikers. Go to the "Hike the Trail" section and follow the "Thru-Hiking" link to "Workshops," listed in the "Preparing for a Thru-Hike" section.

TRAIL MAGIC

Trail magic is the little acts of kindness that people perform for hikers and is one of the best things happening on the AT. This is a great practice that always brings happiness to tired and hungry hikers. Trail magic is administered by "trail angels," who are often long-distance hikers themselves. These acts span the whole gamut of good deeds, from free food to shuttles and hot showers. Basically, trail magic is any wonderful happening, stroke of luck, or act of kindness on the trail, and can be deliberate or serendipitous. Sometimes, trail magic is the little push that a discouraged hiker needs. It's a great way for the AT community to show that they're there for one another and are invested in everyone's hike.

Trail angels leave water in dry stretches, coolers full of treats, and informational notes about trail conditions as a part of their work. Some trail angels, such as Pastor Karen Nickels of the Presbyterian Church of the Mountain in Delaware Water Gap, dole out trail magic of a more spiritual nature, giving hikers encouragement and words of advice along with free hostel accommodations. The "Cookie Lady" near Dalton, Massachusetts, hands out a steady supply of freshly baked cookies to hikers. There's even a board game devoted to trail magic! Trail magic is a wonderful way to rediscover the kindness of people and is the glue that binds the Appalachian Trail community together.

ROMANCE ON THE TRAIL

Ask any hiker and he or she will tell you that, while on the trail, there are but a few major thoughts running through his or her head on a day-to-day basis: mileage, food, water, shelter, and, of course, love. The AT has spawned a number of romantic relationships, some resulting in marriage. For those not already hiking with a significant other (many honeymoons have been celebrated on the trail), the quest for love or even a little lust can be an all-consuming internal obsession to help wile away the miles.

Though it's moving toward the trend of stabilizing, the ratio of men to women on the trail is lopsided, with male hikers greatly outnumbering females. *Pink-blazing* is the somewhat derogatory term applied to hikers who alter mileage and generally bastardize their itinerary to stay on the same schedule as a romantic interest. Once love is achieved, mileage drops even further as frequent town stays become an integral part of the romantic routine. While pink-blazers may get grief from other hikers about their decisions, the trail is all about following your heart.

THE PEGGY POST OF THE AT: TRAIL ETIQUETTE

One might think that the AT offers a lot of personal space. In some ways it does, though it also adds social pressures not encountered off the trail. The great thing about long-distance hiking is the fact that hikers develop a camaraderie and comfort with one another. But tensions can arise when people share space, food, and other resources. The AT, with all of its farting and filth, is certainly no place for Peggy Post, but you do need to keep in mind that you're sharing the trail with others and should practice good trail etiquette. On the Appalachian Trail, especially during northbound thru-hiker and spring break season in the south, shelters may seem like Grand Central Station at rush hour. Many hikers may share a shelter and tenting area in Georgia in the months of March and April.

The Appalachian Long Distance Hiking Association is concerned with maintaining good relations between hikers and the towns and services close to the trail. As a part of this effort, they created the Endangered Services Campaign. This campaign works on the same principles as the Leave No Trace movement, encouraging hikers to treat towns and businesses with the same respect they would have for the wilderness. As one of the ALDHA flyers states, "Just because you live in the woods, doesn't mean you can act like an animal." The Endangered Services Campaign advises hikers to be courteous and respectful of the businesses and communities that help long-distance hikers in order to ensure the continuation of these services.

GREEN-BLAZING AND HANGOVERS:
THE DARK SIDE OF THE TRAIL

The use of alcohol, tobacco, and illegal drugs occurs with some frequency on the AT. The mere presence of substances on the trail, such as marijuana and moonshine, seems to invite hikers to develop unsavory habits. Some hikers get bored of walking day after day and seek ways to alleviate their

Some hikers carry loose tobacco and even light-weight plastic cigarette-rolling machines because regular packs of cigarettes are expensive and can be easily crushed and ruined in a pack.

boredom with substance abuse. No matter what you do, be aware of the law, practice moderation, and respect those who abstain.

Life on the trail is generally very easy-going, and hikers are an accepting group. The phrase "hike your own hike" applies to much more than just hiking style—it is a catch-all for reminding us to be appreciative and tolerant of each others' quirks. Every once in a while, hikers run into hostility from business owners or locals, but these episodes are few and far between. Seldom is there animosity or serious rivalry between hikers, perhaps because at the end of the day everyone's simply too exhausted to fight.

When you hike the AT, walking is but a small part of the journey. For many hikers, the most memorable aspects of the trail aren't the big-mile days and tasty AYCE (all-you-can-eat) buffets. Rather, the best memories come from the families you develop on the trail and the wonderful people you connect with on your way.

13

Hygiene (or Lack Thereof)

. . . if dirt was trumps, what hands you would hold!
—Charles Lamb

Leave the deodorant at home; you've entered the realm of privies and antibacterial gel baths. With an aroma that alerts people to their completed mileage, long-distance hikers learn to give up on being clean and pristine. There *are* ways to stay somewhat civilized, however, and a certain level of hygiene is necessary for good public hiker health. Staying clean without running water or soap can be a real challenge, and keep in mind that your definition of clean changes as you rack up the miles. Some hikers even find the lack of showers, deodorant, and hairbrushes liberating.

PERSONAL CLEANLINESS: TRICKS TO COMBAT THE FILTH

The average long-distance hiker typically showers once a week (sometimes even twice or sometimes less). There are lots of showers within easy reach of the AT. Some hotels, motels, and hostels allow you to shower for a small fee without having to get a room for the night. When showering in town, share shampoo with other hikers to save money. Any remaining soap or shampoo can be left in a hiker box for someone else to use, cutting down on waste and providing another hiker with a nice gift. Always wear camp shoes in the shower since fungal infections are spread through skin contact with warm, damp areas such as shower floors.

When a shower isn't available, clean up near a lake or stream, carrying your water at least two hun-

So, should you carry soap on the trail? There are a number of environmentally friendly, phosphate-free biodegradable soaps on the market. Soaps such as Dr. Bronner's are great to have if you want to wash up out of doors (just make sure to stay at least two hundred feet away from drinking water sources when doing so). Carry your soap with you in your pack or bounce it ahead to towns where you plan on getting a room and a shower.

dred feet away from its source and using a bandana to take a sponge bath. On the trail, a bandana or camp towel can be used in place of a standard terrycloth towel, which is too bulky to carry in a pack. For when there's no shower or it's too cold to clean up in a stream, use baby wipes or even antiseptic/alcohol wipes for mini bathes. These are a great way to clean up between showers, especially when water is at a premium. You can cat bathe with these in the privacy of your tent, and their smell helps to tame hiker stink. Gentle, hypoallergenic wipes made especially for the face are good for people with sensitive or acne-prone skin. Biodegradable wipes are now available for backpackers and other travelers.

Most hikers choose to skip deodorant. If they do use it, it's usually in town after a shower. After a few hours of hiking, no deodorant's effect lasts, and it only takes up room in the pack. You may want to use a deodorant crystal or powder, or a small travel-sized stick of deodorant if you really feel the need to carry it for use on zero days in town.

Consider carrying a comb or small brush if you have long hair. Brushing helps to distribute hair oils and helps hair look cleaner. It also helps you to avoid knots that may have to be cut out later. A small travel brush or comb can be used in lieu of a full-sized hairbrush to cut down on weight.

Some hikers refuse to shave, feeling that long beards (for men) and hairy legs (for women) are a badge of hiker credibility. Whether or not you carry a razor is up to you and your level of comfort with your body's primitive side. If you choose to shave, you can keep a lightweight disposable razor in your pack or leave it in your bounce box. If your beard grows overly long, trim it with scissors before shaving to extend the life of your razor.

Laundry is an essential part of staying clean on the AT. Typically, a long-distance hiker does laundry every time he or she is in town taking a zero. Follow instructions on clothing labels and use the dryers on low to avoid melting synthetic materials. Tech clothing is notorious for retaining smell. Use Febreze to combat hiker stink (it is especially good on pack straps and the shoulder areas of shirts and jackets). Carry a large freezer bag to store stinky laundry (particularly socks) in your pack to cut down on the smell between trips to the laundromat.

HEALTH AND HYGIENE

Taking care of your teeth is a lot more important on a long hike than on a weekend trip. Cavities can form just as easily in the woods as they can at home and getting one when days away from dental care can be horrific. A child-sized toothbrush, travel toothbrush, or if you're an ultralight fanatic, a brush with a sawed-off handle works well. Toothpaste comes in small travel-sized tubes that can be shipped in your mail drops or purchased in town. Baking soda is an alternative cleaning product to toothpaste (it doesn't smell and is gentler on the environment than toothpaste and soaps) and can also be used to clean pots and pans.

Most hikers get sick from a lack of cleanliness rather than from exposure to contaminated water. Always clean your cookware and use an alcohol-based hand sanitizer to clean your hands, particularly before cooking and eating (sanitizers such as Purell come prepackaged in half-ounce and one-ounce containers). Practice common sense when sharing food with other hikers to keep the spread of germs to a minimum. Colds and other contagious illnesses pass through parties of hikers like wildfire. Avoid sharing food and drink with other hikers and don't eat out of unsealed containers of food found in hiker boxes as they may have encountered a lot of handling by dirty fingers.

> When you make town visits, you may find the overwhelming smell of soap and perfume on people more offensive than your week-old unwashed hiker armpits. As a matter of etiquette, try to clean yourself up as much as possible before hitching and going into town. Not only does this leave a better impression on non-hikers, it sometimes facilitates better service at places like restaurants.

HOUSEKEEPING IN THE MOUNTAINS

Cleaning your pots, drinking containers, and utensils is essential. Many hikers get sick from bacteria growth on dirty pots and dishes. Cleaning up after a meal is not the most pleasant thing when running water and soap are at a premium, but there are some tricks to making the job easier. If backcountry dishwashing isn't your forte, you may opt to cook in freezer bags or disposable, microwave-safe Tupperware (you can even pour hot water straight into your morning oatmeal packet to spare cleanup hassles). Cooking meals with a little extra water helps to cut down on burnt-on grime on the pot's surfaces. The same goes for using a dollop of olive oil to keep food from sticking. Both techniques are effective, even if you use a pot coated with a non-stick surface. And, of course, keep an eye on your pot and don't allow food to burn and leave a difficult mess to clean up after.

After cooking, scrape your pot thoroughly, add a little water, and rinse it out using your fingers as a dish rag. Lightweight pot scrapers are great

Some hikers make a hot after-dinner drink, allowing boiling water to kill germs and remove leftover food particles in a dirty pot. As long as you don't mind bits of ramen floating in your hot cocoa, this is an efficient way to kill two birds with one stone.

for getting every last bit of food out of cooking pots (a cheap alternative is to use a spatula with the handle removed). You can drink rinse water or dispose of it far enough away from camp to keep food smells and hungry animals at bay. Ideally, you should use a little biodegradable soap and a small square of a scouring pad stored in a plastic bag (Scotch Brite or a piece of plastic onion bag works well for getting the tough stuff off, and these materials dry quickly). Periodically rinse your pot with a little water and a drop or two of bleach. Avoid using sand and other materials to scour your pot as this can introduce contamination and is harmful to your pot. Also, always use treated water to clean your pot since untreated water may introduce harmful organisms into your food. Most harmful organisms die after exposure to the air, but it is best not to take a risk.

THE TAO OF POO

Places to go to the bathroom are seemingly unlimited in the woods as long as you stay away from fragile vegetation and more than two hundred feet away from water sources and campsites. Since urine is sterile and doesn't hurt the environment (it may, however, attract animals because of the salts in it), solid waste is the primary concern for environmentally friendly privy visits.

The following are a few guidelines for going to the bathroom out of doors:
- Go at least two hundred feet from the trail, water sources, and campsites.
- Bury your solid waste at a depth of six inches or more in a "cat hole" (some hikers leave waste above ground and cover it with twigs and leaves, believing that it decomposes more quickly this way).
- Pack out your used toilet paper and hygiene products.
- Some hikers opt to use baby wipes in lieu of toilet paper. Most wipes are not biodegradable and must be packed out.

Most serious AT hikers do not carry a shovel to dig cat holes with. Use a stick, trekking pole, or lightweight tent stake instead. Go to the bathroom in an area that won't be used by other people since there's nothing more unpleasant than stepping in another hiker's waste. Packing out solid waste in a sealable container is a practice used in more remote backcountry areas and is not typically practiced on the AT.

Typical AT privy

FOR WOMEN HIKERS ONLY

For women, privy time is further complicated by menstruation. Pack out tampons and sanitary napkins with regular trash, and never dispose of these materials in a privy. Hygiene materials do not biodegrade quickly and cause a lot of extra unpleasant work for the shelter maintainers who care for the privy. Use a heavy-duty freezer bag to contain the waste and dispose of it when in town. There's no hard evidence that bears are attracted to the smell of used sanitary materials, but women should bear-bag feminine hygiene waste along with other smellables such as garbage.

A few crushed tablets of aspirin can be added to your sanitary waste to neutralize the smell.

Some female hikers use menstrual cup products such as the Diva Cup (www.divacup.com) or The Keeper/Moon Cup (www.keeper.com) in lieu of sanitary napkins and tampons. These products are reusable, internally worn silicone or latex cups that catch menstrual flow and can then be emptied and reinserted, eliminating backcountry waste. Menstrual cups are convenient as they eliminate the need to purchase and pack bulky sanitary products.

14

Leave No Trace

*When we see land as a community to which we belong, we may
begin to use it with love and respect.*
— Aldo Leopold, *A Sand County Almanac*

Leave no trace is the catch-all phrase used to describe a set of responsible behaviors for backcountry areas. Federal agencies such as the United States Forest Service, National Park Service, and the Bureau of Land Management initially labeled this ethical approach to backcountry behavior as wilderness manners, wilderness ethics, minimum-impact camping, or no-trace camping. The AT is a heavily used trail that is in danger of being loved to death, meaning that irresponsible use could injure it to the point of no return. There are seven main tenets of the Leave No Trace philosophy. In order to responsibly use backcountry areas, hikers must carefully plan their trip, travel and camp on resilient and designated surfaces, properly dispose of waste, leave the forest as they found it, practice prudence with fire building, respect wildlife, and treat other visitors with respect. For further information on leave no trace principles, visit the Center for Outdoor Ethics at www.lnt.org, or call 800-332-4100.

Have respect for the wilderness in which you hike and also for the hikers who will be enjoying it after you have passed through. Hiking is a great way to cut down on waste—you use less water, no electricity, and generate less trash. However, the waste you do create has a greater impact on the environment because the woods are not equipped with incinerators, water treatment plants, and other means of dealing with it. By following Leave No Trace principles, you can make as small an impact as possible on the environment, preserving it for generations to come.

Puncheons in northern New England

LEAVE NO TRACE TIPS

- Stay on the trail to prevent erosion and damage to plant life. Do not cut through switchbacks, make alternate trails, or walk around muddy or wet areas. If the conditions are wet, avoid the urge to tramp around big puddles. This harms plant life and causes erosion and other long-term damage.

- Always remove your bear-bag cord from trees when you're done using it.

- Pick up litter off the trail when possible. If every AT hiker were to pick up one piece of litter, that would equal millions of fewer wrappers, bottles, and cans in the woods. It only takes a second to do this and is a way of paying respect to the trail and those who use it.

- Don't bury or burn trash; always pack it out with you. Many materials, such as plastics, won't fully burn and may create toxic fumes when heated. Carry heavy-duty freezer bags for packing out trash.

- Do not bathe, eat, or cook closer than two hundred feet to water sources to avoid polluting them.

- Use an environmentally friendly biodegradable soap, such as Dr. Bronner's, on the trail.

- Pack out all of your used toilet tissue. Bury waste at least six inches deep and never void closer than two hundred feet from a water source. Women should pack out hygiene products—do not leave them in the privy, as they do not decompose properly and create more work for the caretakers of the shelter.

- Don't take souvenirs from the woods. Leave all plants, rocks, and other things where you found them to minimize the human impact on an area. If you must have a reminder of your hike, take photographs.

- Only build campfires in designated areas. Aside from making an area unattractive, campfires kill vegetation and create pollution. They can also be a forest fire hazard if the conditions are right. If you do build a campfire, use dead wood from the ground, leaving standing trees and other vegetation alone. Some states on the AT, such as Connecticut, have banned campfires.

- Do not feed or harass the wildlife. Bears have become a nuisance in areas such as the Smokies and Shenandoah because people feed them and they come to associate hikers and campers with a free handout. Unfortunately, when people feed animals, animals become bothersome or dangerous and may have to be relocated to another area or even humanely destroyed.

- Only camp in designated areas. If you absolutely have to camp in an area that isn't designated for tenting, make sure to remove all traces of your stay before you leave.

- Don't use radios, electronic games, or cellular phones louder than the volume of an average human conversation. It's a good practice to use these devices away from other hikers.

- Consider the garbage you'll be generating while you hike and try to pack items with as little packaging as possible.

15

Safety on the Trail

It's when you're safe at home that you wish you were having an adventure; when you're having an adventure you wish you were safe at home.

—Thornton Wilder

Many non-hikers feel that long-distance hiking is a dangerous sport, but the AT is safer than most urban areas. In fact, it is statistically safer to hike long distances through the mountains than it is to drive a car. However, there are issues hikers need to be aware of when out on the trail. Injury, attack from animals or other humans, petty theft, and other dangers do exist on the trail. Elements such as drifters, dangerous weather, and aggressive wildlife deserve respect. Practicing common sense and caution can keep a hiker safe in most any situation.

SAFETY IN NUMBERS

There are many benefits to hiking with a partner or group. Partners provide companionship and, above all, safety. For long-distance hikers, hiking alone is never advisable but is often unavoidable. However, traveling solo on the AT is unlike hiking alone on other trails since the AT is typically well-populated. In all but the harshest weather and most remote areas, there is usually another hiker, trail angel, or area of civilization close by. If you travel during peak seasons, particularly if you're a thru-hiker, it's usually pretty easy to hook up with a crew of other people en route.

Share your itinerary with fellow hikers, including alternate routes that you may take. Use the shelter registers to keep track of other hikers and to let others know of your status. Registers are a good way to let people know of your whereabouts and also to warn hikers coming in the opposite direction of problems such as aggressive bears, poor trail condi-

If you're looking for a hiking partner, one can be found by advertising in *Appalachian Trailways News* or on web sites such as trailjournals.com or whiteblaze.net.

tions, and other dangers. If you leave an important message for a hiker, make sure to put the date and time of the message in the register. It's a good idea to always enter the date of your entry in the register so others know when you've passed through.

PLAYING IT SAFE AROUND TOWN
Being close to civilization gives hikers a sense of safety; it represents the prospects of good food, a hot shower, and a bed to sleep in for the night. Many locals are friendly and supportive of hikers, but civilization does not come without its risks. For example, in Tennessee there is an area infamous for hostility toward hikers. This section of the trail was taken by the government through eminent domain, something that didn't sit well with some of the locals. There have been incidences of vandalism (including shelter arson), physical attacks on hikers, and tampering with the trail (one area was reported to have been strung with fish hooks hung at eye level to catch unaware hikers). The Appalachian Trail Conservancy has worked very hard to improve relations and the area is safer now than it was in the past. While towns are a safe haven in most instances, you need to exercise caution when traveling through populated areas.

Many long-distance hikers find themselves in a situation where they have to hitchhike into towns to resupply. Hitchhiking is usually easy to do in trail town areas where the locals are aware of the hiking community and are willing to help out with shuttles to and from town. However, it's not the safest way to travel. You may opt to call ahead for a hostel-, hotel-, or outfitter-provided shuttle instead of hitching. If that's not possible, try to hitch in a group rather than alone. Try to avoid hitching at night, and stay well off the road to avoid being hit by passing traffic when looking for a ride. Hitchhiking is illegal in some states, and hikers have been issued fines for hitching. Check your guidebook or ask local authorities such as rangers or ridge-runners before you hitch to avoid fines.

Be careful at road crossings and at shelters and campsites close to roads or heavily populated parks. Some shelters close to roads, such as the Governor Clement Shelter in Vermont, have an unfortunate history of vandalism and hiker harassment problems. Never leave your pack unattended for prolonged periods at shelters or near road crossings as pack theft occurs year after year. Your pack is your life support system—an expensive and well-tailored one that is difficult to replace. If you have to leave your pack, hide it in the woods off the beaten path. Secure cash, I.D., and credit

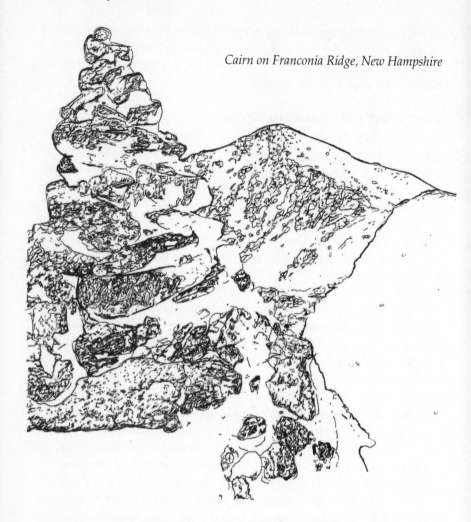

Cairn on Franconia Ridge, New Hampshire

cards while in town, and remember that, unfortunately, petty theft can occur anywhere on the AT.

If you encounter problems on the trail, notify local law enforcement agencies and submit a report to the ATC. Emergency numbers are listed in guidebooks and are posted at most shelters. When calling for help, keep in mind that cellular reception is usually best at higher elevations, not in hollows where shelters are typically located. If there are trail-specific problems such as vandalism, let the ATC know about it by calling 304-535-6331 or e-mailing them at incident@appalachiantrail.org. While it's good to be cautious, don't treat every person and situation with mistrust. One of the best aspects of trail life is its general safety and openness.

RIVER CROSSINGS

Fording the Kennebec River in Maine is extremely dangerous, and hikers have lost their lives attempting it. Fortunately, the Maine AT

Avoid carrying weapons such as guns or knives. Pepper spray is an acceptable self-defense tool if you travel alone and feel more comfortable with it. Carrying a whistle is also an option for the cautious hiker (the distress signal is three sharp blasts).

club and the ATC provide free ferry service to hikers. Information on the dates of operation of the Kennebec Ferry may be found at www.riversandtrails.com and are posted in the trail shelters on either side of the river. Some ultra-purists feel that it's unfair to take the canoe ferry across the Kennebec River, but crossing it on your own is *extremely* dangerous and the ATC strongly discourages fording Kennebec due to its erratic flow from the upstream power station.

HUNTING SEASON IS NOT OPEN SEASON FOR HIKERS

Hunting is permitted on or near the AT in many areas along its length, and a portion of the AT is made up of state game lands. Hunters sometimes hunt on property where hunting is prohibited due to ignorance or through purposeful actions, and it's important to alert hunters of your presence by wearing blaze orange (orange pack covers and vests are available at many outfitters) or by making noise such as talking and singing.

Both hunters and hikers can enjoy the outdoors in safety and harmony. Bear in mind that hunters compose a significant group of advocates for protecting land and often share similar environmental concerns with the hiking community. Try to avoid hiking during hunting season, and if you're planning a hike that coincides with hunting season, check with the local agencies governing hunting regulations such as the local state fish and game commission.

Rely on common sense and knowledge of the areas you hike in for safety. Listen to your instincts about where to sleep for the night and who to talk to, and, when in doubt, err on the side of caution. Avoid hiking alone, at night, or while wearing headphones, and

For hikers traveling during hunting season, a helpful link is provided on the Appalachian Trail Conservancy web site (www.appalachiantrail.org) under "Hike the Trail"/"Plan a Hike"/"Hunting and the AT." This link provides updated information on hunting season dates in each state.

never abuse your ability to call for help. Carry gear that you are familiar with, which is appropriate for the seasonal conditions you'll find yourself in. Have a working knowledge of the local flora, fauna, terrain, weather, and other factors, and be prepared to deal with situations as they arise. A little knowledge and a lot of common sense can go far in making your journey a safe one.

16

Injuries, Illnesses, and First Aid

He who limps is still walking.
—Stanislaw J. Lec

Hiking is generally considered to be part of a healthy lifestyle; it provides one with fresh air, exercise, and a break from the many stresses of the everyday world. However, with a physically demanding long-distance hiking trip comes the risk of certain health problems. The human body is elegantly designed to walk, yet walking excessive mileage while carrying weight is not natural and sometimes results in injuries. While on the trail, you'll be susceptible to physical conditions ranging from dehydration and allergic reactions to exhaustion. Though many of the more horrific ailments are rare on the AT, it is valuable to be aware of

> While this book gives information on treatment and prevention, it is in no way a replacement for professional medical care. If you encounter a medical condition or emergency on the trail, it is strongly advised that you seek professional care.

the symptoms, precautions, and treatments associated with them. With a proper awareness of the potential health hazards of the trail (and some luck), hikers are usually able to complete their hikes without major problems.

PREVENTATIVE HEALTH CARE FOR HIKERS

The human body is an amazing thing and can adapt rapidly to extreme physical conditions. A state of continual adaptation occurs in the body after about six weeks of hiking. At that point, a hiker's body produces more plasma, which in turn causes more blood cells and capillaries to be created to transport it. Bone mass increases as a response to the added pack weight and the impact of taking steps. Despite your abilities, it's important to listen to your body and provide it with rest, proper nutrition, and hydration. Rest is probably one of the most important and overlooked preventative health care measures a hiker can take. Making

Before your hike, visit your doctor and dentist for a complete checkup in order to avoid preventable medical emergencies on the trail, and to develop strategies for managing existing conditions (such as asthma) while on the trail. Also update your vaccinations against diseases such as tetanus.

demands on your body day after day is the number one cause of injuries, and it also weakens your immune system, leaving you more susceptible to illnesses.

GENERAL FIRST AID

It's a good idea to be knowledgeable in basic first aid before starting your hike. It's easy to find inexpensive or free first-aid courses, which can teach you skills such as CPR and how to deal with injuries. These can be found through organizations such as the American Red Cross (www.redcross.org) or at an outdoors school such as NOLS (www.nols.edu/wmi/).

FIRST-AID KIT

Create a first-aid kit tailored to your hiking needs. Your first-aid kit may contain everything from your daily prescription medicines to antibiotic ointment. A freezer bag or travel soap container makes a great waterproof, lightweight container for a basic first-aid kit. See the sidebar on the next page for suggestions on what to include in your kit.

CPR

Knowing CPR (cardiopulmonary resuscitation) can save lives. It's a fairly simple procedure that allows oxygen to circulate artificially until help can be found. CPR is best learned through a course taught in an environment where it can be practiced on a dummy under the watchful eye of a professional instructor.

If a hiker is not breathing, begin CPR. If there's access to a cell phone, call for help. Often, shelters provide a listing of emergency numbers. An emergency dispatcher will be able to direct you over the phone in helping the victim. If there's no way to call for help, send a hiker to the nearest road crossing for help. It's important to seek medical help, since CPR is merely a time-saving device meant to keep the victim alive until medical treatment is available.

With the victim on his or her back, tilt the head back slightly and listen for signs of breathing. Using your fingers to sweep out the mouth, make sure that the airway is cleared of foreign objects. Pinch the nose shut and blow into the victim's mouth with a quick, short breath until you see

Hikers should carry some sort of first-aid kit containing some or all of the following:

Analgesic cream—Creams such as Aspercreme are great for use on sore muscles and even hurting feet.

Antibiotic ointment—This is indispensable for basic cuts and scrapes.

Antifungal cream—Use on Athlete's foot and other fungal infections of the skin.

Antihistamine—Over-the-counter medicines such as Benadryl are useful in treating everything from hay fever to insect-bite reactions.

Antiseptic wipes—These wipes are great for cleaning abrasions and lanced blisters.

Band-aids—Bring a variety of sizes of band-aids. Use the waterproof and flexible-fabric "sport" type.

Bandage—You can use products such as trainer's tape or vet wrap (a flexible, self-adhesive material used primarily on horses). Regular ace bandages are also an option but are bulkier and not as durable.

Duct tape—Duct tape adheres well to perspiration-soaked skin, keeps debris out of cuts, and helps to eliminate blistering and chafing.

Electrolyte replacement powders—These are useful in combating dehydration.

Gauze—This is effective for more severe lacerations.

Identification card—Carry a laminated card listing your emergency contacts, allergies, prescriptions, existing conditions, primary care physician, insurance information, treatment restrictions due to religious beliefs, and any other vital information.

Moleskin—This is the luxurious alternative to duct tape used for covering blisters.

Multi-tool—A tool with scissors, knife, and tweezers is indispensable for removing ticks and debris from cuts and for cutting bandages and tape.

Nonsteroidal anti-inflammatory medication (NSAIDS)—These are over-the-counter drugs that help reduce inflammation and pain. The most popularly used on the AT is ibuprofen, known by hikers as "vitamin I."

Prescription medications—Your fist-aid kit is a great place to safely store the medications you use on a regular basis. Be sure to keep these medications safe from humidity and crushing (some pharmacies offer individual dose packets, which are convenient for hikers).

Stomach medicine—Over-the-counter chewable tablets are good for treating nausea and diarrhea.

Tea-tree oil—This oil is a natural antiseptic and is especially effective against fungal infections.

Witch hazel—This is another type of natural antiseptic with many uses. Like tea-tree oil, it is effective against foot fungus. You can find witch hazel wipes at some larger drugstores.

the chest rise. If there's no sign of breathing, use chest compressions. Push on the chest (between the nipples) at a rate of a little over one thrust per second for thirty compressions. Vomiting sometimes occurs with victims. If this happens, turn the victim's head to the side, clear the mouth out with your fingers, and continue CPR once the mouth and throat are clear of obstructions. Continue this process of blowing two puffs of breath into the victim's mouth and administering chest compressions until the victim is breathing independently or help arrives.

Heimlich Maneuver

The Heimlich maneuver is a first-aid treatment designed to use abdominal thrusts to help victims with airway obstruction caused by choking or asthma. If a hiker is choking, wrap your arms around him or her, placing your fist (thumb side in) below the ribcage and above the navel. Using your other hand, hold the fist and thrust it into the upper abdomen. Repeat until the victim's airway has cleared. If victim is unconscious or can't sit up, you can perform the Heimlich with the victim lying on his or her back. Use the heel of your hand placed below the ribcage and above the navel to deliver thrusts to clear the airway. You may perform the Heimlich maneuver on yourself using the edge of a picnic table or similar surface placed between ribcage and navel to deliver thrusts to the abdomen. A hiker who requires a procedure such as the Heimlich maneuver should always seek professional medical help as soon as possible, even if lingering problems or symptoms are absent.

OI, MY ACHIN' BOWELS: DIGESTIVE DISORDERS

Digestive disorders are some of the most dreaded but common afflictions for hikers. There are a variety of causes for stomach disorders on the trail. Exposure to contaminated water and spoiled food (surprisingly enough, food poisoning appears to occur more in towns rather than out on the trail) makes hikers sick, and viruses can easily spread throughout shelters and hostels.

Water sources (particularly those close to human- or livestock-inhabited areas) can contain a toxic cocktail of bacteria causing giardiasis and cryptosporidiosis, among other disorders. Proper treatment of water using chemicals or filters is an effective way to avoid such disorders. Giardiasis is not as prevalent a problem as people make it out to be, though you should still exercise caution. Not all people demonstrate symptoms of giardiasis, and a few lucky hikers may even develop immunity to it.

Cleverly nicknamed "beaver fever" (because of its spread through water in beaver ponds), it is an illness caused by a tough germ known as *Giardia intestinalis*, or *Giardia lamblia*. This parasite has the potential to appear in water sources all along the AT and spreads through the feces of contaminated people and animals. Keep in mind that an infected hiker who fails to wash his or her hands can spread the disease to others. Giardiasis causes symptoms such as diarrhea, gas, stomach cramping, nausea, and fatigue, which appear a week or two after exposure. If you think you have giardiasis, seek professional medical help to obtain diagnosis and prescription treatment.

Other bacterial infections from *Salmonella* and *Escherichia coli (E. Coli)* may create digestive problems but are less of a hiker-specific threat. To prevent these illnesses, practice good hygiene, handle food safely, and try to be discerning about where you eat while in town. If you have a digestive disorder that involves diarrhea, be sure to drink plenty of fluids to stay hydrated, and seek medical assistance if symptoms persist or are severe. Many digestive disorders disappear naturally with rest and hydration.

Constipation is also common on the trail. This condition may stem from physical causes (such as a lack of fiber in the diet) or psychological conditions (an aversion to going to the bathroom out in the open or in privies). The psychological causes for constipation typically disappear after a week or two on the trail, while the physical causes call for a hiker to incorporate more fiber into his or her diet to clear up the problem.

FOUR EYES ARE BETTER THAN TWO: EYEGLASSES AND CONTACTS

The trail is a place full of visual wonders. Not all hikers have good vision, and many need to carry some form of prescription glasses or contacts. There are a number of options for hikers with less than perfect vision. When deciding on what's best for you, consider essentials such as ease of use and safety.

With all of its pollen and dirt, the trail is a minefield of debris for contact wearers, and it's difficult to remove a contact, clean it, and reinsert it when in the backcountry. In the woods, with no hot water and soap, putting your fingers into your eyes and handling contacts can be an open invitation for infection. Use treated water and antibacterial gel to clean hands before handling a lens, and remember to allow the alcohol in the gel to evaporate before putting your fingers near your eyes and lenses. Never use untreated water to wash your hands, as this may introduce serious infections to the eye. Some hikers have successfully used extended-wear lenses. These are lenses that don't need to be removed and cleaned on a daily basis. This allows hikers to wait until town stops to handle lenses in a clean environment. There are some health risks associated with these types of lenses, and you should discuss them with your vision care provider.

The alternative to contact lenses is glasses. Glasses have their pros and cons. While they eliminate the worry of eye infections, they are bulky and easily get covered in rain and fog, obstructing vision. An anti-fog cloth, such as Smiths No-Fog, or paste, such as Cat-Crap anti-fog lens cleaner, can help to repel moisture and reduce condensation problems. Synthetic materials predominantly found on the trail make terrible cloths to use for cleaning glasses.

> There's the chance of losing a contact, rendering you partially blind until you find replacements in town. It's a good idea to carry a spare contact or pair of contacts with you in your pack or in a bounce box. Have your prescription stashed safely at home where a family member or friend can mail it to you in a pinch.

Carry a small scrap of glass-cleaning cloth designated only for cleaning glasses in your pack. If you get a new set of lenses before your hike, look into the variety of protective coatings available. You may want to opt for a scratch-resistant or UV protection coating. Eyeglasses can easily be broken, and it can be difficult to keep them safe, especially in crowded shelter environments. Make sure your lenses are shatterproof to avoid injuries if you happen to break your lenses while wearing them.

INJURIES AND CHRONIC CONDITIONS

One of the main reasons that a hiker fails to complete a hike is an injury or flare-up of an existing condition. While the non-hiker may see bears and lightning as the main threats on the trail, a hiker knows that the real enemies are stress fractures, shin splints, and other injuries. Hiking is hard on the body. Carrying a pack puts a lot of extra weight on your back—weight that humans aren't designed to carry. The entire length of the AT involves elevation changes that equal sixteen ascents of Mount Everest. These elevation changes are rough on the entire body, particularly the knees. The rocky and lumpy terrain lends itself to twisted ankles, bruised heels, and other complications.

Injuries often occur from pushing too hard—doing too many miles, hiking too fast, not getting enough rest, or carrying too much weight. They may also occur during the early stages of a hike when a hiker is in poor

Hikers on Hump Mountain, North Carolina

physical condition. Injuries tend to build on other injuries. A simple blister may lead to a serious soft-tissue injury if a hiker favors the foot with the blister, throwing the balance of the body off to a disastrous degree. Injuries may occur from trauma, such as a fall, or through repeated abuse, such as walking up and down hills with too much weight on your back.

Though there is no surefire way to fully prevent injuries, there are some precautions you can take to protect your body. Soft-tissue injuries are some of the more common injuries on the trail. "Soft tissue" refers to parts of the body that are non-skeletal, such as tendons and cartilage, and these sorts of injuries include strains, sprains, and torn ligaments. If you have a preexisting condition, have it checked out by a specialist well before your hike. Your body may require the use of orthotics, footbeds, knee or ankle braces, or other devices during your hike. You may also want to

If you feel tired, give your body a rest. The body goes through its healing processes when at rest. If you experience soreness, don't push yourself too hard until the condition resolves itself.

take vitamins and supplements such as chondroitin, glucosamine, vitamin E or C, iron, or calcium to promote good joint health. Make sure you aren't allergic to any of these before taking them on a regular basis, especially before using them on the trail. Eat as well as possible and stay hydrated, keep your pack weight down to a minimum, and, above all, listen to your body and rest as needed.

FOOT PROBLEMS

An old horseman's saying states, "no hooves, no horse." The same stands true for a long-distance hiker. Human feet are wonderfully designed and can withstand a lot of abuse. The infamous hiking duo of the Barefoot Sisters, Isis and jackrabbit, did a yo-yo hike of the AT predominantly in bare feet. While footwear is recommended for proper protection and support, the Barefoot Sisters' hike demonstrates the amazing abilities of feet (for an interesting approach to the powers of bare feet, check out the Barefoot Hikers web site: barefooters.org/hikers). There are a large number of products on the market designed to cradle, buffer, and generally smother feet with comfort. Baby your feet at every opportunity and they should serve you well. Some hikers go so far as to give themselves foot rubs. Taking small precautions, such as changing your socks, wearing camp shoes at the end of the day, and monitoring hot spots, helps to ensure that your feet go the distance.

Blisters and Calluses

Blisters are one of the most common foot complaints on the trail. Pay attention to your feet and rest often, especially at the beginning of the hike and during terrain and temperature changes. If you feel hot spots or tenderness in your feet, stop and look for signs of blistering and chafing. It's easier to prevent blisters than to treat them and wait for them to heal. If you know that you're prone to getting blisters on certain parts of your foot, tape that area when you first start hiking and give it time to toughen up. Wear two layers of socks, a liner and an outer sock, to reduce harmful chafing on your foot's skin.

Gaiters are a good investment as they keep pebbles and other debris from getting into your shoes or boots. A foreign object in your boot, no matter how small, can become a large problem after hiking a number of miles. Keep your toenails trimmed but avoid cutting them too far back, as this may cause ingrown nails. Some hikers soak their feet in Epsom salts or give them alcohol baths to toughen them. Other hikers feel that by keeping feet soft with Vaseline, Bag Balm, or other products, blisters may be kept at bay.

Some hikers combat the swampy foot conditions that lead to blisters by using Gold Bond or other foot powders. The best way to keep feet in good condition is to give them rest and fresh air at the end of the day and during breaks. Having an extra pair of dry socks or wearing roomy camp shoes can make a huge difference in how your feet perform for you. Always keep your feet as dry and cool as possible since hot, wet socks and shoes lead to blisters as well as other foot problems such as fungal infections.

While band-aids work well for some skin abrasions, many hikers use duct tape on their feet because it's inexpensive and adheres to skin better. Duct tape prevents chafing, and, at the end of the day, should come off the foot fairly easily. Moleskin, Micropore Tape, 2nd Skin, Spyroflex, and Compeed are also effective products for dealing with blisters. They function on the principle of creating a synthetic, skin-like layer to protect tissue from further damaging abrasion. Use a layer of duct tape over these products to help keep them in place.

If you get a blister that is painful enough to impede your hiking, you may want to consider lancing it. First know that you should never lance a blister that is blood-filled or appears to be infected. Also keep in mind that by opening the skin you are making it vulnerable to infection. You're putting your feet at risk. To lance a blister, use a sterilized needle to puncture and drain it. Wipe the area with an antiseptic pad before and after puncturing. Apply antibiotic ointment and cover with a bandage after lancing. Another option is to draw a sterilized piece of thread through the blister with a clean needle, leaving a long tail hanging out. The thread wicks the fluid out of the blister, preventing you from having to lance it multiple times. Be sure to change the thread frequently and to keep the area covered with a sterile bandage. Keep the blister covered and padded with moleskin, gauze, and duct tape until it's fully healed. Lancing a blister reduces the pain and makes it possible for you to hike while the blister heals. If ignored, blisters may turn into serious and debilitating infections requiring antibiotics and can take you off the trail indefinitely.

Calluses usually form after a few weeks of hiking and generally help to cushion the foot against abrasion. Calluses may crack in certain conditions. To prevent cracked calluses, use a lotion such as Vaseline or Bag Balm to soften the skin. A callus is made of dead skin and can't heal. Eventually, it sloughs off, but it may cause pain in the living skin contiguous with it. Some hikers use Superglue to bond calluses and prevent skin cracks from becoming deep or infected. Thoroughly clean the area, then apply glue to the crack and hold it shut until the glue dries. This is a good temporary fix until feet can be moisturized, softened, and healed.

Plantar Fasciitis

Symptoms of plantar fasciitis often crop up with long-distance hikers, but this condition isn't always identified or treated correctly. The plantar fascia is a piece of thick, fibrous tissue that runs along the bottom of the foot from the heel bone to the metatarsal bones in the ball of the foot. Its basic function is to help maintain the arch of the foot. Plantar fasciitis is a condition where this piece of tissue becomes inflamed, usually due to a repetitive trauma such as heel impact from hiking day after day. Hikers may be more prone to getting this disorder if they have flat feet; very high arches; a tendency to walk on the toes, pronate or supinate; or a family history of the problem. Poor arch support in shoes or wearing poorly sized shoes can also lead to plantar fasciitis. And, as with many other injuries, being in poor physical shape can be a culprit as the more rapid a change in activity level, the more likely a person is to develop plantar fasciitis.

Plantar fasciitis causes soreness, swelling, and heat. It is often felt when first walking in the morning and then subsides as the body warms up. Symptomatic pain generally begins in the heel and may increase in area and intensity after a period of time. If it is a severe case, it can cause bone spurs. This condition usually heals without surgery, but, if necessary, surgery is a fairly straightforward procedure and can be done on an outpatient basis. Anti-inflammatory drugs, heat or ice, stretching, rest, orthotics, heel cups, steroid injections, and night splints are the usual non-surgical methods of treatment. An over-the-counter, one-time-use (it lasts for a few days) device called Heel-Aid is helpful in controlling plantar fasciitis. If you are diagnosed with plantar fasciitis, always wear shoes to provide arch support for your feet.

It may take anywhere from weeks to months for plantar fasciitis pain to go away, and it's important to seek medical treatment as soon as possible as it can become a chronic condition if left unchecked. Symptoms of plantar fasciitis may be similar to certain types of stress fractures or nerve or collagen disorders, so it's important to get a reliable diagnosis. Certain stretching exercises may help to alleviate or prevent plantar fasciitis. Stretching the calf, heel, and Achilles tendon using a wall, stair step, or curb is helpful for relieving pain. You may roll your foot over a tennis ball, which can help stretch the foot. Or you can do a toe-tapping exercise, keeping the heel on the floor while raising the front of your feet and alternating between tapping your four little toes and the big toe on the ground. There is also a method of using trainer's tape to relieve plantar fasciitis pain.

Heel Spurs

Heel spurs often occur in tandem with plantar fasciitis and are sometimes given the generic misnomer plantar fasciitis. However, heel spurs are bony overgrowths in the bottom of the heel bone and are not a condition of the plantar fascia. Heel spurs occur when the damaged plantar fascia irritates the heel bone and more bone is formed as a natural defense mechanism. Heel spurs result from carrying too much weight, wearing poorly fitted shoes, or having pronation problems. They are detected with X-rays and treated with many of the same techniques as plantar fasciitis, including orthotics, ice, and heat.

Stress Fractures

Stress fractures are a common result of repetitive stresses placed on bones. Stress fractures are associated with high-impact and repetitive sports such as running and hiking. Repetitive abuse doesn't give bones a chance to repair themselves, allowing tiny painful fissures to appear in the bone. Stress fractures most commonly occur in the weight-bearing lower extremities (feet and ankles), though one can get stress fractures in other places.

Stress fractures hurt when bearing weight. Depending on where the stress fracture is, the area around it may develop swelling or bruising. X-rays won't typically be able to show stress fractures, and a bone scan may be required to make a diagnosis. An untreated stress fracture may turn into a fully broken bone, so seek medical help and rest right away if you display symptoms. Many stress fractures heal on their own in a matter of weeks if allowed to rest, but some cases requires splints, casts, or even surgery for complete recovery.

A hiker should have a decent level of fitness and rest as often as possible to help reduce the risk of stress fractures. Tired or underdeveloped muscle can fail to support the impact of hiking, allowing bones to absorb the destructive shocks and jolts. Covering too many miles with too much weight before your body is in shape can easily lead to stress fractures. For a few older hikers, stress fractures may be a sign of deteriorating bone density.

Pronation and Supination

Your physiology plays a large role in how injury-prone you are. The way your body is put together and how you use it determines to a large extent how physically sound you'll be on your hike. Many chronic problems start with the feet. The shape of the foot and the way the foot falls when walking affects the stresses put on the joints of the body all the way up through the back. Pronation and supination occur because of conditions of the foot that affect the way you walk.

The term pronation describes when the arch of the foot flattens out when the foot strikes the ground, causing the ankle to tilt inward. A small amount of pronation is normal and necessary to help absorb shock and maintain balance. Overpronation can cause a host of problems, affecting the inside of the foot, the muscles of the lower leg, and the knee. Supination (also called underpronation) is when the weight of the foot is directed toward the outside of the foot, and the ankle has a tendency to roll toward the outside. Minor supination is normal and necessary to provide stability during the part of a stride where the toe is ready to leave the ground. Supination may cause ankle-rolling and problems with the lower leg muscles and ligaments, as well as tendonitis and plantar fasciitis. Both pronation and supination can affect the hips and back.

So how can you tell if you have a pronation or supination problem? If you're having pain that might be associated with these abnormalities, your doctor will assess your gait and see if pronation or supination is to blame. You can check the bottoms of your shoes for excessive uneven wear to see if you have these tendencies. If you overpronate, the inside edges of your shoes' heels wear down faster than the rest of the shoe, and if you have a supination problem, the outside edges will show excessive wear. It's a good idea to take a pair of worn athletic shoes with you to the podiatrist, since heel wear can give the doctor clues about your condition.

Excessive pronation or supination may be treated using specially fit corrective orthotics. These differ from footbeds purchased at an outfitter (though those may be helpful for more minor cases of pronation or supination). A podiatrist makes a cast of the feet and, from that cast, creates a stiff shoe liner that compensates for the foot's natural tendencies to roll in one direction or the other. Orthotics are expensive and, for some, uncomfortable. Some hikers feel that the stiffness of the orthotics' material is detrimental to the foot because it affects the arch's ability to absorb shock. However, for many hikers afflicted with pronation or supination, orthotics may be a hike-saving device.

Athlete's Foot

Athlete's foot is a relatively common fungal infection that affects the foot, particularly the area between the toes. This condition causes dryness, flaking, cracking, blistering, and even bleeding of the skin. An afflicted foot becomes painfully itchy and may swell. There are four main types of fungus that cause athlete's foot and a variety of manifestations of the condition. Ulcerative athlete's foot is characterized by cracking skin; "moccasin foot" by a red rash and thick, dry skin; and inflammatory or vesicular infections by itchy bumps and ridges. Athlete's foot may also create a rash reaction on the hands as a part of an immune response.

The fungi that cause athlete's foot breed in wet, warm places such as shoes, locker rooms, and around swimming pools. Athlete's foot is spread through skin contact with areas where the fungus grows, such as the floors of shower stalls. To prevent this condition, keep your feet as dry and clean as possible and wear flip-flops or some sort of shoe in the shower to avoid direct contact with infected surfaces. Use well-ventilated camp shoes when you are not hiking to give your feet a chance to air out. Changing your socks and sock liners on a regular basis also helps to keep fungal conditions at bay. If you have athlete's foot, avoid spreading it by following the same precautions. The fungus can also spread through contaminated bedding and socks, so keep the affected areas covered and clean.

If you suspect you have athlete's foot and it doesn't go away after a week or two, consult a general physician or a podiatrist. The doctor will make a diagnosis based on visual appearance, microscopic examination of skin cells taken from a scraping, examination under a UV light, or through growing cultures. Athlete's foot may be treated with topical fungistatic chemicals, which inhibit the growth of fungus in the more superficial layers of the skin. Over-the-counter drugs such as Lotrimin can be applied to the skin to fight infection. There are also over-the-counter pills and medications that come in multiple forms (spray, powder, or cream) such as Desenex and Tinactin. Witch hazel is a great natural cure for more mild fungal infections. Oral medicine may be prescribed for cases that have penetrated deeper layers of skin (specifically in areas with thick calluses). Bacterial infections sometimes take advantage of damaged tissue and, if this is suspected, oral antibiotics are prescribed.

Ringworm

Ringworm, named for the ring-shaped patches it leaves on the skin, is another contagious fungal skin disorder that hikers catch. It affects all areas of the body (including the scalp, nails, and feet; on the feet, it is also sometimes referred to as athlete's foot). Ringworm can be spread through direct skin contact or contact with objects that have been used by an infected person. It thrives in warm, moist conditions and affects skin that has suffered minor scratches and abrasions. As well as being passed between humans, this condition can be caught from pets.

A physician can diagnose ringworm with special lighting or by examining skin scrapings, and it's fairly simple to treat with antifungal medicine. If you are diagnosed with ringworm, be careful not to share clothing, sleeping bags, sleeping pads, or anything else with other hikers. Try to stay as clean and dry as possible, changing your clothing and washing your sleeping bag liner often. In the hiking environment, it's difficult but necessary to take these precautions and minimize contact with others.

Trench Foot

Trench foot (also known as immersion foot) is a disorder that occurs when the feet are cold and wet for long periods of time. Trench foot was so named because of the large numbers of soldiers experiencing this disorder in the trenches during World Wars I and II. This disorder is fairly uncommon but has affected some hikers. It causes constriction of the skin capillaries and may result in damage to the skin if allowed to persist for twelve hours or more. Trench foot can occur in relatively mild temperature conditions. The disorder is characterized by numbness, redness and eventual loss of color, leg cramps, slow pulse in the foot, blistering, and swelling. If left unchecked, trench foot can lead to sores, infections, and even gangrene. To prevent this disorder, try to keep feet dry and warm. If you think you may have trench foot, elevate and massage feet, and take NSAIDs for swelling and pain. Consult a physician as soon as possible.

Toenail Damage and Loss

Toenail damage and loss is a sad (and gross) reality of long-distance hiking. It can result from ill-fitted footwear, repetitive concussion of the toes, fungal infections, or trauma. Nails may become blackened (darkened in color as a result of bruising) and fall off completely. Typically, nails grow back, but treat lost nails as a symptom of a larger problem, such as ill-fitting footwear. Blackened toenails result from repeated and prolonged episodes of concussion to your toes when your feet slide around in loose-fitting footwear. It also occurs from pressure caused by swelling of the feet in overly small shoes or boots. Sometimes, pressure from a blister under the nail causes the toenail to separate from the toe. This condition can be fairly painful but doesn't cause permanent damage. If blackened toenails continue to give you problems for days on end, seek medical advice as this condition can lead to serious infection if left untreated.

To prevent this condition (and a host of others), make sure your shoes or boots fit correctly. You need to strike the perfect balance between having enough room in the shoe to accommodate the foot when it swells (it can increase by a whole shoe size) and having a snug enough fit to keep the foot from sliding around too much. It's essential to have a well-fitted toe box to avoid blackened toenails. In the toe box, you need room on the sides as well as below and above the toes. Lace shoes tightly enough to keep the heel firmly in the heel box, but leave enough play for swelling and circulation.

Paresthesia

Paresthesia is a neurological disorder that can occur in the feet of long-distance backpackers. Characterized by an initial sharp pain followed by a change in skin sensitivity, tingling, and numbness, the physical sensations that accompany paresthesia are similar to the pins-and-needles feeling when a limb falls asleep as a result of prolonged pressure to nerves. This condition may be caused by a host of illnesses, such as diabetes, but, for backpackers, is most often the result of pressure put on the nerves from ill-fitting footwear. If there are no other symptoms (such as dizziness) accompanying the nerve sensation, there should be little worry about the condition indicating a more serious illness. Usually, paresthesia goes away after a month or so of rest, with no lingering effects. If you feel the onset of tingling, check to see if your shoes are optimally fitted. If your problems persist and cause discomfort, you may need to decrease your mileage. NSAIDs help with pain management, but the disorder will heal itself with rest and properly fitted footwear. If symptoms of paresthesia persist after you are done with your hike, consult a doctor as this may indicate tarsal tunnel syndrome (a disorder similar to carpal tunnel syndrome). Permanent pressure to the nerves in the foot can usually be controlled with orthotics and properly fitted footwear.

Stone Bruises

A stone bruise on the foot is different from an ordinary contusion on another part of the body. Stone bruises (also known as bone bruises) are fairly common heel injuries for long-distance hikers. These bruises occur from hard impact with stones and other sharp or uneven objects on the ground. An inflammation occurs in the skin that covers the heel bone and causes mild to moderate discomfort when pressure is applied to the area. A stone bruise will go away with rest, and NSAIDs may be taken to relieve pain. Footwear made for hiking should have special supports and puncture-resistant plates to help prevent stone bruises.

SHIN SPLINTS

Shin splints, more formally known as medial tibial stress syndrome, are a common though sometimes debilitating injury with which many long-distance hikers deal. As with many of the injuries associated with hiking, shin splints result from the repetitive concussions created by walking. This condition is characterized by a pain on the inside of the shin, a pain that can be merely annoying or even crippling. The repetitive stress of walking many miles day after day affects the fascia, sometimes leading to stress fractures. The risk of shin splints increases with the toughness of the ground (packed dirt, for example, is tougher on the legs than grassy, springy footing).

Shin splints cause a hiker pain that may initially be walked off as the day progresses. If the hiker does not rest and the condition is allowed to worsen, pain from shin splints can increase and plague a hiker every step of the day. Shin splints are accompanied by a local pain along the shin and possibly mild swelling. If you suspect you have shin splints, try to rest your body as much as possible: take zero days, slack-pack, or decrease your daily mileage until the condition ceases. Use the R.I.C.E. method of caring for shin splints by resting, icing, compressing (wrapping with a bandage), and elevating (above the heart). Take NSAIDs to reduce swelling and manage pain. Rest generally cures shin splints, but seek medical help if there is pain while at rest or if the pain is severe. Either of these symptoms may indicate a stress fracture.

Traditional stretches for calf muscles help to reduce the risk of shin splints. Using a tree, shelter wall, or other vertical surface to lean your hands against, place one leg a stride length in front of the other. Lean forward, keeping your heel on the ground while allowing the back leg's calf muscles to stretch. Make sure that the knee on your forward leg doesn't extend beyond the toe as this can cause injury. Switch legs and repeat with the other heel on the ground.

Proper shoes that fit well and provide plenty of shock-absorbing padding help to deter the condition, but sometimes it occurs due to a hiker's unique physiology (high, rigid arches and flat feet both decrease shock-absorbing abilities and may lead to shin splints; those who pronate are also more susceptible).

If you have known foot abnormalities or pronation issues, using orthotics can reduce the risk of getting shin splints. Avoid shin splints by stretching and, during the initial phases of your hike, taking it easy until your body grows used to the demands.

SORE MUSCLES

Muscle soreness results from damage inflicted on the muscle but is a natural part of the strengthening process. All hikers experience sore muscles from time to time, no matter how conditioned they are. This is especially true at the beginning of a hike before your body grows accustomed to the demands of daily hiking. There are ways to manage soreness to make it more bearable. First of all, stay hydrated. Along with helping to combat general fatigue, being hydrated helps to maintain the body's balance of electrolytes

It used to be a common belief that muscle soreness was due to lactic acid content in muscle tissue, but that belief has been disregarded and post-exercise muscle soreness is now attributed to mechanical damage to the muscle fibers. Lactic acid, however, can be blamed for the "burning" sensation you experience while hiking up a big hill.

and helps muscles recover more easily from labor. Stretch and begin your daily hiking at a slow pace until your body is warmed up. If you are extremely sore, use NSAIDs for pain management. Icing and gentle massage may also help alleviate pain. Soaking legs in cold streams (well downstream from where hikers collect water) is a great on-trail therapy for sore muscles.

Pulled Hamstrings

The hamstring muscle is actually a generic name for the large group of muscles in the back of the thigh that work to extend the hip and flex the knee. When this muscle group experiences tearing, it is said to be pulled. An injury of this sort results from sudden movement, typically acceleration for aggressively climbing a hill, for example. A pulled hamstring may also result from sudden impact to the muscle, though this is more typical in contact sports rather than hiking. A pull may be as mild as a small microscopic tearing, or it may entail a full-blown rupture that requires surgery to repair. A pulled hamstring creates pain in the back of the thigh, buttocks, or belly, and may be accompanied by excessive bruising on the length of the leg, swelling, difficulty contracting the muscles to bend the knee, and muscle spasms. R.I.C.E. (rest, ice, compression, and elevation) are necessary in treating a pulled hamstring. A hiker with this problem should cease hiking and seek medical help if there is severe pain or excessive symptoms such as spasms. A minor pull will repair itself, but a more severe tear may require surgery. To prevent this problem, stretch by doing simple toe touches, don't push yourself through big miles, and never tackle an intense physical task such as a large elevation gain without a proper warm-up.

Bursitis

Bursitis is a general joint injury that some hikers experience. This condition is a swelling of the bursa, a sack filled with liquid that acts as a cushion between tendon and bone. Bursas act as tiny rollers, or air cushions, that allow joints to move smoothly and without pain. Repetitive stress, a fall or sudden impact, arthritis, or even an infection of the staphylococcal variety may cause an unhealthy swelling and irritation of the bursa. We have bursas throughout the body in many different joints (such as the shoulder, big toe, and hip areas). However, bursitis of the knee is the most common manifestation of this condition in hikers. When the bursa is damaged, it swells and causes pain. This condition is marked with soreness and stiffness (and, in the knee, a swollen lump on the front of the knee cap). Generally, bursitis is successfully treated with rest: low mile days, slacking, or, ideally, zeros. NSAIDs are useful for reducing swelling and managing pain, as is a combination of icing and elevation of the afflicted limb. If bursitis does not go away on its own after a week or so or is accompanied by fever and severe swelling, seek medical help.

Torn Ligaments

Ligaments are the soft tissue that connects bone or cartilage to one another. A torn ligament is a soft-tissue injury that may occur in any area of the body where there are joints, but is most common in the knees (such as a torn anterior cruciate ligament tear, also known as an ACL tear). A torn ligament typically occurs from trauma rather than repetitive stress. When a ligament tears, it may make an audible popping sound and can cause a great deal of pain and swelling. A joint with a torn ligament feels unstable, as it's partly the job of the ligament to provide support for the surrounding bones. A minor ligament injury, such as a partial tear, may heal on its own and only require rest and the use of a splint. A severe tear may require surgical repair. If you suspect a torn ligament, seek medical help as soon as possible, especially if there's a lot of pain and instability in the joint. MRIs (magnetic resonance imaging) and other diagnostic strategies can assist in obtaining a correct diagnosis and proposing treatment methods.

Tendonitis

Tendonitis is an inflammation of the tendon and is associated with repetitive stress, especially stress that results from a new exercise routine such as hiking long miles on a daily basis. Along with overuse, physiological and age factors can contribute to tendonitis. Tendonitis may be avoided by taking it easy until your body adjusts to hiking. Ice, NSAIDs, splints and supports (such as the Cho-Pat strap for patellar tendonitis) decrease swelling and help healing.

If you suspect that you may have tendonitis, seek medical help since only a doctor can correctly diagnose this condition. MRIs and X-rays aren't usually necessary for a diagnosis but may be a good idea to rule out other problems. If you are diagnosed with tendonitis, rest is the best course of action to take. A damaged tendon that is not rested is susceptible to rupturing, a much more serious injury requiring surgery.

BROKEN BONES

Broken bones are a fairly common injury. If too much pressure is applied to a bone, it will snap. There are varying degrees of breaks, from small stress fractures to compound fractures where the bone punctures the skin. It's usually pretty obvious when a hiker has a broken bone: the limb is crooked or misshapen; there is intense pain, swelling, and bruising; the limb cannot be moved; and the ends of the bone may even show through the skin. Medical care should be sought immediately when a broken bone is suspected. While waiting for help to arrive, immobilize the afflicted limb with a splint made from tree branches, trekking poles, or whatever materials you can find. Always stabilize the joint before evacuating a hiker. To avoid shock, make sure the victim is kept still and calm. If a break is suspected in the neck or back, *do not* move the person as this can compound problems. If a person has a broken hip, thigh, or pelvis, don't allow him or her to walk or put any weight on the leg. If there is bleeding from a compound fracture, apply a clean dressing and use light pressure to help staunch the flow of blood (never use a tourniquet unless there's a risk of loss of life due to blood loss). The amount of time a broken bone takes to heal varies depending on the size of the fracture and where it's located, but generally it's a month to six weeks.

DISLOCATED BONES

Dislocated bones (also known as dislocated joints) occur when a bone is forced out of its natural setting in a joint. Most commonly dislocated are shoulders. This condition results from trauma and may be accompanied by nerve and ligament damage. Anyone suffering from a dislocated bone should seek medical help. The symptoms of a dislocated bone are very similar to that of a broken bone but may be loosely diagnosed based on its proximity to a joint. Treat a dislocation the same as a fracture; immobilize the injury and seek immediate medical assistance. As with a broken bone, do not attempt to straighten out the limb or pop the joint back into place. This only causes more damage. A dislocation usually takes three to six weeks to heal.

SPRAINS AND STRAINS

A sprain is a common traumatic injury that involves tearing or an unhealthy amount of stretching of a ligament. A strain is different from a sprain in that it's damage to muscle or tendon. Like a sprain, it results from overstretching or complete tearing of tissue. Both sprains and strains most commonly occur in the ankles due to the amount of pressure and movement that area of the body is prone to experiencing. Sprains and strains are characterized by swelling, pain, and bruising. Depending on how severe the injury is, a person may lose functionality of the joint. If the injury is mild, treat it with rest, ice, compression, elevation above the heart, and ibuprofen. Usually, a sprain or strain heals on its own and may be functional though tender. Severe manifestations of these injuries may require surgery for treatment. Seek medical help for sprains and strains that don't heal quickly or are accompanied by a lot of pain, numbness, or loss of functionality.

Always have injuries checked out. Never ignore them. Injuries tend to create a snowball effect, with one injury leading you to walk differently to alleviate the pain, which creates another set of stresses on the body. Some injuries are easily reversed when treated right away but can become serious problems if left unchecked.

CHAFING, CUTS, AND BRUISES

Chafing, scrapes, cuts, and bruises are common yet annoying injuries experienced by long-distance hikers. Typically, these are minor problems and don't require expert medical help. You do need to pay attention to skin wounds, though, as they're especially prone to infection and irritation on the trail. And if you experience wounds that don't disappear on their own, continue to bleed, bleed excessively, or cause a lot of pain, seek medical treatment.

For cuts, flush out the wound with potable water or alcohol wipes. Remove debris with tweezers cleaned with alcohol wipes or sterilized over an open flame. Apply antibacterial ointment and cover with a band-aid or clean gauze. Always clean wounds with water that's treated since bacteria can enter the body through the wound, causing infection. Don't blow on a cut since that spreads bacteria. Change the gauze or band-aid at least once a day or whenever it gets wet or dirty, and make sure your tetanus shot is up-to-date.

Bruising usually occurs when trauma causes damaged capillaries to bleed into surrounding tissue. The colors of a bruise are created by the breakdown of hemoglobin. Bruises may also result from conditions such as allergies, viral infections, or septicemia. A person who has a deficiency in vitamin C is more susceptible to bruising. If, for some reason, you suspect you have bruises that don't result from trauma, seek medical help as bruising may be symptomatic of a larger problem. Minor bruises aren't typically a problem, and pain can be managed with NSAIDs and icing to help control the swelling. A large, painful bruise resulting from a fall or blow may indicate a fracture or internal bleeding. If a bruise is accompanied by severe pain, have it checked out by a doctor to rule out fractures or other serious injury. Usually, a bruise will heal in one to two weeks.

Chafing is an unpleasant but fairly harmless problem encountered by long-distance hikers. It usually occurs from clothing or skin rubbing on skin and is aggravated by heat, salt deposits from sweat, and dampness from humidity or sweat. It's easier to prevent chafing than to treat it. Stay hydrated, wear properly fitted clothing made of breathable fabrics (make sure there are no annoying exposed seams that can damage skin), change into dry clothing as often as possible, and use talcum powder or a lubricant such as BodyGlide (www.bodyglide.com), Bag Balm, or petroleum jelly. If you experience chafing, wash the affected skin in cool water and apply a thin layer of antibacterial ointment. Diaper rash ointment (such as A + D, Desitin, or Balmex) is useful in treating itchiness and acts as a lubricant to prevent further chafing. Depending on where the chafe is, you may want to apply a bandage to help prevent infection.

SEASONAL ALLERGIES

Seasonal allergies are a problem for some hikers. If you are prone to having allergies, be sure to bring antihistamines with you in your first-aid kit.

Through being exposed to different regions and their accompanying allergens, hikers can experience allergies for the first time while out on the trail. Fortunately, it has been shown that exercise probably helps to decrease allergic reactions from hay fever, so your daily mileage may work in your favor. For hikers requiring special medical care for their allergies (such as inhalers or allergy shots), consult your guidebook for the availability of doctors and pharmacies in towns along the trail. Take preventative measures if you are allergy-prone. There are prescription medicines in pill and nasal spray forms designed to work without causing drowsiness or dizziness. Talk to your health care provider about what options are best for you. You may want to try a homeopathic approach to allergy relief such as stinging nettle, an herbal remedy taken to prevent hay fever problems.

WOMEN'S HEALTH CONCERNS

Women have some specific health concerns on the trail. As well as having to deal with menstrual cycles, they are more prone to certain joint and bone problems because of their physiology and bone-density-loss issues. Urinary tract infections, calcium loss, and other female-specific issues can be dealt with effectively while on the trail.

An average woman experiences her menstrual cycle about five times during a thru-hike. One would think that, with the lack of privacy and indoor plumbing, this may be a hassle. However, it's fairly simple to deal with this natural event. Always make sure to carry a supply of sanitary products with you on the trail. Extreme exercise can alter a woman's cycle, creating unpleasant surprises if one is not prepared. Use tampons (ones with applicators for sanitary reasons) rather than pads as they trap blood internally, cutting down on unsanitary conditions. Store these in a strong plastic bag to keep them safe from dirt and moisture. Carry a small pack of baby wipes with you to clean yourself (you may want to use these on an everyday basis after privy visits as well). Store used sanitary supplies in a heavy-duty freezer bag that you can pack out. Never leave tampons or pads in a privy because they won't decompose.

Women hikers may also have to deal with vaginal yeast infections while out on the trail. These infections result from the overabundance of *Candida* or *Monilia.* These yeasts are always present in small numbers but may multiply in a number of different scenarios. Infections are marked by itching, burning, and sometimes a thick discharge similar in consistency to cottage cheese. Antibiotics are one of the major causes of yeast infections; so if you go on antibiotics for any reason, you may want to take precautions to avoid getting an infection. Acidophilus is a "good" bacteria that helps to keep yeast levels down. Ingesting it in pill form or by eating plain yogurt is a good precautionary measure to take. You also want to pay attention to what you wear from the waist down. Make sure you wear breathable pants or shorts, or a skirt. Women who are prone to getting yeast infections are commonly advised to wear cotton underwear. Because this isn't a realistic or comfortable option on the trail, you may want to wear breathable tech underwear or no underwear at all to maximize air flow and comfort. If you've had a yeast infection before and you recognize the symptoms, you can purchase an over-the-counter medication at most any pharmacy. If symptoms fail to clear up in a few days, seek medical help.

Urinary tract infections, more commonly known as UTIs, are another problem for female hikers (and some male hikers, too). Because of the way the female urinary tract is designed, women are more prone to getting this type of infection than men. The best precaution against UTIs is to drink plenty of water to flush out the urinary tract. A UTI is primarily characterized by a strong and constant urge to urinate that can't be relieved. Sometimes, with a more severe infection, blood may appear in the urine. Be aware that blood in the urine may also be symptomatic of an internal injury, typically caused by an ill-fitting hip belt. If you get an infection, seek medical help immediately as the infection could spread to the kidneys. Doctors typically prescribe antibiotics, which alleviate symptoms within a day or so.

TREATING SHOCK

Shock is a secondary result of a major accident. It can be brought about through blood loss or an extreme lowering of blood pressure, an intense psychological state, severe dehydration, or infection. It results from not getting enough blood flow to the major organs of the body. Shock can manifest itself in patients in a number of ways, such as nausea and vomiting, sweat, paleness, vertigo, fatigue, faintness, shallow breathing and pulse, or unconsciousness, and it may create permanent damage if left unchecked. A shock victim has cold, clammy appendages and pale, bluish skin. If you encounter a hiker in shock, lay him or her down and cover with a sleeping bag to help the body retain heat. Raise the feet above the head to encourage blood flow to the major organs. If the shock is bad and the victim stops breathing or loses a heartbeat, perform CPR. A person in a state of shock should receive professional medical assistance as soon as possible.

EVACUATING AN ILL OR INJURED HIKER

If you are feeling sick, tell other hikers about your condition. That way, there'll be people paying close attention to where you're at on the trail. And if you get very sick, go into town as soon as possible. There's nothing worse than being caught in the middle of nowhere with a nasty illness. If a town isn't close and you're unsure if you can walk, stay put at a shelter or designated campsite on the trail. More often than not, other hikers will come by and be able to assist you.

If you have to evacuate a sick or injured person from the woods, leave a note with the victim containing pertinent information about his or her illness or injury (such as how and when he or she was hurt, if they have any specific conditions, and so on). Leave information about the time you went for help and how to reach you (if you or someone you're traveling with has a cell phone or if you're going to a specific place to get help). This information will help rescuers when they reach the victim.

17

Lightweight and Ultralight Backpacking

Less is more.
> —Ludwig Mies van der Rohe

The environmentalist John Muir is considered by many to have been a lightweight backpacker. He wanted to be unencumbered in order to better enjoy nature and felt that the less he carried into the wilderness, the better he appreciated his experience. One well-known contemporary advocate of going light, Ray Jardine, promotes carrying less as a part of his philosophy for similar reasons. When one thinks of ultralight backpacking, a harrowing image of a shivering and haggard hiker sleeping on bare ground with a sawed-off toothbrush may come to mind. However, with the advent of new high-tech materials and designs on the market, minimalist gear is becoming more of a practical reality on the AT.

Why opt to go lightweight or ultralight? I prefer to travel light and utilize a number of strategies for keeping my pack weight low. There are a variety of reasons for why I pack light. These range from a pragmatic need to take weight off my injury-prone knees and a deeper, philosophical need similar to Muir's. The reduction of excess weight makes hiking easier on my body, allows for quicker miles, and generally makes the act of hiking from place to place more enjoyable. With the beautiful simplicity it advocates, the lightweight and ultralight movement in backpacking is an admirable manifestation of what the AT experience is all about.

WHAT IS LIGHTWEIGHT AND ULTRALIGHT BACKPACKING?

The term *pack weight* accounts for the total weight of a pack at the start of a trip. This includes food, water, and other consumable items such as fuel, sunscreen, and insect repellent. The *base weight* of a pack is the weight of the pack minus consumable items. The definition of base weight may vary a little from hiker to hiker and is called *dry weight* in some circles. This weight includes storage sacks and, for the very exacting, the clothing worn on the hiker's body (known as *skin-out base weight*). Traditional pack weight can range from thirty to forty pounds or more. A lightweight backpacker's pack is in the twenty-some-pound range, and an ultralight backpacker can have pack weights dipping down into the teens and even single digits.

To calculate the weight of your pack, do not rely heavily on the manufacturer's listing for its product's weight. The manufacturers' weights aren't always accurate and may exclude items such as stuff sacks and spare parts, skewing your weight data. You can also get an idea of your base weight by weighing yourself on a bathroom scale with and without your pack, subtracting your weight without the pack from your weight with it to get your pack's weight. The average hiker can get a reasonable sense of his or her pack weight without using a postal scale, but those wanting to account for every ounce will benefit from this fairly inexpensive device. You may also use an online backpacking weight calculator (www.chrisibbeson.com/pages/GearWeightCalculator.html). Designed by Chris Ibbeson, this computer program allows you to calculate and tweak your pack weight before physically packing for a trip.

> One elaborate system defines base weight in terms of ratios: ultralight is descriptive of those products within the top fifth percentile of gear available on the market, lightweight includes weights in the twenty-fifth percentile, and traditional weight covers gear in the fiftieth percentile. The definition of ultralight and lightweight gear changes annually as manufacturers produce lighter designs and materials.

TRIMMING THE FAT OFF OF YOUR PACK

When considering the level of lightness you'd like to achieve with your gear, consider the minimal amount of gear you require for relative comfort and, most importantly, safety. This changes from season to season and with the terrain (for example, your gear needs in summertime Maryland are a lot less complex than in the demanding winters of Maine's Mahoosuc Range). Ultralight is a great way to go when hiking in warm conditions, but becomes difficult when hiking in cold weather because of the extra clothing, fuel, and sleeping bag weight required.

When looking to reduce weight, hikers often focus on the big three essential items of gear including the pack, sleeping bag, and portable shelter. Some hikers also add their cooking system to this equation to account for primary pack weight. The most important of the big three is the pack. A small, lightweight pack automatically reduces what you can carry, minimizing your overall pack weight and volume. After the big three come the little necessities, which can really add up, such as additional clothing, a first-aid kit, toi-

A hiker wanting to reduce his or her pack weight usually does so at the cost of comfort in the camp. The most obvious way to lighten one's load is by getting rid of luxury items like full-length inflatable mattresses and additional clothing, books, and other items that make time spent in camp more enjoyable.

letries, and other odds and ends. Focus on the big three first when reducing weight, then move on to the smaller items afterward. Little items can add up to mere ounces, while changes to the primary essentials can literally shave pounds off your weight. Backpacking.net offers a couple of sample lightweight and ultralight gear lists in the "Gear Checklists" section (http://backpacking.net). These lists show you where weight can be sacrificed and give you a good idea of what weight to look for when you purchase gear.

When lowering your weight, take your footwear into account. Heavy-duty boots aren't as necessary for support when you carry a lighter pack, and you may want to consider switching to lightweight trail runners or hiking shoes. Reducing the weight of your footwear can have a significant impact on your performance. A single pound on the foot equals five or six pounds in the pack because the weight of footwear is not carried near your center of gravity and requires more effort to move. For footwear, you need to strike a balance between something that is lightweight yet provides adequate support for your foot.

Materials and design have a large impact on the weight of gear. High-tech materials such as carbon fiber and titanium are cropping up in many backpacking products from cookware to trekking poles. While these materials don't compromise strength for the sake of weight, they do tend to cost more than traditional materials such as stainless steel and aluminum. Being weight-savvy about materials and design doesn't have to entail spending lots of cash. For example, instead of using a heavy and pricey Lexan water bottle, opt for a recycled sports drink or soda bottle.

Successful weight reduction typically happens gradually, though the weight-loss learning curve can be pretty steep on a long-distance hike. Many veteran hikers on the AT, including employees at outfitters, are more than happy to help you go through your pack with a fine-tooth comb to reduce excess weight (Mountain Crossings at Walasi-Yi Center in Georgia offers free pack shake-downs primarily catering to northbound thru-hikers in the early stages of their hike). With experience comes a sense of what is and isn't necessary to take on the trail. That said, some old-school hikers carry heavy packs because they are comfortable with their gear or don't want to spend the money to upgrade to lighter-weight items. Quite often, inexperienced hikers pack everything but the kitchen sink, and AT hikers have carried everything from bottles of perfume to bulky camp chairs. After the first week of hiking, these excess items usually find themselves stranded in hiker boxes.

There are a couple of strategies to lightening your load. The first one involves finding equipment capable of multi-tasking to eliminate redundancies in your gear inventory. Using this strategy can save you money as well as pounds. A great example of this is using a tarp tent that incorporates trekking poles into its rigid support system, eliminating the need to carry the extra weight of tent poles. During the day, the trekking poles are in use and aren't acting as dead weight in your pack. If you choose to cook, use only one pot for all of your frying, boiling, and simmering needs, rather than carrying a collection of skillets and pots. A poncho that also acts as a shelter is another example of multi-tasking gear, as are packs that utilize closed-cell sleeping pads as framesheets.

Another weight-loss approach is to use gear that is very specific to your needs. Typically, this accounts for seasonal gear such as tents, clothing, and sleeping bags. There's no need to drag a three-pound sleeping bag around in the summer when the night temperatures are balmy. Instead, mail your cold-weather bag ahead and use a lighter summer bag (these bags can weigh less than a pound and usually have temperature ratings in the mid-forties). Tents may be replaced with light hammocks in warm weather, and cold-weather clothing can be bounced ahead for later use. When taking this approach, be careful not to rid yourself of your cold-weather gear too early. Many a hiker has been caught in a late spring snowstorm with a forty-degree bag because he or she tried to lighten the load prematurely.

There are many hikers who make their own gear. This began as a response to a market that didn't initially provide light enough equipment. A cottage craft industry sprang up around these innovators, spawning companies such as AntiGravityGear and Ultralight Adventure Equipment (ULA). There is a wealth of online information, including patterns and directions, for making lightweight and ultralight gear (Gossamer Gear's "Make Your Own" page at www.gossamergear.com is one such

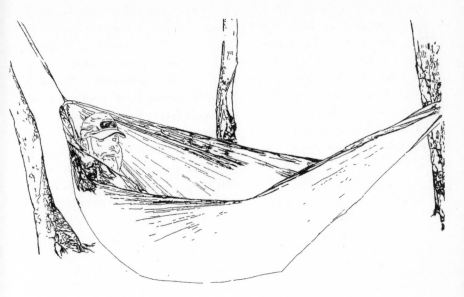

A hammock-hanging hiker

example). Along with being a rewarding activity and a great way to streamline gear to suit your specific needs, making your own gear can be surprisingly inexpensive.

Lighten your pack by becoming logistically smart about water sources. Become more aware of water sources and resupply locations so you aren't obligated to carry as much. Mind you, it's always a good idea to carry *some* extra water in case of unforeseen circumstances. Water weighs 2.2 pounds (or one kilogram in metric) per liter. A standard hydration bladder holds about three liters—that's over six and a half pounds of weight! By carrying only enough water to make it from source to source, you can cut down on a lot of excess weight. How much water you'll need varies from person to person, but a few days into your hike you should have a good sense of how much you drink, enabling you to carry only as much as you need. Some hikers prefer to carry their water in clear bottles rather than a hydration bladder so that they can better ration their intake by keeping visual tab on how much they're drinking. Cooking and camping at sites with water sources helps you to avoid carrying excess water as well.

A popular technique used to avoid carrying excess water is called "cameling up," named so because of a camel's ability to store water in his body. This practice involves rehydrating primarily at water sources to reduce the amount of water you have to carry on your back. Chugging a liter at a water source will enable you to avoid carrying that liter's weight on the trail.

Food needed for a single day of hiking typically weighs around one and one-half to two pounds, which can really add up if you go many days between resupply. Planning for resupply takes effort as it involves taking time-consuming side trips off the trail. Don't resupply at every available town in the name of carrying as little as possible, since this can add time and cost to your overall trip. However, be strategic about how you resupply depending on what region you're in. For example, in Shenandoah National Park there are many opportunities to eat a hot meal at a restaurant or wayside on nearly a daily basis. If you don't mind spending the money, pack one less meal per day, saving yourself quite a few pounds of pack weight. Focus on packing healthy foods with a high calorie content to reduce the amount of weight you have to carry. Read nutrition labels to see which foods give you the most caloric value per ounce.

When shopping for lightweight or ultralight gear, be watchful for manufacturers who stretch the definitions of light. Instead, look at the product weight listed by the manufacturer and, better yet, check out a review. The weight of a specific product may vary from year to year, and variations such as size and capacity affect weight. Lightweight or ultralight pack weight is never achieved through buying lightweight gear alone. Commit to carrying less, regardless of weight. Gear currently on the market is much lighter than it was years ago, and there's a lot of competition between companies to make the lightest gear. Even standard-weight gear is significantly lighter than it was just ten years ago, as manufacturers have recognized the importance of shaving off the ounces.

Some ultralight fanatics do everything they can to save weight, such as trimming the excess edges off of their maps or sawing off the ends of their toothbrushes. These folks are referred to as "gram weenies." Since ultralight backpackers carry so little weight, the amount of weight saved by these activities is proportionately high. For the more traditional hiker trying to save a few pounds, this is not a reasonable approach.

Reducing your weight doesn't necessarily entail hiking and camping in discomfort. Hikers have lived happily in the woods for months with only a tarp or a bivy sack for shelter. On a less extreme level, saving weight may involve leaving your bulky camera at home or not carrying a hard-

PRACTICAL WAYS TO SAVE WEIGHT

- Carry items that work double-duty, such as dental floss, which can be used for flossing or as thread for repairs.
- Use products (such as toothpaste and sunscreen) sold in travel-sized rather than full-sized containers.
- Remove additional pockets, lids, and excess straps from your pack.
- Use stuff sacks that are just large enough to hold their contents.
- Carry only what you need between resupply locations—this particularly applies to fuel.
- Use lithium batteries—they last longer and you won't have to carry as many.
- Pump excess water out of your filter before packing it. Along with reducing weight, this is a good practice in chilly conditions to keep the filter from freezing and cracking.
- Reduce the amount of fuel you need to carry by presoaking food, using a windscreen, cooking with the pot's lid on, and using a pot cozy.
- After resupply, eat your heaviest meals first.
- Use recycled sports drink or soda bottles instead of heavy Lexan bottles for carrying water.
- Eliminate the need for a stove, pot, and fuel by opting to eat only cold food (keep in mind that some cold food tends to be heavier, possibly offsetting the weight-reducing benefits).
- Use a tarp tent, hammock, or bivy sack in place of a traditional tent to slash the weight of your big three.
- Opt to use titanium cookwear and a homemade beverage-can stove in lieu of heavier cooking gear.
- Hike with a partner or group to share the weight of necessary gear. Two or three hikers are able to share a water filter, tent, and stove, reducing the weight in everyone's packs.

cover birding guide. You don't have to leave all of the luxuries at home if you're looking to go light, but you do need to prioritize when selecting what to put in your pack.

With a change in gear comes an overall change in a hiker's mentality. If you want to go light, be willing to abandon the emotional security of your extra gear. Hikers are attached to their gear and often find it difficult to shed the pounds because of psychological reasons. Backpackers who are successful at going light are typically comfortable in the trail environment and have well-developed backcountry skills. Quite often, nascent hikers make up for a lack of confidence by loading their packs with excess gear that acts as a security blanket. While contingency planning is necessary, gear can be streamlined when a hiker knows what to expect out on the trail and is able to solve on-trail problems with minimal gear. As with all gear changes, it's a good idea to test out any new items or configura-

LIGHTWEIGHT AND ULTRALIGHT GEAR MANUFACTURERS

AntiGravityGear: www.antigravitygear.com

GoLite: www.golite.com

Gossamer Gear: www.gossamergear.com

Granite Gear: www.granitegear.com

Jacks 'R' Better: www.jacksrbetter.com

Six Moon Designs: www.sixmoondesigns.com

Ultralight Adventure Equipment (ULA): www.ula-equipment.com

tions on a short weekend trip. That way, if something doesn't work, you're not committed to it for any excess amount of time. To help shave off extra ounces, keep notes on what you use or don't use on shakedown hikes.

There are many great print and electronic resources for hikers wanting to reduce their pack weight. There's a magazine devoted to the art of ultralight and lightweight backpacking called *Backpacking Light* (the online version may be found at www.backpackinglight.com). This is an innovative and helpful magazine providing product reviews, a gear store, and articles on reducing your gear weight, which caters to backpackers possessing a variety of levels of experience. Backpacking Lightweight (www.backpacking.net) is a web site offering links, a forum, and gear checklists for hikers interested in going lighter.

Conclusion

I did it. I said I'll do it, and I've done it.

—Emma "Grandma" Gatewood

Often, a long-distance hike occurs during a transitional period for people. It comes before graduate school or after retirement, always at a time between the usual phases of life. And, for hikers, hiking hundreds or even thousands of miles of the AT is such a daunting task that many have a difficult time imagining life beyond it. As a result, many find themselves nearing the end of their trek with no idea what to do at its completion. Many long-distance hikers experience unease after the hike is over when they rejoin the real world. There are many ways to stay involved in the trail community and live the hiker lifestyle, even when the big hike is over. Providing trail magic, participating in volunteer opportunities, and attending hiker festivals are but a few of the many ways to stay involved with the trail.

For hikers who have completed the entire AT, the Appalachian Trail Conservancy acknowledges their status as "2,000-milers." After completing all of the AT's miles, hikers need to fill out and mail a form provided by the ATC. This form may be picked up at the Katahdin Stream Campground at Baxter State Park, the Walasi-Yi Center in Neels Gap, at Amicalola Falls State Park, or at the ATC Visitor Center in Harpers Ferry. An electronic form can be downloaded off the ATC web site (www.appalachiantrail.org, the form is entitled "Appalachian Trail 2000-Miler Application"). The ATC verifies the completed forms and adds hikers to their official 2,000-miler roster, giving them a patch and certificate from the ATC. In the spirit of the "hike your own hike philosophy," the ATC recognizes section hikes and thru-hikes with equal respect, and it doesn't matter if you finish the trail in one year or ten. Fully supported, leapfrog, flip-flop, and other types of hikes are respected on equal terms.

Once your hike is completed, you may opt to do another long-distance hike. The 700-mile International Appalachian Trail and the 1,300-mile

Florida National Scenic Trail serve as bookends to the Appalachian Trail and as an extended hiking opportunity for those who are truly mad about walking in the woods. The International Appalachian Trail runs from the northern terminus of the AT to Cap Gaspé in Forillon National Park in Quebec, Canada. This trail is fairly wild and unpopulated by other hikers and is known to be muddy and bug-ridden during the warmer season. Starting in Everglades National Park and ending near Pensacola, the Florida National Scenic Trail is less rugged than the IAT. The FT is prone to flooding in the southern sections and, unlike the AT, lacks abundant opportunities for hikers to resupply and stay in hostels. The Long Trail, running parallel to the AT for about one hundred miles, is America's oldest long-distance trail, and is a popular trip option for AT graduates. This trail runs from the Massachusetts/Vermont border up to Canada and crosses Vermont's highest peaks en route. The brewing company, Long Trail Brewing, Co., is named after it.

You may want to become a *triple-crown* hiker, which is someone who has hiked all three of the United States' premier long-distance trails: the Pacific Crest Trail (PCT), the Continental Divide Trail (CDT), and the Appalachian Trail. The Pacific Crest Trail is a 2,650-mile-long, well-graded trail running from Mexico to Canada, which passes through California, Oregon, and Washington. This trail is more logistically challenging and remote than the AT and travels through a wide array of landscapes ranging from desert to rainforest. More information about hiking the PCT may be found at www.pcta.org or in Jackie "Yogi" McDonnell's book, *Yogi's PCT Guide* (www.pcthandbook.com). The Continental Divide Trail is a much more rugged trail than either the PCT or AT. It runs along the backbone of America, passing 3,100 miles through Montana, Idaho, Wyoming, Colorado, and New Mexico. At this time, the CDT is more of a corridor than a trail, meaning that a permanent blazed route has not been created for the entire trail. Because of this, strong map, GPS, and compass skills are needed to navigate. For more information on the CDT, check out the Continental Trail Alliance at www.cdtrail.org. Both the CDT and the PCT are challenging in terms of logistics, wildlife encounters, weather conditions, altitude, and navigation and are a great next step for an accomplished AT hiker.

For someone who's hiked a long distance on the AT, a return to his or her old lifestyle can be unimaginable. A long-distance hike can change you, shaking you to your core. After the hike is over, it's your responsibility to take everything you've gained from the trip back into the world with you.

Many hikers find themselves leading different lifestyles post-hike, and some search for different employment or pursue education related to the environment or outdoors.

> The following is a list of organizations offering volunteer and paid work opportunities and/or education you may want to consider when your hike is over:
>
> - Appalachian Mountain Club (www.outdoors.org): AMC is America's oldest non-profit conservation and recreation organization. A number of employment opportunities, such as croo and ridge-runner positions, are available through AMC.
> - The AT is always in need of helping hands, and volunteers contribute millions of dollars worth of labor every year. Check with your local AT maintaining club for maintenance volunteer opportunities.
> - There are a growing number of schools offering education in outdoors knowledge and leadership. This sort of education can provide a person with solid footing to enter jobs as backcountry guides or educators. Schools such as the National Outdoor Leadership School, more popularly known as NOLS (www.nols.edu); the Appalachian Mountain Club (www.outdoors.org/education/); and Outward Bound Wilderness (www.outwardboundwilderness.org) offer courses in backcountry sports, survival, and leadership.
> - A large number of parks, adventure touring companies, and outfitters seek experienced employees. You may consider putting your backcountry knowledge to use in one of these fields.
> - Outward Bound (www.outwardbound.org): Outward Bound is a great resource for outdoor-oriented employment and education. Experiences with this organization include anything from sailing instruction to leading urban kids on hiking trips.
> - Habitat for Humanity (www.habitat.org): Habitat for Humanity provides opportunities to travel abroad or work in the U.S., helping others by providing services such as construction or education. Check out the "Habitat Jobs" link for information on volunteer and salaried jobs in the U.S. and abroad.
> - Peace Corps (www.peacecorps.gov): The Peace Corps offers opportunities to work abroad, assisting in agriculture, technology, public health, and other projects in developing countries.

Governor Percival P. Baxter (for whom Baxter State Park is named) stated that, "Monuments decay, buildings crumble, and wealth vanishes but Katahdin in its massive grandeur will forever remain the mountain of the people of Maine." The permanence and significance of the Appalachian Trail's impact on humanity and environmentalism is visible all along the trail. The trail is more than a monument or park, more than a recreational diversion. It is the place where complete strangers take hikers in for the night, where hikers tackle obstacles they never imagined they could overcome, where one of the final vestiges of American wilderness is safely tucked away and protected from development. No person can undertake a long-distance hike on this trail and not be changed by it. As an AT hiker, you've entered a community of people who care for the environment, along with its challenges and beauty, and the great memories of your hike will remain with you forever.

Virginia Appalachians

Trail Organizations

The Appalachian Trail is the result of a collective volunteer effort. Integral to the work accomplished on the trail are the many non-profit organizations that help to maintain the trail on a local level. I recommend joining a local trail club before your hike. These clubs offer educational, recreational, and social experiences for the hiking enthusiast. Clubs also provide an important liaison between the hikers and the rest of the community by offering outreach programs and educational literature. The following is a listing of clubs that actively participate in the care of the AT:

Allentown Hiking Club
P.O. Box 1542
Allentown, PA 18105
www.allentownhikingclub.org
info@allentownhikingclub.org

American Hiking Society
Membership Department
1422 Fenwick Lane
Silver Spring, MD 20910
1-800-972-8608 ext. 207
www.americanhiking.org
Membership@AmericanHiking.org

Appalachian Long Distance Hikers Association (ALDHA)
10 Benning Street
PMB 224
West Lebanon, NH 03784
www.aldha.org

Appalachian Mountain Club (AMC)
AMC Main Office
5 Joy Street
Boston, MA 02108
617-523-0655
www.outdoors.org

Appalachian Mountain Club Berkshire Chapter
964 South Main Street
Great Barrington, MA 02130
413-528-6333
www.amcberkshire.org
chapterchair@amcberkshire.org

Appalachian Mountain Club Connecticut Chapter
96 Merritt Valley Road
Andover, CT 06232
860-742-8243
www.ct-amc.org

Appalachian Mountain Club Delaware Valley Chapter
1180 Greenleaf Drive
Bethlehem, PA 18017
www.amcdv.org
chapterchair@amcdv.org

Appalachian Trail Conservancy (ATC)
Membership Services
P.O. Box 807
Harpers Ferry, WV 25425-0807
304-535-6331 ext. 119
www.appalachiantrail.org
membership@appalachiantrail.org

Batona Hiking Club
6651 Eastwood Street
Philadelphia, PA 19149
www.members.aol.com/Batona
bobleo@aol.com

Blue Mountain Eagle Climbing Club
P.O. Box 14982
Reading, PA 19612-4982
610-326-1656
www.bmecc.org
info@bmecc.org

Carolina Mountain Club
P.O. Box 68
Asheville, NC 28802
www.carolinamtnclub.com

Cumberland Valley AT Club
P.O. Box 395
Boiling Springs, PA 17007
www.geocities.com/cvatclub/
wbohn@paonline.com

Dartmouth Outing Club
P.O. Box 9
Hanover, NH 03755
603-646-2428
www.dartmouth.edu

Georgia Appalachian Trail Club
P.O. Box 654
Atlanta, GA 30301
404-634-6495
www.georgia-atclub.org
trailssupervisor@georgia-atclub.org

Green Mountain Club
4711 Waterbury-Stowe Road
Waterbury Center, VT 05677
802-244-7037
Fax: 802-244-5867
www.greenmountainclub.org
gmc@greenmountainclub.org

Maine Appalachian Trail Club
P.O. Box 283
Augusta, ME 04332-0283
www.matc.org

Mountain Club of Maryland
7923 Galloping Circle
Baltimore, MD 21244
410-377-5625
www.mcomd.org
paulives2@aol.com

Mount Rogers Appalachian Trail Club
24198 Green Spring Road
Abingdon, VA 24211-5320
www.geocities.com/Yosemite/Geyser/2539/
emdg@naxs.net

Nantahala Hiking Club
173 Carl Slagle Road
Franklin, NC 28734
www.maconcommunity.org/nhc/

Natural Bridge Appalachian Trail Club
P.O. Box 3012
Lynchburg, VA 24503
www.nbatc.org

New York–New Jersey Trail Conference
156 Ramapo Valley Road (Route 202)
Mahwah, NJ 07430
201-512-9348
www.nynjtc.org
info@nynjtc.org

Old Dominion Appalachian Trail Club
P.O. Box 25283
Richmond, VA 23260-5283
trailguymike@aol.com

Outdoor Club of Virginia Tech
P.O. Box 538
Blacksburg, VA 24060
www.outdoor.org.vt.edu

Philadelphia Trail Club
741 Golf Road
Warrington, PA 18976
http://m.zanger.tripod.com/
Kenna@comcat.com

Piedmont Appalachian Trail Hikers
P.O. Box 4423
Greensboro, NC 27404
www.path-at.org

Potomac Appalachian Trail Club
118 Park Street, S.E.
Vienna, Virginia 22180-4609
703-242-0693
Fax: 703-242-0968
Activities tape: 703-242-0965
www.patc.net
info@patc.net

Roanoke Appalachian Trail Club
P.O. Box 12282
Roanoke, VA 24024-2282
www.ratc.org

Smoky Mountains Hiking Club
P.O. Box 1454
Knoxville, TN 37901-1454
865-693-9795
www.smhclub.org
mark.shipley@townoffarragut.org

Susquehanna Appalachian Trail Club
120 Kock Lane
Harrisburg, PA 17112
717-657-8281
www.satc-hike.org
athikerjb@aol.com

Tennessee Eastman Hiking and Canoeing Club
P.O. Box 511
Kingsport, TN 37662
www.tehcc.org

Tidewater Appalachian Trail Club
P.O. Box 8246
Norfolk, VA 23503
www.tidewateratc.com

Wilderness Volunteers
P.O. Box 22292
Flagstaff, AZ 86002
www.wildernessvolunteers.org

Wilmington Trail Club
P.O. Box 1184
Wilmington, DE 19899
www.wilmingtontrailclub.org
membership@wilmingtontrailclub.org

York Hiking Club
2684 Forest Rd
York, PA 17402
717-244-6769
www.yorkhikingclub.com
president@yorkhikingclub.com

Trail Terminology

aqua-blazing. Taking an over-water route instead of the AT. Some hikers opt to aqua-blaze on the Shenandoah River rather than hike Shenandoah National Park.

AYCE. An acronym for all-you-can-eat buffet, one of the high points of the hiker dining experience.

bald. A mountaintop without plant coverage larger than small shrubs and grasses.

bandit camping. Camping in restricted areas on the sly.

base weight. The weight of your gear minus food and water. See also **dry weight** and **skin-out base weight**.

bear-bagging. The art of hanging your food to protect it from bears.

blaze. Marker used to indicate the location and direction of the trail.

blow-downs. Fallen trees from storms and high winds.

blue-blazing. Taking the alternate blue-blazed trails instead of the official AT route.

boil time. The amount of time it takes a stove to boil a liter of water at sea level.

bouldering. Free rock climbing. There are a few good bouldering sites along the AT.

burn time. The amount of time a stove will burn with a standard unit of fuel (such as a canister).

bushwhacking. To travel through the woods off the trail, creating your path as you go.

cairns. Stone piles marking the trail above tree line and in other areas where trees for blazing are absent.

cameling up. Drinking a lot of water at its source to reduce the amount you have to carry in your pack.

cat hole. A six-inch-deep hole in which you bury your waste.

circuit hiking. When a hiker completes the trail in two or more large sections, continuously hiking in the same direction (such as southbound).

class (as in, AT class of 2007). The annual group of AT hikers, much like high school seniors, are referred to as a class.

croo. The summer staff employed to run the AMC huts in the White Mountains.

deacon's seat. An additional short wall built across the front entrance of a shelter designed to keep out porcupines.

denier. Indicates the weight in grams of the material that 9,000 meters of fiber weigh.

dry weight. The weight of your pack minus "wet" items such as food and water. See also **base weight** and **skin-out base weight**.

fast-packing. Traveling light and fast; typically an ultralight phenomenon.

fill power. This number indicates the volume of space filled by an ounce of down and determines the warmth of a down bag—the higher the number, the warmer the bag.

flip-flopping. Walking from one terminus of the trail to a halfway point, then walking to the same point from the other terminus.

framesheet. The internal structure found in packs that provides support.

gap. A noteworthy dip between two mountains. When you see "gap" in your guidebook, prepare for a big hike down and then up.

gear head. Those hikers obsessed with gear.

General Delivery mail. A service provided by the United States Postal Service that allows travelers to pick up mail addressed to them at any post office destination.

ghost-blazing. Following old blazes on parts of the AT where the blazes have been painted out after trail relocation.

gorp. "Good old raisins and peanuts," the venerable and popular trail snack.

gram weenie. This is a somewhat derogatory term for an ultralight backpacker who is obsessed with shaving grams off his or her pack weight.

green-blazing. This term can either refer to the act of bushwhacking or of smoking marijuana as you hike. Sometimes the two inadvertently occur in tandem.

greenway. A broad swath of protected land through which the trail runs.

hiker boxes. Boxes left at hostels, outfitters, and other places that act as repositories for unwanted gear and food.

hiker midnight. An absurdly early hour in the evening (eight or nine o'clock) when exhausted hikers generally go to bed.

hut. AMC-governed hostels in the White Mountains of New Hampshire.

HYOH. Abbreviation for "hike your own hike," a philosophy of acceptance of others' hiking styles.

knob. A geographical feature that describes a small yet prominent area of elevation. Features of the AT with the word "knob" in the name may be subject to many delightfully lewd jokes.

lean-to. The term used to describe AT shelters in the New England states.

leapfrogging. Skipping large sections of the trail and returning to hike them at a later date.

Leave No Trace. This is the catch-all phrase used to describe a set of responsible behaviors for backcountry areas.

loft. The thickness of the insulation in a jacket or sleeping bag.

nero. A day of walking almost no mileage, a combination of the words "near" and "zero."

northbounder. Otherwise known as a NOBO, a thru-hiker who travels in a northbound direction from Springer Mountain to Katahdin.

notch. See **gap**.

NSAIDs. An abbreviation for over-the-counter nonsteroidal anti-inflammatory medications such as ibuprofen.

pack sniffer. Someone who isn't a hiker but likes to spend time with hikers and live the trail lifestyle at festivals, hostels, and shelters near road crossings.

Pamola. The Native American god believed to inhabit Katahdin.

pass. A low-lying valley going between two mountains.

peak-bagging. An activity usually undertaken by the hiker who wants to own claim to climbing any number of peaks. AT hikers inadvertently "bag" some peaks, but are usually more interested in bagging dinner in town.

pink-blazing. The act of throwing your itinerary to the wind to chase a romantic interest.

post-holing. The demoralizing act of wading through deep, unbroken snow on the trail, leaving post-hole-looking depressions with your legs.

power hiking. An aggressive high-mileage, low-weight approach to hiking.

privy. The outdoor restroom facilities provided along the AT. Privies usually consist of a shack located over a hole dug in the ground, though some interesting variations thereof exist along the trail.

PUD. An acronym for "pointless ups and downs." This term describes stretches of the trail that consistently lose and gain elevation without an obvious purpose such as water sources, road crossings, or views.

puncheons. The wooden bog bridges that traverse the marshy areas of the trail, especially in New Jersey, Vermont, and Maine.

purist. A hiker who refuses to deviate from walking past each and every white blaze on the trail.

rainbow-blazers. Those hikers who follow blue, yellow, and other blazes on their hike.

relos. Short for "relocations": areas where the official AT has been relocated due to storm damage or property issues.

resupply. Visits to town to restock food, medicine, and other necessities. Resupply can be short-term (a quick dash to a country store for a handful of noodles and candy bars) or long-term, involving more planning.

second-growth. A renewed wilderness area where the trees are the product of re-growth occurring after the original forest was cleared for lumber or farmland.

section hiker. A hiker who hikes the AT in smaller sections.

shelter. The generic name for the three-sided buildings at campsites along the AT.

skin-out base weight. The weight of your gear including the clothes on your back and footwear. See also **base weight** and **dry weight**.

slack-packing, slacking. Hiking with only a day pack while a support crew carries your supplies to your destination via car.

southbounder. Otherwise known as a SOBO. A hiker who walks in a southerly direction, from Katahdin toward Springer Mountain.

Springer fever. The hiking madness that puts hikers' eyes in a glaze every spring and sends them out on the trail. It's similar to spring fever, with a dash of AT mania thrown in.

stealth camping. See **bandit camping**.

step-kicking. A method of breaking trail in deeper snow.

thru-hiker. A hiker who walks the entire length of the Appalachian Trail during the course of one calendar year.

trail angel. A person who does kind things for hikers, such as offering them shelter, food, or water.

trail magic. The serendipitous acts of kindness performed by trail angels.

trailway. Indicates the area dedicated to a hiking path. This includes a buffer zone of land on either side of the trail as well as the trail itself.

tree line. Also known as timberline. This is the line marking the border of the habitat where trees are able to grow.

triple crown. The achievement of hiking all three of America's most noteworthy long-distance trails: the Appalachian Trail, the Pacific Crest Trail, and the Continental Divide Trail.

2,000-miler. A hiker who has hiked the entire length of the AT (coined by Ed Garvey in the 1970s).

vitamin I. A nickname for ibuprofen, the sore hiker's best friend.

watershed. An area whose rain runoff and snow-melt travels toward a certain body of water.

white-blazing. The act of following the white blazes of the AT.

widow-makers. Dead limbs in trees that can blow down or fall off, crushing whatever is underneath them.

yellow-blazing. Originally, yellow-blazing was a description for walking along the road. Now it more commonly applies to hitchhiking.

Yogi-ing. Yogi-ing is begging without begging—receiving food and other favors without blatantly asking for them (named after the cartoon character, Yogi Bear).

yo-yo-ing. Hiking the entire trail and then turning around and hiking it once more for good measure.

zero day. Also known simply as a "zero." A day of rest where no AT mileage is accomplished.

Suggested Resources

Books

Allnutt, Rick, MD. *A Wildly Successful 200-Mile Hike*. Beavercreek, OH: Wayah Press, 2005.

Amato, Joseph A. *On Foot: A History of Walking*. New York: New York University Press, 2004.

Anderson, Kristi, and Arleen Tavernier, eds. *Wilderness Basics: The Complete Handbook for Hikers and Backpackers*. Seattle: The Mountaineers Books, 2004.

Anderson, Larry. *Benton MacKaye: Conservationist, Planner, and Creator of the Appalachian Trail*. Baltimore, MD: Johns Hopkins University Press, 2002.

Atlanta Journal-Constitution staff. *Appalachian Adventure: From Georgia to Maine: A Spectacular Journey on the Great American Trail*. Atlanta, GA: Longstreet Press, 1995.

Axcell, Claudia et al. *Simple Foods for the Pack: More Than 200 All-Natural, Trail-Tested Recipes*. San Francisco, CA: Sierra Club Books, 2004.

Backer, Howard D., MD, MPH, et al. *Wilderness First Aid: Emergency Care for Remote Locations*. Sudbury, MA: Jones and Bartlett Publishers, 2005.

Berger, Karen. *Advanced Backpacking: A Trailside Guide*. New York: W.W. Norton & Co., 1998.

_____. *Backpacking and Hiking*. New York: Dorling Kindersley Limited, 2005.

Bryson, Bill. *A Walk in the Woods: Rediscovering America on the Appalachian Trail*. New York: Broadway Books, 1998.

Carline, Jan D. et al. *Mountaineering First Aid*. Seattle: The Mountaineers Books, 2004.

Chase, Jim. *Backpacker Magazine's Guide to the Appalachian Trail*. Mechanicsburg, PA: Stackpole Books, 2005.

Chatwin, Bruce. *The Songlines*. New York: Viking, 1987.

Chazin, Daniel. *Appalachian Trail Data Book*. Harpers Ferry, WV: Appalachian Trail Conference (an updated version is published annually).

Chew, V. Collins. *Underfoot: A Geologic Guide to the Appalachian Trail*. Harpers Ferry, WV: Appalachian Trail Conference, 1993.

Conners, Tim, and Christine Conners. *Lipsmackin' Backpackin': Lightweight Trail-Tested Recipes for Backcountry Trips*. Helena, MO: Falcon, 2000.

_____. *Lipsmackin' Vegitarian Backpackin'*. Helena, MO: Falcon, 2004.

Curran, Jan D. *The Appalachian Trail: A Journey of Discovery*. Moore Haven, FL: Rainbow Books, Inc., 1991.

_____. *The Appalachian Trail: How to Prepare For and Hike It*. Moore Haven, FL: Rainbow Books, 1997.

Curtis, Rick. *The Backpacker's Field Manual: A Comprehensive Guide to Mastering Backcountry Skills*. New York: Three Rivers Press, 1998.

Drummond, Roger. *Ticks and What You Can Do about Them*. Berkeley, CA: Wilderness Press, 1998.

Emblidge, David, ed. *The Appalachian Trail Reader*. New York: Oxford University Press, 1996.

Garvey, Edward B. *Appalachian Hiker: Adventure of a Lifetime*. Oakton, VA: Appalachian Books, 1971.

Hall, Adrienne. *A Journey North: One Woman's Story of Hiking the Appalachian Trail*. Boston: Appalachian Mountain Club Books, 2000.

————. *Woman's Guide to Backpacking*. Camden, ME: Ragged Mountain Press, 1998.

Halpern, Brian. *The Knee Crisis Handbook: Understanding Pain, Preventing Trauma, Recovering from Injury, and Building Healthy Knees for Life*. New York: LifeTime Media, Inc., 2003.

Harmon, Will. *Wild Country Companion: The Ultimate Guide to No-Trace Outdoor Recreation and Wilderness Safety*. Helena, MO: Falcon Press Publishing Co., Inc., 1994.

Hostetter, Kristin. *Don't Forget the Duct Tape: Tips and Tricks for Repairing Outdoor Gear*. Seattle: The Mountaineers Books, 2003.

Hugo, Beverly. *Women and Thru-Hiking on the Appalachian Trail*. Harpers Ferry, WV: Appalachian Trail Conference, 2002.

Jardine, Ray. *Beyond Backpacking: Ray Jardine's Guide to Lightweight Hiking: Practical Methods for All Who Love the Out-of-Doors, from Walkers and Backpackers, to Long-Distance Hikers*. LaPine, OR: AdventureLore Press, 2000.

Jordan, Ryan, ed. *Lightweight Backpacking and Camping: A Field Guide to Wilderness Equipment, Techniques, and Style*. Bozeman, MT: Beartooth Mountain Press, 2006.

Ladigan, Don. *Lighten Up!: A Complete Handbook for Light and Ultralight Backpacking*. Guilford, CT: The Globe Pequot Press, 2005.

Lanza, Michael. *Winter Hiking and Camping: Managing Cold for Comfort and Safety*. Seattle: The Mountaineers Books, 2003.

Lauterborn, David. *Appalachian Trail Thru-Hike Planner*. Harpers Ferry, WV: Appalachian Trail Conservancy, 2005.

Logue, Victoria Steele. *Backpacking: Essential Skills to Advanced Techniques*. Birmingham, AL: Menasha Ridge Press, 2000.

Logue, Victoria, and Frank Logue. *Appalachian Trail Hiker: Trail-Proven Advice for Hikes of Any Length*. Birmingham, AL: Menasha Ridge Press, 2004.

Mass, Leslie, ed. *Appalachian Trail Thru-Hikers' Companion*. Harpers Ferry, WV: Appalachian Trail Conference (an updated version is published annually and an online copy may be found at www.aldha.org).

————. *In Beauty May She Walk: Hiking the Appalachian Trail at 60*. Jacksonville, FL: Rock Spring Press, Inc., 2005.

McCaw, Bob. *The Thru-Hiker's Handbook*. Hot Springs, NC: Center for Appalachian Trail Studies (an updated version is published annually).

Meyer, Kathleen. *How to Shit in the Woods: An Environmentally Sound Approach to a Lost Art*. Berkeley, CA: Ten Speed Press, 1994.

Miller, Dorcas S. *Backcountry Cooking: From Pack to Plate in 10 Minutes*. Seattle: The Mountaineers Books, 1998.

Mueser, Roland. *Long-Distance Hiking: Lessons from the Appalachian Trail.* Camden, ME: Ragged Mountain Press, 1997.

Porter, Yvonne et al. *Beyond Gorp: Favorite Foods from Outdoor Experts.* Seattle: The Mountaineers Books, 2005.

Randall, Glenn. *The Outward Bound Backpacker's Handbook.* New York: The Lyons Press, 1999.

Rubin, Robert Alden. *On the Beaten Path: An Appalachian Pilgrimage.* New York: The Lyons Press, 2001.

Ryan, David. *Long Distance Hiking on the Appalachian Trail: For the Older Adventurer.* Tesuque, NM: New Mountain Books, 2002.

Schlimmer, E. *Thru Hiker's Guide to America.* Camden, ME: Ragged Mountain Press, 2005.

Schneider, Bill and Russ, eds. *Backpacking Tips: Trail-Tested Wisdom from FalconGuide Authors.* Helena, MO: Falcon Publishing, Inc., 1998.

Shaffer, Earl V. *Walking with Spring.* Harpers Ferry, WV: Appalachian Trail Conference, 1998.

Solnit, Rebecca. *Wanderlust: A History of Walking.* New York: Viking, 2000.

Speer, Ed. *Hammock Camping: The Complete Guide to Greater Comfort, Convenience, and Freedom.* Marion, NC: Speer Hammocks, Inc., 2003.

Svien, Sarah. *Freezer Bag Cooking: Trail Food Made Simple.* Napa, CA: Lulu Press, 2006.

Tate, J. R. "Model-T". *Walkin' with the Ghost Whisperers: Lore and Legend on the AT.* Philadelphia, PA: Xlibris Corp., 2006.

Townsend, Chris. *The Advanced Backpacker: A Handbook of Year-Round Long-Distance Hiking.* Camden, ME: Ragged Mountain Press, 2001.

_____. *The Backpacker's Handbook.* Camden, ME: Ragged Mountain Press/ McGraw-Hill, 2005.

Vonoff, John. *Fixing Your Feet: Prevention and Treatments for Athletes.* Berkeley, CA: Wilderness Press, 2004.

Warner, Mark. *The Appalachian Trail: An Aerial View.* Newcastle, ME: Warner Pub., 2004.

Winters, Kelly. *Walking Home: A Woman's Pilgrimage on the Appalachian Trail.* Los Angeles: Alyson Books, 2001.

Wittreich, Paul. *Hike/Bike America: Hike the Appalachian Trail End-to-End, Bike across America Coast-to-Coast.* New York: Writer's Club Press, 2002.

Yaffe, Linda Frederick. *Backpack Gourmet: Good Hot Grub You Can Make at Home, Dehydrate, and Pack for Quick, Easy, and Healthy Eating on the Trail.* Mechanicsburg, PA: Stackpole Books, 2003.

_____. *High Trail Cookery.* Chicago: Chicago Review Press, 1997.

Magazines and Journals

American Hiker
Appalachian Trailway News
AT Journeys: The Magazine of the Appalachian Trail Conservancy

AT Museum News
Backpacker Magazine
Backpacking Light
The Long Distance Hiker
National Geographic Adventure Magazine
Outside

Web Sites and Listservs

American Hiking Society: www.americanhiking.org
Appalachian Long Distance Hikers Association: www.aldha.org
Appalachian Trail Conservancy: www.appalachiantrail.org
Appalachian Trail Museum Society: www.atmuseum.org
AT Listserv, an e-mail list for AT hikers: To subscribe to the list, send an e-mail to at-l-request@backcountry.net. Write "subscribe" in the body of the e-mail.
Backpacker Magazine Online: www.backpacker.com
The Center for Appalachian Trail Studies: www.trailplace.com
The Earl Shaffer Web Page, a presentation of the Earl Shaffer Foundation: www.earlshaffer.com
Live Cam, Mount Katahdin, Maine: www.katahdincam.com
Trail CastPodcasting on Foot (a podcast about hiking): www.trailcast.com
Trail Forums: www.trailforums.com
Trailjournals, an online resource for journaling, forums, photos, and more: www.trailjournals.com
Whiteblaze.net, a community of Appalachian Trail enthusiasts: www.whiteblaze.net

Films

Appalachian Impressions. Flagler Films, 2005.
Southbounders. Southbounders Production LLC, 2005.
TREKA Journey on the Appalachian Trail. Cirque Productions, 2004.
2,000 Miles to Maine. Appalachian Adventures, 2004.
Walking with Freedom. Barking Harley Productions, 2003.

Index